The Soul-Discovery Journalbook

An Intimate Journey into Self

Also by Adriene Nicastro

Little Gifts: The Adventures of a Pigeon Angel

Precious Little Loves

The Soul-Discovery Journalbook

An Intimate Journey into Self

Volumes I - V

Adriene Nicastro, M.S.

Pathways to Freedom Press
Bellefonte, PA

The Soul-Discovery Journalbook: An Intimate Journey into Self

Copyright © 2021 by Adriene Nicastro
All rights reserved.

Cover image: CC0 Creative Commons License
Image: https://pixabay.com/en/girl-mejk-color-rainbow-model-2696947/
Photographer: ivanovgood; https://pixabay.com/en/users/ivanovgood-1982503/

No part of this book may be reproduced or transmitted in any manner whatsoever without the express written permission of the publisher except for the use of brief quotations in critical articles and book reviews.

The advice and strategies found within may not be suitable for every situation and are not a replacement for professional medical or therapeutic treatment.

This book was published in 2018 as five separate volumes and in 2019 as a combined version under Spirit Speaks Publishing.

Pathways to Freedom Press
Bellefonte, Pennsylvania
www.pathwaystofreedompress.com

Library of Congress Control Number: ##########

ISBN Hardback 978-1-7358558-1-3
ISBN eBook 978-1-7358558-2-0

To my children Jackson and Payton and fur babies Ash, Zannah, and Koffee, thank you for blessing me on this great adventure. You make my life so very rich.

To my soul sisters, you know who you are; your friendship is a breath of fresh air and deeper than words.

To the Sacred Garden Fellowship family, your support and teachings have made my own evolution possible; to Rev. Penny Donovan, your love, compassion, and connection to Spirit has inspired me and to Donald Gilbert, whose gifts and guidance encouraged me to be more.

To the challenging characters I've met on my path, thank you for the opportunities to grow.

And finally, to all the spiritual warriors and sacred rebels who allowed me to be part of their growth and soul-discovery, your courage, grace, and authenticity is a joy to behold.

Table of Contents

Letter to the Soul-discoverer

Introduction

Volume I: A Single Step

Setting the Stage...5
  Guidelines on Use..7
  Journaling Suggestions...11
  Using Guided Meditations...13
  Our Sacred Space...15
  Centering..19
  We Are Guided..23
  Setting Our Intent...27

First Glance...31
  Freedom!..33
  Scribbled Reflections...37
  Through the Looking Glass...41
  Our Internal Climate...45
  Thats What I Like..51
  Grrrrrrrrrrr...55
  Create!..61
  Old Habits Die Hard..65
  Dreams...73
  Multi-sensory Memory..77

The Ties That Bind Us 81
Value Park 89
You've Come a Long Way Baby 95

Volume II: Constant Companions

Constant Companions 101
   Attitude of Gratitude 103
   Breathe 109
   Wise Baby Vision 121
   Quieting Our Mind 127
   Thankfulness Tree 139
   The Ego 143
   Spiritual Chutzpah 153
   Laughter is the Best Medicine 161
   Here and Now 165
   Mandala 171
   Mindfulness and Gratitude 177
   Creating Affirmations 183
   Only Love is Real 193
   Your Inside Circle 201

Volume III: Metaphysical Musings

Metaphysical Musings 207
   Our Energy 209
   Beautiful World 217
   The World Sings with You 221
   From Consciousness into Awareness 229
   We Are So Loved 239
   There Is Order 247

Moon Moods 251
In the Heart of the Jungle 267
Wynebgwrthucher 275
Faith in Ladybugs 293
Serendipity and Synchronicity 299
Into the Butterfly 303
Understanding Illness and Healing 309
Karmic Cords 319
Blessings Blooming 329
Let Your Love-light Shine 335
The Substance of Stars 347

Volume IV: A Deeper Gaze

A Deeper Gaze 353
   Love Your Spots 355
   Letting Go 363
   Remembering the Love 375
   The Mysteries of La-La Land 385
   Letter of Love 397
   Joy and Happiness 401
   Shedding Perceived Failures 411
   The Final Frontier 421
   Ho'oponopono 433
   Chagrin 441
   Dearest Friend 451
   Waters Deep and Wide 455

Volume V: Hip Boots and Waders

Hip Boots and Waders	461
Meeting Peter Pan	463
Transforming Drama	471
The Letter That Won't Be Sent	479
Visiting Never Land	485
Snow White and the Evil Queen	499
Message in a Bottle	509
The Merry-go-round	519
Leaving Our Swamp of Judgment	529
The Power of Belief	541
Oh, Merciful Heart!	555
Return from the Looking Glass	565
At Journey's End	569
Thank you	573
Epilogue	575

Appendix
   Resources
   Glossary of Terms

An Intimate Journey into Self

Who in the world am I? Ah, that's the great puzzle.

— *C.S. Lewis*
  (J. Tenniel illustrator)

Letter to the Soul-discoverer

Dear Courageous One,

Welcome to **The Soul-Discovery Journalbook: An Intimate Journey into Self**. Within these pages lies a great adventure….a pilgrimage….soul-discovery as a unique expression of YOU. Some readers may arrive here already feeling like a well-seasoned journeyer, while others may see the path ahead as new and fresh. All of us travel a multitude of routes. In truth, we are but headed to one destination through many, many different trails — a journey to the Self. Your adventure awaits in the following pages through soul-discovery.

While any journey may elicit excitement, anticipation, and joy, perhaps under the surface or even not so hidden lies fear, uncertainty, and anxiety, creating a push and pull inside us. Because this adventure travels within to places many may never have seen or noticed before, the trail may seem like a bumpy mountain path. Often, what we actually discover is less frightening than what we've imagined. We may even realize that fear of our own fear serves as the real root of our nervousness, believing more in the danger of facing the unknown or hidden negative pieces we all carry than in our ability to release or overcome whatever we encounter.

Through this journey, with all its metaphorical deep streams, dense forests, and majestic peaks, I greatly desire that you grow in self-love – the Mount Everest on the Great Path of Life. This very self-love calls to the spark of Life within you. And as you let this journey within peel back the layers of misperceptions that have long skewed the vision of who you really are, may you find the joy, creativity, and peace that is inherently and eternally yours.

I look forward to your metamorphosis, happily imparting what I have learned and remembered from my own twisting and sometimes rocky path. Thank you for taking this journey, for as you grow, we all grow with you. Like the sun, your radiance becomes shared with all.

I hope to hear from you and read the stories of your evolution. Please write to me at www.pathways2innerpeace.com and share your struggles and your triumphs.

May your path be most rewarding and blessed as you intimately connect with yourself and your Self. Be brave, be authentic, and most of all, be loving.

Much love and light,
Adriene

Introduction

We each have the power within us to transform our lives. Our desire to grow brings new opportunities - journeys of metamorphosis that arrive special delivery from the Universe. Through your intentions, the world heard your call, leading you to this book series and the adventures in soul-discovery that lie within its pages.

While there are many paths to personal growth, the **The Soul-Discovery Journalbook** offers a set of distinct tools for personal evolution through what this author calls "soul-discovery" - the unearthing and shedding of limiting beliefs held in our soul memory. While each step herein evolves uniquely for each reader as a journey within, broadly speaking they create an adventure to uncover our True Nature by shining a light on debris and by offering ways to put psycho-spiritual tools into action to release what no longer serves us. As a result, we unblock our path, cleanse our soul memory of misperceptions, and facilitate self-love, all while moving toward the awareness and expression of Self - our ever-present Internal Sun.

The beginning of any change is simple - a desire for movement and growth in our life. Simple, however, doesn't always mean easy. Some of the most potent and transformative aspects of these volumes are the most simplistic in nature. Others may feel elusive or complicated, requiring slow progression and intentional revisiting to assimilate what they offer. Nevertheless, throughout **The Soul-Discovery Journalbook**, everyone is encouraged to find their own distinct path through the gentle nudges to explore, contemplate, experience, laugh, cry, feel, draw, scribble, ponder, process, and practice - expressing with freedom and authenticity.

Traveling through topics, chapters, and exercises, only one key element is required - willingness - perhaps the most important aspect of personal development. **The Soul-Discovery Journalbook** personally invites you to explore through openness, honesty, and a willingness to look...a willingness *to really experience* your internal world, allowing everything that surfaces to move through you, embracing all to progressively and lovingly accept its gifts. This is willingness in action. In turn, opportunities continually unfold to uncover any shadow aspects and put into practice new behaviors, mindsets, and feeling states that ground your growth. Willingness cannot be given to you; each person must reach deeply inside to find their own. Those who do will reap great rewards through lightness of being, transformation, and love. The choice is always yours.

While psycho-spiritual in nature, **The Soul-Discovery Journalbook** is not a substitute for psychotherapy or other modalities of care. Certainly, it provides fruitful, direct, and sometimes side-door gazes at the forces that compel us. It aids those who investigate its pages to understand themselves better, release old struggles, shift perceptions, and grow. What it helps us uncover might urge us toward other ways to heal through therapy and related healing practitioners, or it may serve us in our existing healing process as we embrace what it offers, incorporating the materials and journeys as we are drawn.

Originally envisioned as one, six-section book, **The Soul-Discovery Journalbook's** first publication circulated as five interdependent volumes, each working together to guide readers through progressively deeper soul-discovery. This new version returns to the author's initial intent, housing the five volumes under one cover. It provides the opportunity to easily cross-reference and explore related chapters listed in the comprehensive **Table of Contents**, an **Appendix** that outlines **Resources** as books, movies, and websites supplementing your journey, and a brief **Glossary of Terms** used throughout the series. Additionally, each volume presents chapters within a common theme. Chapters, in turn, introduce a lesson or topic of exploration and follow with one or more exercises called Journeys. Journeys allow for practicing the chapter lessons through frequent use of centering and setting intentions, as well as through a variety of personal and practical explorations in soul-discovery. Even though each section focuses on a general theme, metaphysics, spirituality, mindfulness, and psycho-spiritual tools and lessons infuse the entire book series, blending and weaving concepts and approaches as a comprehensive whole.

Looking across the six sections of the series, we find **Setting the Stage**, **First Glance**, **Constant Companions**, **Metaphysical Musings**, **A Deeper Gaze**, and **Hip Boots and Waders**.

Volume I: A Single Step

Setting the Stage offers important preliminary information; the chapters within paint a significant backdrop to this author's meaning of soul-discovery. Gather valuable tools for self-exploration, the preparation before setting out on the trail with compass and backpack in tow.

First Glance eases into self-discovery by starting the process of exploration and expression to learn new and intriguing ways to uncover feelings, thoughts, and belief systems that inform how we operate in the world.

Volume II: Constant Companions

Constant Companions continues personal exploration, offering tools and perspectives that may be practiced repeatedly. This volume facilitates mindfulness, inner peace, and self-acceptance as vital tools of our evolution.

Volume III: Metaphysical Musings

Metaphysical Musings holds foundational metaphysical and psycho-spiritual gear invaluable for any journey of personal growth, especially a set of core tools to navigate life's daily challenges, as well as a journey to make an intimate connection with Self.

Volume IV: A Deeper Gaze

A Deeper Gaze devotes time to progressively deeper soul-discovery. Dive into layers of self-exploration to uncover the well-worn patterns and old beliefs that hold us back from living in Union with all of life.

Volume V: Hip Boots and Waders

Hip Boots and Waders continues the process of soul-discovery as part of our life-long adventure in getting to know self and Self.

Traveling the pages of **The Soul-Discovery Journalbook**, various volumes may pique your interest. However, regardless of where you feel drawn, the attention and time given to **Setting the Stage** will be time well spent. This section offers valuable information, in the same way that packing before a trip prepares us for the journey ahead. Any adventure missing clean underwear, comfortable clothing, or important toiletries can produce stress along the way and the discomfort can make us think twice about our preparations or haste. So, when allowing for freedom of movement to explore topics and taking what may seem to be a diversion on the trail, this author advises that everyone gathers basic supplies and adequately pack by first exploring **Setting the Stage**. Beyond this section, those compelled to skip around must remember that some chapters present a deeper, more complex version of others; what you may bypass could hold foundational material needed for future exploration and chapter comprehension. In any event, set the intent that moving too quickly ahead ignites an inner guidance to slow-down, refocus, or return to earlier missed chapters to regain your bearings.

Additionally, the nature of this work at times employs the benefits of repetition, which offers opportunities of more comprehensive experiences, diving deeper into the layers of our soul with each pass-through. At other times, it pays homage to growth as a way to witness and celebrate our evolution. At best, the simple idiom, "practice makes perfect," can transform into a new mindset; repetition gently sheds the layers that we no longer need to reveal the perfection of the Self within. So by all means, repeat when it feels right, and know that each time we revisit a theme, idea, or lesson, it can help us progress on the path.

Staple foods for growth, navigational tools for life's daily challenges, faithful traveling companions, dependable lanterns, indispensable adventuring gear...these are what you, my soul-discovery friend, find within these pages. May they serve you well.

Many, many blessings on your path.

The Soul-Discovery Journalbook

An Intimate Journey into Self

Volume I

A Single Step

A journey of a thousand miles begins with a single step.

— Lao Tzu

Setting the Stage

Welcome to the very first step of soul-discovery! The tools contained within this section help you prepare for your journey. **Setting the Stage** includes important tips about navigating the work, valuable journaling suggestions, ideas on creating a sacred space, helpful ways to use guided meditation, steps to call in your Divine helpers, and how to set your intent.

Treasured information lies within these beginning pages that aid in making the most out of your experience with **The Soul-Discovery Journalbook**.

Happy trails!

Guidelines on Use

The materials before you create a journey. Well really, each of you creates the journey; these pages provide the food, tools, lantern, and map to assist and help guide the way in soul-discovery.

While some may interpret a journey as a paced walk over time, others may see it as a sprint. Our inclination to mesh with a fast-food culture brings an instant gratification mentality to our life and day-to-day living, but this book series is not a sprint, nor can you learn everything within these pages all in one big bite. Let me say that again. **The Soul-Discovery Journalbook** series *is not a sprint, but a marathon.* If approached in a fashion that strives and rushes - a "want results now" mindset - expect frustration, exasperation, and discouragement. Moreover, hurrying the process and movement through these exercises may lead to emotional overload. So, take the time to progress naturally… organically…and trust that your process and progress is perfect for you.

While some of this soul-discovery may seem quite foreign, if thought of as a new way to approach life challenges and situations, we find a common thread. ALL of us face challenges in this great adventure called life, and knowing the tools that help us navigate these difficulties more smoothly, deeply, and meaningfully is what this author endeavors to provide.

Reading and working within these pages often affords more than a once-and-done opportunity. Like new ways to condition the body give rise to a stronger, healthier physical state, this material embraces the same vision. While a new Pilates pose or interval training regimen provides many gains, we certainly cannot expect to do either only one time or for a single day to demonstrate improved stamina or muscle tone. The same applies to soul-discovery and personal evolution. Even though this author doesn't presume to know how much or how often the treasures and tools within these pages need to be read, as well as traveled to experience benefit, the changes will be highly individual and vary from person to person. Some changes will be immediately incorporated, expressed as a new attitude or mindset to practice, growing in strength with each passing day. More commonly, revisiting exercises may feel like peeling an onion, as readers uncover deeper and deeper layers of misperceptions, negative beliefs, or old habits. Still other opportunities to apply new ways of being - employing the help of constant companions - aid readers in navigating challenging situations and thus make the path lighter, clearer, and filled with ease. Regardless of how each journey unfolds, trust that your "personal prescription" is in perfect order, giving room for practice, visiting and revisiting wherever and whenever drawn. Remember, every leg of your journey differs slightly, even though it might seem like the exact same lesson or exercise. However seemingly repetitive or similar circumstances or lessons appear, we change with each experience, each journey, each chapter navigated. As such, growth occurs in sometimes immeasurable ways, yet most certainly through observing, living through, shedding, and understanding one step at a time as we put what we've learned into action.

Inherent in soul-discovery, some exercises also provide immediate shifts in the form of less tension, lower anxiety, more peace, greater understanding, or the proverbial "ah-hah" moment. Other exercises palpably increase anger, sadness, frustration, and nervous tensions as buried emotions surface for examination, expression, and ultimately release. Becoming easily overwhelmed by emotions especially happens when feelings routinely get ignored, stuffed, or bypassed, so be gentle. Give room for movement and breaks, time to process and experience, time to express and transform. Know that all things come to pass and that accepting whatever internal state presents itself heralds a place in the transformative process. Again, every step is progress.

For many, **The Soul-Discovery Journalbook** guides readers through newly charted waters. Others may find themselves in familiar seas. In general, anything new can feel strange because we are creatures of habit, so what's unfamiliar often breeds discomfort. Remember all of life and living, whether pleasurable, unusual, or challenging, provides valuable opportunities for growth.

Knowing that self-discovery may feel challenging or uncomfortable (in life or in a journey within these pages), what is a good benchmark for constructive navigation? Simply said, work within a manageable range. What is manageable? Well, that varies from person to person and experience to experience. Most importantly, when we live mindfully by paying attention to the body, feelings, thoughts, and behaviors, all reveal valuable information. Take time to express, reflect, sit with, witness, journal, draw, feel, bawl your eyes out, meditate, laugh like crazy, walk, talk with a friend…using whatever processing tools and pace that is workable. And remember, discomfort is where the magic happens, especially as we allow it to help us transform what no longer serves our highest and best.

If, however, you feel increasingly overwhelmed to the point that days or weeks are consumed by a negative internal state, consider counseling or therapy. A widely accepted misperception says that we must be sick, weak, crazy, or unable to heal to seek help. Our world holds so much assistance. The mere desire for a guide to light our path or to help develop tools currently beyond our awareness provides a hand to cross a deep and swollen river of challenges - perceived obstacles need not obstruct our journey forward with so much help available.

As a teacher and therapist, student and client, my beliefs firmly rest with getting assistance to learn, heal, and grow, instead of continuing to struggle on our own. When we wait until the stresses of life reach a critical mass and we feel that we are breaking, we block our own development. Many may even stretch beyond that point into depression, anxiety, or disease states that not only impair living, but also thwart Life - an expansive expression of Divine force that flows through us with love, joy, and peace.

Most important of all, our True Nature, exposed through soul-discovery, forever remains our internal compass. Within each of us lies this soft, intuitive urging…a feeling…a voice that always guides us toward our highest and best. It leads us Home to the Self that whispers, "Remember Me."

Journaling Suggestions

There are no right or wrong ways to journal. The process itself is a very personal and individual one. The suggestions intended within this section offer a guide to make the most out of journaling and the journeys within these pages; quick references, helpful tools, and useful reminders assist and enhance your personal journaling process.

For this author, journaling is much more than a log of events. It is a place to process thoughts, feelings, emotions, situations, and reactions as a multi-sensory and multi-media experience. Drawings, descriptions, and pointed notes coalesce to illuminate limiting beliefs, unhelpful patterns, and habits of our ego-based personality. As our internal climate unfolds before us, it can be examined non-judgmentally, giving room to align with our true Self.

Listed below are general journaling suggestions for this book series, as well as journaling beyond these pages. While some appear self-explanatory, other specific suggestions/exercises unfold in the chapters to come, deepening the practice and understanding of particular topics. So, if a suggestion appears cryptic or elusive, know that relevant exploration lies in subsequent chapters.

- Create a safe, quiet place to write, free from distractions, foot traffic, and curious eyes whenever possible.
- The blank canvas for the journeys within each chapter may not provide enough room to complete what you are processing. Consider a separate journal for additional space, one in lieu of writing within these pages, some combination of the two, or another creative solution to comfortably navigate these exercises.
- If choosing a journal, consider one that offers the space to draw, write, color, and paste items. Whether you create one out of your own paper or discover another that feels right, all journals help to honor and observe your progress.
- Find a private place to keep this book series and/or your journal to give you the mental and emotional space to write freely - freedom from the concern that anything shared may be exposed without your permission.

- Be generous and loving - "gift" yourself the time to spend with *you* writing, exploring, and being.

- Log events that you experience or imagine and your accompanying thoughts, emotional reactions, and behaviors in response to those experiences.

- Give yourself permission to express all thoughts, emotions, and feelings, freeing yourself from censoring. This may mean swearing, scribbling, yelling, punching a pillow, running, crying, etc.

- If you have difficulty identifying or reaching elusive emotions and thoughts, props like music, photos, videos, and movies facilitate expression, bringing to the surface what may be suppressed, compartmentalized, hidden, or stuffed.

- Use gratitude and affirmations freely to promote the flow of positive energy, manifestation, and creative growth.

- Consider writing out an action plan, where appropriate, to assist the development of new patterns of behavior, thoughts, emotions, and feelings, even if that plan is simply to observe yourself and your world. This particularly helps when writing about situations that seem problematic.

- Be prepared to shred and/or burn pages when you feel the need or as a means of letting go of old energy, emotions, thoughts, or situations. Even when we have a safe location for our journal, sometimes the mere thought that others could somehow discover our hiding place inhibits our writing. Remember, shredding or burning pages is always an option to give us the space to freely express.

- Encourage and remind yourself to develop the habit of non-judgmental self-observation, seeing anything that surfaces not as "good or bad" but as an opportunity for change and growth.

- As often as possible, consider the broader context of what you uncover through each journey; examine how current circumstances are part of a bigger picture that feeds personal patterns in life relating to other situations, work experiences, family, or community interactions.

- Remember that this is a path…a journey…and *all* it holds is for *you* and not for someone else, even though *everyone* in your life benefits from your growth.

- Affirm that you deserve to have the time and space for growth, self-development, and soul-discovery.

- Most of all, enjoy your soul-discovery as much as possible. Life is an adventure and you are journeying to YOU!

Using Guided Meditations

Throughout **The Soul-Discovery Journalbook** series, various journeys make use of guided meditations. Just as notes create melodies, guided meditations use words to create mental images and multi-sensory experiences. Like painting a picture in the mind, colorful descriptions build vivid landscapes where readers travel to places and states of consciousness. Images, feelings, and thoughts move through the reader or listener producing relaxation, reflection, introspection, and/or revelation - an alternate universe of the astral plane rich with opportunity, solutions, and inner peace.

Generally, the imagery of guided meditation takes us to a tranquil setting to lower stress and cultivate calmness. This priceless passport into the ethers enables us to leave our chaotic world behind so we may rest in alignment with our Self. As we follow along, allowing our imagination to flow, we may find our five senses alight with the mere suggestions of wind, sunshine, or fragrant flowers. Additionally, the language offers suggestions to the conscious mind but may hold deeper, subconscious meaning. For example, water (symbolic of emotions and cleansing) identifies or clears away old emotional debris.

Guided meditations, however, offer much more than wrapping us in a gentle blanket of comfort. Within this book series, they aid in the discovery of our mind's hidden corners, the excavation of internal states forgotten or veiled, and the recreation of situations to discover more loving solutions.

Sometimes when navigating a guided meditation, we experience internal states (thoughts, feelings, images, etc.) that differ from the presented language. At these junctures, what surfaces may demonstrate our mind's wandering nature, our personal discomfort, or a consciousness beyond our awareness attempting to reveal its secrets. These points of seeming digression can serve as food for deeper understanding. Giving permission for ourselves to experience whatever arises, we can trust that valuable clues to our inner world are being shown, the very clues needed to navigate soul-discovery.

Readers will find the guided meditations within these pages written out, as well as recorded for those who desire a digital version for easy listening. Recorded meditations can be found on www.pathways2innerpeace.com on the OM page, which is linked through the QR code next to each written meditation. Some readers may find reading the meditations suitable, retaining the essence enough to re-create the mental imagery without the step-by-step language. Others may desire the help of a trusted friend or partner to read the meditation out loud. Most will find the recordings provided through this author's website calming and simple to use, generating the visual cues desired. Playing "Goldilocks", like the beloved, golden-haired, curious, storybook child of yesteryear, offers the opportunity to try out different approaches to determine what feels best.

Simply said, we can remember the following:

- Follow the description in the guided meditations and allow the imagery to unfold in your mind's eye.
- Let the experiences move through you and flow instead of grabbing or wrestling with any specific words or descriptions.
- Observe what you experience by paying attention to surfacing images, feelings, emotions, thoughts, and body sensations.

Our Sacred Space

What comes to mind when thinking about a sacred space? Is it a location…a pillow-filled room lined with candles, plants, and an inviting rainbow of soothing colors, smells, and sounds that feed us on all levels? Maybe we imagine an empty room, bereft of detail and things to distract; instead, its clean lines and surfaces feel simple and uncluttered. Whatever we envision, all can benefit from a room, corner, or little hideaway from the world - a place to temporarily remove ourselves from the responsibilities and demands of this earth adventure. A physical sacred space provides the place to journal, center, meditate, contemplate, do soul-discovery, and just be, taking a break from everything that pulls us in twenty different directions.

Let's stop for a moment and contemplate a sacred space. How do you feel about creating it? Using it? Some may envision a space perfect for them but immediately dismiss its creation as a wild fantasy, feeling as if the time, physical place, or an overall lack of freedom makes it impossible. Others may immediately consider expense or practicality. Some may question whether they deserve the time to go there. Regardless of your mindset, I encourage all who travel these pages to create a sacred space that helps quiet the mind, rest the body, and feed the soul. Remember, it doesn't have to be large or fancy or cause more burden to an already busy life.

In the beginning of my journey, I used a corner of my bedroom where I placed a small, portable stereo and a chair. My intent set the energy. Centering and meditating in the space grounded and infused it with my desire for personal growth. With some boundaries for my children like "Don't interrupt unless there's an emergency," and "If you want to join me, you must be quiet and sit still; if not, please find something to do until Mommy is done," I established a sanctuary oriented to self-care that grew into its own room filled with plants, healing crystals, spiritual books, and an abiding climate of peace, harmony, and healing.

I know you might be thinking, "A space is great, but what about the mental and emotional freedom to center, express, and be me?" Only you can give yourself the time and space for self-nourishment, as well as the permission to express your thoughts and feelings honestly and openly. When you allow it, the tools and exercises in this book series will lead the way.

So, let's first intentionally select a physical space designed to cultivate peacefulness, a place to do your inner work, center, meditate, and remove yourself from the world, if only briefly.

Most importantly, a sacred space has:

- freedom from foot traffic and interruptions;
- freedom from phones, computers, or TV noise, or has devices that can be silenced;
- a comfortable chair or floor cushions and a cozy blanket;
- pens, pencils, markers, crayons, paint, paper, a journal - materials to allow for self-expression;
- incense or sage to clear unwanted, heavy energies (see Wynebgwrthucher); and
- a candle for comfort, to draw angelic help, and to represent your eternal light.

The following can be added as you are drawn to provide support on your path:

- music and/or white noise like a fan or small fountain;
- plants or flowers to infuse your area with nature, cultivate beauty, and honor life;
- an altar with objects and images to represent your growth;
- crystals that resonate with you; trust the ones that draw your attention; and
- mindful reminders such as quotes, images, and photos that support you on your journey.

Remembering that self-care makes us better caretakers of everyone and everything in our lives, even small breaks and respite from busyness, chores, or chaos nurture us through our day. Thirty minutes, two or three times a week, gifts us the opportunities for the personal feeding of mind, body, and spirit, which facilitates growth and soul-discovery. As we honor ourselves and allow for the exploration of our inner climate through a sacred space in geography and time, we grow awareness of our most important self - our sacred space within.

Journey:
Creating Sacred Space

Review the list of qualities of a sacred space.

Make your own list of essentials for a little sanctuary in your home or apartment. What feels vital to support the ways you desire to travel soul-discovery and your personal growth? Remember, this is the place where you'll go to do your inner work, center, and meditate, cultivating inner peace.

Collect and arrange the items from your list in your sacred space.

Journal about the process of creating it including any reactions or challenges along the way.

How do you feel having a special place just for you, dedicated to your soul-discovery and the journeys in this book series?

Now you're ready for centering!

Centering

A common practice to many traditions (yoga, martial arts, spiritual studies, mindfulness), centering may be used anywhere and anytime to gain clarity, calm the mind, soothe emotions, and/or bring a sense of peacefulness. We center to rest in a consciousness beyond our focus on the external world and our internal climate. When desired, it segues to meditation.

Centering, defined as a gathering of our energies to shift of our attention inward, is meant to quiet all our layers - physical, mental, and emotional. As we do this, we first notice our body sensations. How our body feels - current aches and pains, general health, lack or abundance/quality of sleep, restlessness, etc. - affects our centering. When our body hurts or doesn't feel well, for example, much of our attention may go to that discomfort. Bypassing those sensations often requires time or practice; we can even choose to wait until we feel healthier or employ centering to move past our physical discomfort.

Equally challenging, our mental chatter appears as a busy brain, clamoring and begging for notice as lists, chores, or conversations replay in our mind. At other times, our ranges and fluctuations of feelings may dominate, as emotions about unresolved situations create an internal unrest that makes sitting and our inward focus even more uncomfortable.

Our inner static can often feel difficult to ignore; if we forcefully dismiss it, engaging in a battle of sorts, it behaves like a wayward child demanding attention. This becomes particularly evident with our mind, which moves constantly in varying degrees, even when we remove our active attention from it. As such, our mental activity consistently runs in the background, much like a computer with multiple programs open but invisible. As it joins with our physical and emotional state, even what appears as seemingly silent operation taxes our system. Thus, the noise of our little self accumulates and compounds with other external busyness, creating discomfort and turmoil. No wonder we experience so much stress and dis-ease, especially when we ignore our needs or can't seem to give ourselves a gentle respite.

Here's the good news...when we address the inner static of the little self, it presents a roadmap to the lessons we are here to learn. As we gently observe (our body, thoughts, and emotions), we can learn to step back and watch what we're experiencing as a neutral bystander - non-judgmental observation. Through this process and what it shows us, we become adept at allowing experiences to move through us without attachment. As such, we can transition to meditation, which guides us to hear the soft voice of our Higher Self - the core of peace within us as an innate facet of our True Nature. Because the Higher Self's voice for peace lies within us, through meditation we have a path leading to It; however, we need a resolute willingness to move past the distractions of our body, navigate the jungles of our mind, and clear away the overgrown vines and weeds of our emotions so we can rest in the comforting arms of Self. With consistent centering and meditation, combined with transformation through soul-discovery (the journaling, reflecting, and releasing), we are led from an external space to the inner jewel - a Sacred Space within, Union with our Higher Self.

As we progress in soul-discovery, the dedication and practice of centering breeds a skill set, enabling us to center among environmental energies like noise and people. That does not mean that our space at home will no longer serve us but rather that we expand our scope of practice beyond our own walls, making it portable to other times and places to gently assist us in our growth.

So, if you already have an established practice, great! If not, refer to the centering journey on the following page. As often as possible, allow the time for centering before each journey. This practice prepares all of us to gain more from every experience, whether it's learning, self-exploration, or soul-discovery. For additional guidance, refer to **Breathe** and **Quieting Our Mind** in **Volume II**.

Journey: Centering

The following QR Code provides the recorded version of this centering exercise on www.pathways2innerpeace.com via the OM page. If you have no access to the internet, find a friend or partner to read this guided imagery to you. The following journey incorporates aligning your subtle bodies and chakras and progressively relaxes you into the whole of a centering practice.

Use your created sacred space or find a temporary location, making it as free from noise and distractions as possible. Sit comfortably with your feet flat on the floor, hands resting comfortably on your lap while your core muscles remain supported by using good posture to give space for your lungs to fully expand. If drawn, place your palms facing upward in a position to receive.

Close your eyes and take three slow, deep breaths. Allow your attention to withdraw from all outside stimuli. Just let everything from your surroundings gradually fall away, bringing your awareness inward. Breathe slowly and comfortably.

Ask to be aligned completely on every level of your being where every chakra and subtle body operates in perfect synchronicity and symmetry in accordance with your True Nature. Ground your energy by envisioning large, thick roots that travel from the bottoms of your feet into the earth. These roots travel through all levels of the rich soil, reaching deeply within our sacred Mother who nurtures and helps sustain your physical body.

Now inhale and envision a bright stream of light from above you, entering the top of your head, filling your body. As you exhale, this light pushes out any tension, mood, or thoughts that are not for your highest and best. You see and feel the light cleanse and release any negativity, heaviness, or constrictions, first in your head, then your neck and shoulders. It moves into your arms and hands, cleansing all tension. The warmth continues into your chest and torso as you breathe in. Now the light moves into your hips and you take a deep breath to help it along its path. It continues down the rest of your form into your thighs…knees…calves, down into the ankles and feet. Every part of your body feels relaxed and cleansed in this light as it fills every cell of your being. Breathe in and feel its presence. This spiritual light from Source feeds you on all levels, making your journey here possible. It surrounds you and all of life and is an integral part of your Divinity, drawn to you by your intent and grounded by the deep earth roots from your feet. The two energies meet to make your journey here loving, nurturing, and powerful.

Extend the time as you desire. As you rest in this place, relaxed and whole, stay centered in the light and in the awareness of your rooted sustenance. Should you drift off and lose focus, bring yourself back to being in the light. Remember to be gentle with yourself, as your thoughts may wander over and over again.

Continue with this centering journey for a few moments and allow any thoughts, sounds, or sensations that interrupt to just fall away. When ready, return your awareness to the room, opening your eyes. Take a nice deep breath. Give yourself a few moments to rest with eyes open before rising to your feet.

You're ready to meet whatever lies before you.

We Are Guided

Past the veil between our physical world and the next - a consciousness just beyond our normal five senses - helpers, passed loved ones, spirit guides, and angels call to our hearts to accept their loving assistance. All they require is our willingness to receive what they offer. This help, our personal, spiritual GPS, remains eternally available. As we reach out, even in our darkest hour, know that Divine helpers wait patiently for our outstretched hand to comfort, support, guide us upward, counsel, and facilitate growth.

We may feel that only those imbued with "special powers" gain access to the other side. Our Divine helpers don't require us to possess special sight (clairvoyance), psychic hearing (clairaudience), or feeling their presence (clairsentience) in order for us to acquire and accept their aid. All they offer remains ever available, though we can consciously open the channel and better attune to our spiritual GPS for help and guidance.

The following is a brief list that facilitates aid from our Divine helpers in a direct way:

1. an intent (thought fueled by feeling) or desire;
2. an openness to receive what may be offered;
3. trust - a knowing that as we ask, the Universe replies;
4. raising our vibration to align with spiritual and personal evolvement; and
5. centering and meditating to open to our Higher Self, our True Nature.

> ...in situations, you have to go within yourself and know the force, the power of Spirit. Now when you do that, angel help comes in instantly, for that's what we're there for. We come and we hold that vibration of spirituality around you and we see you through every bit of it.[1]

Our Divine helpers support us constantly, aiding us in all our day-to-day earthly tasks, as well as in our climb inward and upward. They work diligently to provide

---
[1] Donovan, Rev. Penny (2017). *Angels, Spirit Guides & Other Beings: Selected Lessons from an Archangel.* Albany, NY: Sacred Garden Fellowship.

information in ways that are personal and meaningful through people we encounter, songs on the radio, little coincidences on our path, and other seemingly insignificant signs that beg for our eyes, ears, and hearts. Their assistance can even come to us more easily as we clarify our desires and remember the importance of our intent; intent must be specific enough to address our aspirations and yet broad enough to allow for the Universe to reveal its gifts. Additionally, we can ask based on the talent or jobs of our helpers.

The following offers a general overview of our Divine guidance team:

- Angels are created with specific purposes and operate accordingly. Angels of Healing or Angels of Teaching serve as examples. Generally speaking, angels always assist us from the spiritual outlook of any situation. They provide support, guidance, strength, and love.

- Guides, entities who have spent time incarnated on Earth, understand the inner workings of our world. They help with life duties, chores, and activities, like finding a parking spot, locating keys, or writing a letter.

- Passed-over loved ones may understand our life's current influences or direction based on perspectives from their most recent incarnation combined with time in Spirit. They may offer guidance on areas where we could benefit from healing or growth.

- Our Higher Self knows beyond our three-dimensional existence the Truth of our being and unerringly guides us to that Truth.

Regardless of where we direct our attention - to soul-discovery, solving life's problems, or finding our keys - many opportunities for help and guidance lie before us. Below are some examples of how we might ask for what is ever-present, tapping into our personal spiritual GPS:

- I ask my _____ (angels, guides, Higher Self) to help me remember what is only for my highest and best.

- I ask my _____ (angels, guides, Higher Self) to help me pay attention to when my ego sabotages me in my actions, thoughts, and emotions.

- I ask my _____ (angels, guides, loved ones, Higher Self) to show me what I need to understand about _____ (name the situation) for my highest and best. I desire to heal this situation. I thank you for this guidance.

- I ask my _____ (angels, guides, loved ones, Higher Self) to help me find the courage, compassion, love, understanding, peace, forgiveness, etc. toward _____ (name persons) in this _____ (name the situation) for my highest and best.

- I ask that the Divine, Cosmic, Universal power of Pure Love work through me to transform this situation for my highest and best and for all involved.

One way I consciously open the door happens before sleep. Intentionally asking for guidance at this time often creates vivid dreams that fill the night hours; some I remember in detail while others linger in wisps. Whatever transpires, I'm sure to journal as much as possible immediately upon waking. Though at times the messages remain cryptic, the symbolism often holds personal significance.

By welcoming Divine helpers to our journey, we can consciously practice asking for assistance and pay attention to all that unfolds before us. Opening to their love around us, we can become more familiar with their energy through simple exercises such as asking for help in finding objects, for guidance on journaling exercises, and for assistance with centering. The more we practice, the more ease we find in attuning to the help. Expanding from simple requests to more complicated endeavors, know that no task is too small. As always, remember to thank these dedicated helpers along the way with thoughts of gratitude, flowers, or some small colorful tokens of appreciation. Angels especially love our words and gestures of thanks for their constant and unending dedication.

For more information on this topic, see **Only Love is Real** in **Volume II**, and **We Are So Loved** and **Let Your Love-light Shine** in **Volume III**.

Journey: Spiritual GPS

Consider all the situations where you can ask for Divine helpers to guide and assist you. List them here.

Write out your personal invitation for help, journaling a request for each item of your list using the examples provided to assist you.

How do you feel knowing you are so loved and guided?

Setting Our Intent

Our life unfolds based on our intent - the energy we put forth to fulfill desires, wants, and needs as thought activated by the power of our feelings. Intent arises from the levels of our conscious mind, as well as from our subconscious, infusing and fueling every situation.

Because setting intentions frames and shapes life experiences, let's take a moment to clarify your intent for this journey as a liberating, non-judgmental adventure of self-discovery and transformation aligned only with your highest and best. As we consciously affirm a path of growth through theses energies, any subconscious opposition becomes more easily noticed and released. Furthermore, the general acceptance we extend to ourselves allows us to be where we are at any given time, trusting in the process and most of all ourselves.

Below are suggested intentions. Each may operate as a template or a guide:

- I embark on this journey to grow on all levels, cultivating joy, peace, and love in my life.

- I intend to allow my inner child to play throughout my experiences.

- I intend to uncover and allow all aspects of my personality to be revealed.

- I intend to examine, accept, and ultimately let go of anything that no longer serves me.

- I intend to reveal the Truth of my being by connecting with my Higher Self.

- I intend to use what I discover only as a tool to grow and not as a source of judgment to criticize myself.

- I intend to develop trust in myself and to accept that I am doing my best at any given moment.

- I intend to accept and trust that all things beyond my understanding will be revealed in perfect timing.

- I intend to do no harm nor be harmed by what I may experience or write about myself or others; I ask that all negative emotions be released and transformed, replacing their absence with love.

- I allow my mind and my heart to open to all possibilities, knowing that this openness will only help me move toward Truth, understanding, and self-acceptance.

Journey I:
Setting Your Intent

Retreating to your sacred space, take a moment to rest quietly and center.

Reflect on the journey you desire. How would you like to navigate this multi-volume adventure in soul-discovery?

Create your intentions and write them down, using the examples in the chapter as a guide.

Journey II: Reflections

Now take a moment to read your intentions out loud. Allow yourself to connect with them, feeling the power they hold.

Imagine yourself healthier, happier, more loving, and abundant.

Reflect by journaling on your experience, considering the following questions: How did you feel writing your intentions?

Did you notice any thoughts about the experience?

How did you feel while reading your intentions to yourself or out loud? After?

Continue imagining yourself healthier, happier, more loving, and abundant as your soul-discovery unfolds.

First Glance

You're off to a great start! In **Setting the Stage**, you've gathered some vital tools to start your adventure. Let's journey on.

First Glance intends to help you wet your toes in the lake of self-reflection. In this section, each chapter and its accompanying journeys create a wonderful opportunity in exploration! This gentle opening to soul-discovery, **First Glance**, offers new ways to uncover you.

As you navigate these chapters, know that topics covered more deeply in future volumes await your arrival. Patience! Great value lies in this beginning section, providing the mildly sloping trail to gain strength and to practice looking within. With each step, you collect more tools for your pilgrimage, and what you seek shall reveal itself in perfect timing.

Trust the path ahead and trust in yourself, allowing your mind and heart to lead the way for your highest and best.

Freedom!

Disobedience is the true foundation of liberty.
— Henry David Thoreau

Life is an expansive sea of self-expression, rich with endless possibilities and limited only by our own imagination and grit. In truth, we are expression - a vibrant light igniting an intelligent mass of cosmic dust. Regardless of the form we take, we have the freedom to choose the how, what, where, and when of our expression; easy for some but for others, a bit more challenging.

The very nature of this book series hinges on expression, one of the core principles of navigating soul-discovery. Experimenting with expression and its various forms helps us discover new ways to witness our internal climate and the lessons presented in our lives. The journaling processes within these pages allow energy to flow from us and onto the page to be observed, aiding our investigation. At times, what we've held securely within our mind can even take on new meaning when revealed in front of us. What happens will be as personal as we allow it to be.

Throughout these pages are repeated prompts to pay attention - to notice emotions, thoughts, behaviors, body sensations, compulsions, and reactions. What surfaces in us - from the moment our eyes touch the first chapter or journey to the point when we lift our pen from the page, and even days or weeks beyond - feeds, informs, and aids our growth. In these spaces, betwixt and between, an unveiling, a discovery, a revelation occurs. All present a wonderful opportunity to know ourselves more each day.

The Soul-Discovery Journalbook

Journey: Freedom!

Set aside time in your sacred space, centering before you begin.

For some, this exercise will seem silly, juvenile, and absurd. For others, liberating and relaxing. Remember, there are no right answers or right reactions, only YOUR answers and reactions... uniquely yours. What you experience represents a place that is exactly where you are meant to be - right now, this moment, pen in hand.

Let's set the energy for freedom - the freedom of expression. Break the rules of convention. Scribble away! Yes, you read correctly. Use this page and/or another to scribble or doodle your heart out. Allow yourself to express what you're feeling, what you've been holding in, what seems to be against the rules, what may seem unproductive or silly.

Pay attention to all your thoughts and feelings from moments ago to the end of this journey, then move onto the next chapter to continue.
Go for it! Let YOU out!

More scribbling!

Scribbled Reflections

*Don't be satisfied with stories, how things have gone for others.
Unfold your own myth, without complicated explanation.*

— Rumi

Take a nice, cleansing breath. If inclined, stand up and jump around and get that last little bit of energy out. The **Freedom!** journey that started **First Glance** comes to completion in this chapter, though you may desire to revisit the experience to release tension or emotions, or even for fun. **Scribbled Reflections** allows for exploration of the obvious and not so obvious feelings, mental chatter, and trends revealed through the **Freedom!** doodling journey. This process begins a calling forth of our many layers through witnessing, experiencing, observing, and ultimately accepting wherever we are at any given moment.

We are each a beautiful crystal with many facets - some pure, brilliant, and colorful… others cloudy, occluded, and unwanted. These parts blend uniquely into a whole, representing a consciousness that evolves with the work. Looking through the veil of what seems to obscure our perfect beauty, we discover the clear precious gem that shines at the very heart of each of us. Many opportunities lie ahead to explore these facets and discover our gem, one small journey at a time.

Let's travel on, setting the pace that works for you. Know that whatever you find is exactly where you need to be.

Journey I: Reflections

Write out reflections about your experience, scribbling and doodling from the **Freedom!** chapter.

Consider the following questions, reflecting on the times before, during, and after the exercise:

What thoughts, feelings, and emotions did you experience?

Did you notice any body sensations? Can you describe what you felt?

Did you notice any accompanying emotions?

How did you find the exercise - easy or difficult, ridiculous or fun, embarrassing or freeing? Why?

Journey II: Symbolism

Write out a description of any shapes, patterns, or symbols that emerged in **Freedom!** Make sure to include your feelings and thoughts you noticed about them in the process of scribbling. Now, journal your thoughts and feelings about these patterns, shapes, or symbols as you observe your drawing now. To aid understanding, describe what you see as if having a conversation. Sometimes the words we choose reveal hidden impressions.

Example: "My page has tight scribbles covering half the page. They are perfectly spaced, nearly equal in size, and orderly in rows. The thoughts of freedom with the exercise of scribbling all over the page made me feel a bit anxious."

Research your scribbles using a symbolism dictionary or other resources, journaling what you uncover.

Journal about broader meanings by considering the following: Does what you experienced reveal a trend in how you approach certain situations with activities, relationships, work, or life? How do you feel about these trends?

Example (interpretation of previous example): "Perhaps, I like things predictable and orderly. (trend) When life doesn't neatly fall into place like perfect rows, the chaos makes me anxious." (feeling about trend)

I trust that your "scribble page" resulted in some interesting reflections. Sometimes the simplest of exercises result in some of the most profound and thought-provoking experiences. When doing these exercises with clients and workshop participants, individuals often discover that scribbling and the accompanying emotions and thoughts that emerge reflect current struggles, issues, and/or trends. You may have made similar discoveries. Should this exercise still seem a mystery, don't worry. Many more opportunities of soul-discovery await!

Through the Looking Glass

Everything has beauty, but not everyone sees it.

— *Confucius*

Curiously, in writing this chapter, as I searched for "self-love" synonyms, I came upon a striking conflict that clearly identifies a societal view about this kind of love. Terms like egotism, selfishness, egocentricity, narcissism, self-centeredness, self-interest, vanity, and conceit outnumber the few healthy references to self-love like self-esteem and self-respect. So, at the risk of proposing an unhealthy self-focus, know that this chapter intends to help us truly embrace ourselves whatever size, shape, weight, skin color, and gender expression we wear in this lifetime. Self-love begins with the acceptance of what is, including our physical form. Learning to love and appreciate ourselves as we are illuminates powerful lessons about judgment, appearances, and social or family norms.

Growing up in a house where physical appearance held great value, an importance above all else, messages about body weight, moles, blemishes, and clothing size stood alongside an adherence to wearing well-cared-for, neat, and perfectly coordinated name brand clothing. Coupled with ongoing messages from society and a media barrage focusing on unrealistic body images, anyone could guess how much my self-esteem took a hit. As a result, self-acceptance became a big lesson on my path, as it is for many.

This chapter offers an opportunity to really pay attention to how physical appearance plays out in our life by exploring the feelings and thoughts conjured by our reflection, self-portrait, or photographs. Do we criticize every line, bump, or hair out of place? Can we truly appreciate our physical form with all its perceived nuances? Can we honor and love our masculine, feminine, and/or non-binary presentation and how we share it with the world? And what do these attitudes tell us about our deeper layers…our life experiences? Welcome to the start of self-acceptance and self-love.

Journey I: Selfie

Find a current photo of yourself. A simple image printed on paper is fine.

Now spend time centering in your sacred space or a quiet room.

Next, tape or glue your image in the space to the right or in another journal.

Draw, color, or attach a frame around your image, decorating as you see fit.

Be sure to write your name, nickname, and today's date near the photo.

Journey II: Draw

Draw a self-portrait using any media you desire.

Again, add your name, nickname, and the date.

Journey III: Reflections

Return to your sacred space to relax and center. Ask for assistance from your Divine helpers as you are drawn, calling on them to support, guide, or aid your understanding.

In gentle reflection, pay attention to what thoughts and feelings come to you about the chapter in general.

Now reflect on doing **Journeys I** and **II**. If judgments surface (good, bad, right, wrong labels), pay attention to them, noting all your thoughts, feelings, and experiences.

Now look at your photo and self-portrait. How do you feel looking at yourself?

Note what you like and dislike both inside and out. How long have you felt this way about these qualities or traits? In what ways would you like to change? What aspects of yourself need your love and acceptance?

Our Internal Climate

*The only real failure in life is
not to be true to the best one knows.*

— *Buddha*

As humans, we experience a wide range of emotions and feelings, a seeming reaction or response to what we encounter in our world. Our beliefs, created through how we perceive the vast collection of situations in this lifetime combined with our soul's immense history, trigger our reactions. (See **From Consciousness to Awareness** in **Volume III**.)

Sorting out our internal climate takes patience, courage, and practice. Sometimes our busyness and distractions with life keep us from becoming aware of what's happening inside of us. We may even become overwhelmed by our emotions and feelings or resign ourselves to being fully immersed in the energy of them as they govern us and not the other way around. Giving ourselves the time to be with whatever surfaces and to allow a full reveal is an important part of the soul-discovery process. And as we let the awareness of our internal experiences unfold, we can begin stepping back to witness the situation and our personal climate in an accepting way, ultimately leading to resolution.

At first, just experiencing and observing our feelings and emotions may feel quite foreign, especially if what surfaces motivates us to DO something, like use activity to block the feeling or obsessively focus on our reaction or an event's details. We may even strive to uncover a solution to "fix" whatever we perceive as problematic, to leave the discomfort of our emotional state behind and only operate intellectually. Sure, there will be times and situations that call for action; there always will be. When, however, we can be with ourselves, just BE - moving through the experience and allowing whatever needs to be expressed to flow through us - then everything transforms into an opportunity for healing and growth. This key unlocks our own prison of fixing, overthinking, or frenetically doing.

Additionally, being with ourselves helps keep us from pushing our emotional energy out of our consciousness where it would remain unresolved or hidden. Be cautioned; let's not confuse "being with" with marinating in our emotions. Expressing our emotional energy by giving it a way to move through us is a potent transformational tool. Our allowing and "being with" can help us replace our old tendencies to ignore, push away, wallow, overanalyze, or numb out any uncomfortable internal climate. And while these practices (allowing and being with) remain core principles of soul-discovery, many chapters to come build on this foundation.

As we observe our internal climate and all that it shows us, we may also find that identifying the *intensity* of what we feel to be quite helpful. A simple 1 to 10 scale illuminates just how high our emotions can climb at any given moment. The rating pinpoints how we feel more quantifiably, offering a data point for future observation, as well as a tangible way to log our progress. As we become clearer in recognizing how we feel, we become more adept at healing through soul-discovery, as well as growing through simple self-care activities.

Part of this chapter's healing includes creating a list and subsequent plan for self-care. Use the following guide for self-love ideas to nurture and soothe our ruffled feathers and bruised hearts.

- Journaling (of course)
- Drawing/coloring
- Walking/hiking
- Taking a bath/shower
- Listening to music
- Receiving energy healing
- Meditating
- Getting takeout/dinner out
- Buying yourself a treat
- Having a hot cup of tea
- Getting a massage
- Being in nature

Let's explore our emotions and feelings, unearthing our internal landscape. Four basic emotions - glad, mad, sad, and scared - serve as our guide. Many variations to these fabulous four, our personal barometer put into words, describe the nuances of our reactions and sentiments and help us identify how we experience life.

Let's be brave, real, and present!

Journey I: Create

Retreat to your sacred space, spending time to relax and center.

Create your own resource for feelings and emotions. Begin by making a list of all the feelings and emotions that you can think of.

Consider other sources to help you develop your list. Make the list as comprehensive as possible, providing nuances and variations for each of the four basic states - glad, mad, sad, and scared.

If you feel particularly creative, draw a word cloud or graphic using your word list, placing it here. To create a free word cloud, visit www.wordclouds.com.

Journey II: Feel

Take a moment to center, resting comfortably with each breath as you relax in your sacred space. Invite your Divine helpers to join you on this journey, asking to be shown whatever is for your highest and best.

Taking one emotion at a time, write about an event or situation that "caused" you to feel glad, mad, sad, or scared, including any other variations of the feeling/emotion from your list. Consider allowing your mind to naturally go to situations that stand out as particularly intense or powerful.

Be sure to rate each emotion on a scale of 1 - 10, with 10 for the highest intensity of that emotion.

When journaling each emotion, four different situations may emerge, or one situation where you experienced all four states. Whatever the case, be sure to give each its due attention.

Journey III: Reflections

Journal your reflections about **Journey II**, experiencing each - glad, mad, sad, and scared.

Did any identified emotion lead to another? In other words, when anger was the surface emotion, did you notice sadness under it or vice versa?

Do you notice a trend in how you rated your emotions on a 1 - 10 scale?

Did you experience body sensations while reflecting?

Did **Journey II** help you see any emotion that you experience more frequently than others?

Are there emotions you are more or less comfortable with than others? If so, what fears or concerns do any of them bring? Why?

Journey IV: Self-Care

Navigating a more intense internal climate calls for self-care. Returning to the rating of your emotions in **Journey II**, reflect on what you observed.

As a benchmark, let's consider a rating of 5 and above as the need for self-care. Make a list of what self-care is to you using the list included in the chapter as a guide.

Now create a plan for when you will use it to love yourself back to calm.

Ex: When I reach 5 on my angry scale, I will take a 15-minute walk.

Ex: When I reach 5 on any emotion, I will write about how I feel in my journal.

That's What I Like

Very little is needed to make a happy life;
it is all within yourself, in your way of thinking.
— Marcus Aurelius

Being human, we live and learn through our five senses, which collectively serve as a guidance system that helps us understand and interact with our three-dimensional world. Because our physical survival appears to intimately depend on our sight, sound, touch, taste, and smell, we become undeniably attached to our senses and the ways they inform and aid our interactions.

We need not look far to witness the significance of senses throughout our lifespan. In utero, we respond to our mother's touch (to her own belly) and voice.[2] Months later, as we hatch into a new world to explore as newborns, we arrive in a strange land with foreign people to navigate more experiences. Physically weak, helpless, and dependent, our survival hinges on everyone around us. A giant receptacle of information, we touch everything and explore with our mouth. As our vision sharpens, our eyes follow all, watching, observing, gathering more information. Sounds continue to soothe, intrigue, confuse, and/or startle. Touch lets us know that we are okay, safe, and loved or makes us feel love's absence. Our relationship with food is critical, as hunger feels like pain.

As we grow, language comes and we catalog our world through labels determined by our relationship with the what's, who's, and where's of our life. We apply our five senses to everyone and everything to know what makes us feel good, safe, loved, and happy.

---

[2] Marx, V. and Nagy, E. (2015). *Fetal Behavioural Responses to Maternal Voice and Touch*, PLoS ONE 10(6): e0129118. Retrieved from https://doi.org/10.1371/journal.pone.0129118

And in turn, we find the same for what we want to avoid because it demonstrates harmfulness, an unloving nature, or pain. The hot stove is to be avoided. We squeeze and caress our furry pets because they feel delicious. Maybe we love sweets or pickles or the smell of apples. All our early experiences inform much of how we interact with our world today through connections that may appear elusive and mysterious; some will remain as such while others this chapter hopes to uncover.

The journeys to come offer practice to expand our awareness from the five senses into the great beyond. To reach past our typical experiences into the metaphysical and spiritual realm, we can first attune to our own taste, smell, sight, sound, and touch as a gateway to that consciousness…the very consciousness our logical thinking may fight against. So, let's explore by employing our senses to inform us of what we enjoy, dislike, gravitate toward, or avoid in life. This chapter asks us to acknowledge and record the obvious, subtle, or seemingly hidden pleasures of life as an opportunity to get to know ourselves a little better - what we like, what we don't like, and the associations or connections of both. Just allow the freedom to explore without reasoning away any discoveries. No wrong feelings exist here.

Have fun! Be spontaneous, be childlike, be curious…be you!

Journey I:
Likes or Not

Relax in your sacred space, breathing calmly and naturally to center.

Beginning with eyes closed, pay attention to all senses except sight, one sense at a time. Witness sounds, smells, lingering tastes, and what touches your skin. Be sure to not rush, giving each sense it's due attention. Journal what you witnessed in your world of touch, taste, smell, and hearing.

Now open your eyes and look around your space, taking in what you see.

Make a list of likes and dislikes of what you see around you.

Journey II:
Creative Flow

Allow your creative juices to flow. Expand on your experiences in the world by using imaginative and descriptive language. Write a poem or collection of sentences that describes your world. What do you feel about what you see, hear, smell, taste, and touch?

Ex: I like pink and crimson sunsets after a long, hot summer day.

Ex: I don't like the smell of spoiled milk in a glass peppered with greasy fingerprints.

Journal your experience with this exercise.

Grrrrrrrrrr...

Bitterness is like cancer. It eats upon the host.
But anger is like fire. It burns it all clean.
— Maya Angelou

Irritation, outrage, impatience, resentment, frustration, annoyance, indignation, animosity, and fury are all forms of anger we can encounter throughout our life. A challenging emotion to experience, as well as to express for some, anger remains a normal and very human reaction.

Everyone navigates anger in their own unique way relevant to the themes and experiences of their lives. Specifically, the messages we receive about anger from childhood authority figures, society, the media, and spiritual or religious practices mold our expression of it. How we witnessed anger from others in our childhood, what direct or indirect messages we received about being mad, as well as the consequences of verbalizing or acting out our irritation or annoyance are just a few of the influences everyone faces.

While we may discover our personal brand of difficulty with feeling, expressing, or processing anger, society has distinct ideas about how women and men, girls and boys, should handle and express this emotion. Women, for instance, can experience challenges due to varied gender-biased messages, like the "Good little girls don't get mad" introjects or "Don't" messages. Absorbed as an early mindset, these carry into adulthood to create guilt and anxiety regarding anger. (See **Message in a Bottle** in **Volume V**.) Even when we as females learn to consciously reject these early messages, remnants of them can linger and send tendrils into any of our current behaviors and reactions, creating conflicted feelings about anger or its expression. Additional deterrence may arise through a commonly held mindset in workplace or social interactions where females who express their frustration or annoyance risk being labeled as bitchy, hormonal, or "on the rag".

Anger, my friends, is a human emotion and as such, everyone experiences it. The presence of a uterus does not inherently signify this emotion's absence, regardless of what we are taught. Furthermore, the patriarchal society that appeared to perpetuate the belief that anger stands only as a "manly" attribute will hopefully continue to fade. Regardless, women must get to know their anger, finding the courage and space to clearly look it in the eye. This embraces the archetypal energies of Lilith, the biblical representation of women's equality and the goddess of the Dark Moon, who calls forth the energy of self-assertion and the emergence of our shadow-self.[3,4] As the first wife of Adam, Lilith refused to submit to the missionary position, demanding equality, even in the bedroom. Astrologically, she sings an inspirational song to all women, a potent melody reminding us to stand in our Truth and shine a light on our darkness by urging us to explore the anger that covers the Self.[5] Then, anger truly serves to move us forward, utilizing it constructively, spiritually, and/or vanquishing it to serve our highest good.

Men, on the other hand, impacted by environmental influences like women, encounter messages regarding anger at the other end of the spectrum. Men, in general, expected to embrace anger as an "appropriate" masculine quality, may lean toward or against the messages that communicate that anger equals assertiveness or initiative - a proverbial call to "be a man". As a result, sensitive males, especially boys who behave more gently, quietly, or non-forcefully, may be condemned and labeled as feminine or "sissies", while others who fall into line with an alpha-male mindset may be rewarded for their anger, confusing aggressiveness with assertiveness and force with power.

Regardless of whether we're male or female, the rapid vibration of anger can motivate us to action, to take a stand, or to set boundaries for ourselves when used prudently. At times, it may serve as a virtual passageway, moving us out of a situation that does not serve our highest good. And when anger's time of service comes to completion, we can thank it, release it, and rest in the assistance it provided.

---

[3] Gaines, J. (2018, March). Lilith: Seductress. heroine, or murderer. *Bible History Daily: Biblical Archaeology Society.* Retrieved from https://www.biblicalarchaeology.org/daily/people-cultures-in-the-bible/people-in-the-bible/lilith/
[4] Chilson, Monette (2017). *My Name is Lilith.* United States: A Girl God.com.
[5] Demetra, George (1992). *Mysteries of the Dark Moon: The Healing Power of the Dark Goddess.* New York, NY: HarperCollins.

In general, when transforming anger or any emotion to its highest expression (love), we must be willing to feel however we do in any given moment, accepting where we are. Acceptance helps us connect with how we feel and then subsequently witness any situation as temporary and cleansing. Let's not, however, confuse acceptance with adopting a permanent state of any emotion but rather as an opportunity to understand our perceptions. The way we perceive any situation fuels our reactions. Acceptance of our internal climate and whatever we experience must be embraced as our temporary creation *before* we can release it. And as we acknowledge our feelings and emotions, we can step back to observe our experience and gain a clearer vision of where it is meant to lead us, learning the lessons of life.

So, we begin early within these pages to allow more freedom of expression, intending that what we reveal stands safely bathed in the light of discovery with no harm to anyone. This is a time of pass-through for deeper understanding and transformation.

Welcome to a new residence for hostility, jealousy, irritation, frustration, and rage. May this space serve you well.

Journey I: Grrrrr...

Center in your sacred space to prepare for the next leg of your adventure.

Here we set the intent to express in a way that harms no one, providing the space to allow your anger a safe home.

Consider this page as your place to rant and rave, knowing you can return here again and again as you navigate your soul-discovery.

Scribble, write, color, draw, graffiti, swear, or create a dialogue of all that helps you express anger in whatever way you are drawn to. Use additional pages as you are drawn.

Remember to pay attention to thoughts, emotions, body sensations, and internal chatter as you go.

Journey II: Reflections

Journal your experience with **Journey I**.

Consider the following: How did you feel while you were getting your anger and frustration onto the page(s)?

What experiences did you recall?

How do you feel after?

What old beliefs about anger from childhood authority figures did you remember or hear chattering at you? This may be the voice in your head or negative self-talk that says, "This is silly, wrong, etc."

Can you tell the critics you internalized to stop? Can to tell them that however you feel, it's OK?

The Soul-Discovery Journalbook

Consider using these pages if you find difficulty expressing anger in other exercises. Here you can be free with your emotions in a manner that removes any connections to a specific journey. This is a space for being real, authentic, and open anytime you feel drawn.

Create!

Creativeness often consists of merely turning up what is already there.
— Robert Frost

When we were breathed forth, all the angels rejoiced, celebrating us as amazing, creative beings of light. Creative energy animates our body, flowing from our Divine center, our Higher Self - the pure, loving, and joyful core of our being. In other words, the spark that ignites our creative fire is Spirit, hence the word "inspiration" meaning filled with Spirit or under the immediate influence of Source.

Creativity, awakening, illumination, and inspiration flow from us as an endless expression of our innate energy. As the only entity that creates beyond its own kind - flowers make flowers, dogs produce dogs - we remain limitless, making babies, art, buildings, music, cars...

When we truly enjoy the process of creating, we pour ourselves into it. Whether we make a tasty dessert, paint a mural, design a house, or arrange flowers in a vase, our creative energy pours through us, infusing our creation. As we put our heart into this process and into whatever we create, as we give it our all and feel a sense of joy and unity with what we've made, we experience, as the Greeks say, *meraki*.

So be the creative, inspired, and amazing you! Explore, allowing your beautiful, unique energy pour from your heart onto the page. Bask in the loving feeling of *meraki*. The sky's the limit; your creativity is infinite. Use your imagination. Allow yourself to feel the inspiration; let it to flow through you. You are creation in action!

Journey I: Create

Take a few moments to center in your sacred space, allowing yourself to relax.

Use your creative juices to draw, paint, make a collage, write a poem, create a story. Here lies another opportunity to express.

If you desire other forms of creation that would take place off this page, take a photo of what you create and place it here.

No "right" or "wrong" modalities exist here, so allow yourself to move into the expressive areas that draw your attention.

Journey II: Journal

Journal about your experience creating and expressing.

What thoughts came to mind about the process as you were creating? What thoughts do you have now, as you witness your creation?

How did you feel while you were expressing yourself? About your creation now?

Was this journey easy or difficult? Comfortable or uncomfortable? Why?

Can you find more time for creative endeavors in your life?

How might you benefit by doing so?

Old Habits Die Hard

In any family, measles are less contagious than bad habits.
— Mignon McLaughlin

The repetitive, regular tendencies or practices in daily functioning, those often eliciting our involuntary participation, are known as habits. They become an integral part of our lives as helpful, as well as limiting, entrenchments; the self-care habits that support the health of our physical form stand alongside the pesky, self-sabotage of stress-induced or reactive patterns that become the hard-to-relinquish ruts of daily life.

Habits manifest in all shapes and sizes and are often thought of as an observable behavior. Frequently, our existing habits occur automatically without our consistent or conscious participation, mostly because we lose the need for active focus. Take driving, for example. Once we learn to drive, the methodical thinking through every step to execute the mechanics of operating our vehicle becomes unnecessary. It just organically happens because a habit was formed.

We all have habits of various purpose, creation, and strength - some, borne out of a need for safety, others devised for ease, efficiency, or to fulfill rules or norms. Brushing and washing, for example, live alongside cleaning our room and tidying our home, as well as the larger community care of recycling and maintaining our dwellings and/or properties. Kept in balance, these habits serve to honor our physical temple and proverbial home. Both witness the Divinity within us and all things by loving ourselves, others, and Mother Earth.

As we move beyond our perfunctory and reflexive world to engage in self-reflection, personal growth, and spiritual development, the life of many habits comes to the fore.

Some may be easily seen, while others remain an elusive part of our day-to-day operations and reactions and are a bit trickier to detect. Many have their roots in thought or emotional patterns, like the knee-jerk reaction to a perceived negative comment or our slide into self-criticism when we feel we've done something wrong.

Taking a closer look at the vast array of habits in our life, their origin is one aspect all hold in common; we can trace our habits' literal birth from the womb of our beliefs - a belief about ourselves and/or our world. Returning to driving, for example, the proverbial fuel for this American activity lies in the belief in independence, a teenage rite of passage and an alignment with societal norms. Looking deeper into the habits within habits, we might also discover nervous navigation, road rage, or a compulsion to speed fed by corresponding beliefs in danger, others' wrongdoing, or hurrying through life.

So how can we work with the habits we've developed, especially addressing those that don't serve our highest good? Traveling on the road to discovery and change, we can free ourselves from old habits through examination and relinquishment. Other interventions require intentional re-patterning. Calling, for example, on the Japanese practice of *datsuzoku* - the freedom from habit, daily routine, or the ordinary - opens us to the new by transcending convention and our personal ruts. Applied, it is the choice to "do something differently", to break the steps of our routine, or think out of the box in an innovative way and move past our typical ways of operating.

Working at a deeper level we can examine the belief that created our habit in the first place, asking if the habit serves us or we're serving it. As beliefs that find voice through the patterns of our limiting attitudes become discovered, we can intentionally allow them to fall away because we see how they block us from living freely in alignment with our True Nature. And while releasing these kinds of beliefs moves us forward on our path, the accompanying patterns and habits often remain scored into our psyche like a well-traveled hiking trail until we re-pattern or completely release them, too. In other words, as we liberate ourselves from constraining beliefs, it's often the habits and patterns that remain intact to plague us, feeling as if they pull our mind and heart back to the ways we left behind, though not nearly as potently as when the attached belief remains active. As we invest energy into new, healthy behaviors instead of our outdated habits, the heavily worn trail of these entrenched neural patterns grows grass again to blend once more with the mossy forest floor of our psyche. Removing all energy from old habits or merely acknowledging any diversion as a tug in the "old direction", we also practice *datsuzoku* to move forward on new and exciting paths.

Changing habits, because of their nature and ours, often feels challenging and uncomfortable. But know that discomfort serves as a marker to demonstrate our progress, a sign that we are just where we need to be, even in the midst of change. So, hang in there! Remember that habits take approximately eighteen months to form, so their dissolution and/or re-patterning takes time, too.

Listed on the following page is a partial inventory of behavioral, thought, and emotional habits. Those that appear helpful, sustaining, or growth-enhancing remain alongside those that may not serve our highest good. While incomplete, this list shines first light on that which we tend to ignore or do automatically, demonstrating that nearly any behavior, thought pattern, or emotional recurrence may indicate a habit needing our conscious attention. Because we tend to categorically label patterns or habits as "good" or "bad" influenced by our judgment-driven world, in the journeys to come, let's broaden our scope and instead consider how each habit may be serving our highest good. Are they growth-promoting, health-based patterns, which demonstrate our self-love? Or are they a call to examine what is unhealthy or inhibiting - a notification to shed light on the work yet to be done? For a deeper look, we revisit this topic in **Letting Go** in **Volume IV**.

Here lies the opportunity to witness whatever the Universe calls us to observe, re-balance, or shed to be the master of our world, lovingly caring for ourselves on this big, beautiful rock floating in an infinite sky.

Habit List

Healthy eating	Word choice	Emotional self-care
Caffeine addiction	Swearing	Staying centered
Praying	"Seeing" a silver lining	Loving attitude
Meditating	Positive thinking	Reacting dramatically
Driving a car	Assuming "bad" outcomes	Consistent irritation
Good hygiene	Being bossy	Feeling inferior
Deep breathing	Looking for "the culprit"	Blaming others
Smoking	Complaining	Worrying
Hurrying	Apologizing	Defaulting to frustration
Physically isolating	Overly independent	Shutting down
Nail biting	Needing to be right	Nervousness
Nose picking	Poor hygiene	Sadness
Scratching/picking skin	Feeling superior	Perfectionism
Doing, doing, doing	Cleaning	Feeling victimized

Journey I: Datsuzoku

Spend time in your sacred space, centering. When ready, fold your hands together naturally, fingers laced between one another; allow one hand to hold the other like the photo on the right. Look down at your hands to see which thumb and fingers rest on top. Make a mental note. Carefully switch positions so that your fingers and thumb from the opposite hand are now resting on top; by weaving the fingers together, make sure you change the order of your hands.

Pay attention to how uncomfortable switching positions feels. Did you have to really think and pay attention to the change in positions? How do you feel this applies to letting go of habits or practicing *datsuzoku*?

Journal your experience, witnessing all this journey reveals.

Continue over time to practice folding your hands with the new position. How long did it take to make the experience comfortable? What might this say about practicing *datsuzoku*, freedom from other habits?

Journey II:
Habit Inventory

Retreat to your sacred space. Ask for guidance from your Divine helpers for this journey if you are drawn.

Carefully review the reference list of habits, identifying those you practice. Expand the list as you are able.

Journal about the habits and patterns present in your life.

Which of these serve your highest good? Which don't? Why?

Moving forward, what steps will assist you in managing or changing habits that don't serve you?

Buddhist monks set aside exactly 20 minutes for cleaning in a practice that's called *soji*. Unlike common cleaning practices, this activity is two-fold. First, when the time ends, stop, even if the job isn't finished. And secondly, cleaning is done for the sake of cleaning as a kind of mindful meditation, where focus remains on the task with no attachment to the outcome. This journey offers an opportunity to practice current work habits in a new way - staying in the flow, being present with a simple task, and releasing any concerns about the results.

Journey III: Soji Life

Chose a simple household task like sweeping the floor, washing the dishes, or folding clothes. Set a timer with an audible bell for 20 minutes.

Using mindfulness, stay present. In other words, focus only on the task, bringing the mind back to the job as it drifts into other realms.

Let go of all expectations and attachment to the how, when, where, and how much of your chore. When the bell rings, stop the job and move onto journaling.

What did you notice about this journey - thoughts, emotions, beliefs, opinions, judgments? How do these influence other aspects of your day, tasks, or life, esp. in relation to *datsuzoku*?

Dreams

Every great dream begins with a dreamer.
Always remember, you have within you the strength, the patience
and the passion to reach for the stars to change the world.
— Harriet Tubman

Dreams and aspirations pave the way to manifesting what we desire. What are your dreams? In the space below, describe a dream - dream job, dream relationship, dream vacation, etc. Let your mind wander…your imagination soar! Remember to connect with what "feeds" you, what you love, and what inspires you. There are NO LIMITS here, so allow all possibilities to enter and stay with you through this journey. Go wild!

Journey II:
Feeling Dreamy

Write about your experience creating your dream.

How do you feel about your dream?

Can you connect with the feeling of having, being, or fulfilling the dream?

Journey III: Manifest

You're on the road to manifesting!

Imagining your dream is one of your most powerful tools to creating it. Writing it down helps ground the energy of making the dream become a reality on the physical plane.

What intentions will you set toward making your dream a reality?

Remember to ask your Divine helpers for guidance and support.

Return here to log your progress along the way, writing about how your dream comes to life over the following weeks or months.

For more information on manifesting, see **Our Energy** and **Faith in Ladybugs** in **Volume III** and **The Power of Belief** in **Volume V**.

Multi-sensory Memory

Sometimes you will never know the value of a moment until it becomes a memory.

— Dr. Seuss

From the time we are small children, we learn to categorize our world by label and function to understand everything around us, as we first discussed in **That's What I Like**. Through our earth-based monitoring system - our five senses - we learn about our world, piecing together and assigning meaning to our interactions. Immersed in our physical consciousness, touch, taste, sight, smell, and sound influence how we feel and think about everything. Initially, our multi-sensory experiences help us make sense (no pun intended) of life. In other words, how we perceive *anything* results from interpreting our world through early sensory experiences. Over time, these experiences accumulate and combine with our moment-by-moment consciousness. Because we are typically unaware of the databank behind any current happenings, our memories become a strong subconscious influence on our perceptions.

How does this multi-sensory memory work day to day? Let's imagine a situation from childhood as an example. Say we were having a great time playing house with our dolls or making an imaginary city out of blocks the first time we smell cookies baking. As a result, our general association with cookies and/or the smell of baking cookies would be pleasurable and fun; in other words, we make a positive connection with the multi-sensory experiences of playing and smelling cookies. If, however, the baking cookies occurred during a family fight, the accompanying yelling and witnessed anger would join with our own reaction of fear to create a negative association with the cookies in a subconscious alignment with the situation. Bring either of these multi-sensory combinations to the present and we find memories that color our perceptions and reactions in vastly different ways. Our current mood, physical state, and the day's events add even more layers to our reaction.

Multi-sensory memories create a complex web that often unknowingly affects our life. Because our senses operate continuously, unless we have a disease or dysfunction that limits our faculties like blindness or hearing loss, our experiences become intrinsically tied to all senses, informing and causing us to label everything in categories of pleasant or unpleasant, or somewhere in between.

So, let's take the opportunity to become more acquainted with our multi-sensory life as it helps us be more in tune with ourselves.

An Intimate Journey into Self

Journey I: Survey

Retreat to your sacred space for time to relax and center. Spend a few moments with each of the five senses below, listing pleasant, neutral, or unpleasant smells, sounds, tastes, touches, and sights for as many sensory experiences as possible. Begin with your strongest reactions, as these are often the easiest to identify. Using the examples as a guide, rate each experience on a scale from -10 to +10 as you travel through your multi-sensory memory.

	Unpleasant – 10	Neutral 0	Pleasant +10
Smell		+1 cinnamon	
Taste			
Touch			+10 kittens
Sight			
Sound			+10 Yo-yo Ma

Journey II: Associations

Reflect on your survey from the previous page, paying attention to senses demonstrating your strongest reactions (-7,8,9,10 or +7,8,9,10).

What associations can you make to any of the senses listed? What specific memories do you find linked with your strongest reactions? Describe the memories and how you feel when recalling them.

Reflect and journal about how your memories are tied to your senses then and now.

Have you found any associations or memories that surprised you? Any reactions that now make more sense because of your combined multi-sensory memory?

The Ties That Bind Us

The meeting of two personalities is like the contact of two chemical substances: if there is any reaction, both are transformed.

— C.G. Jung

Relationships weave a beautifully complex tapestry. They are the energetic ties that connect us like interlacing threads - some strong and thick, others seemingly tenuous and fragile. All relationships vary in intensity, connectedness, and importance. In truth, we are in relationship with all of life as an intricate dance of interactions with everything and everyone. Only through our perceptions do we become tricked into believing that we are separate from the world, seeing life apart from us and outside ourselves. We are, however, eternally linked with our world, even through our minds, but what we've been taught would say otherwise.

> Relationship is what exists between one thing and another. It is not a third thing in terms of being a third object, but is something separate, a third something. You realize that a relationship exists between your hand and a pencil when you go to write something down, but it is a relationship you take so completely for granted that you have forgotten that it exists. All truth lies in relationship, even one so simple as this.
>
> — A Course of Love, C:5.6

A Course of Love beautifully illuminates the very nature of relationships with ourselves and our world. To illustrate, we can apply this premise to the moment at hand; each of you currently reading this is in relationship with this book, with the words on the page, and with yourself immersed in this journey...just as my hands are in relationship with the computer keyboard as I type, with my thoughts, and with a vision of the reader. Relationships abound.

Though we may be oblivious to the varied and unique nature of our relationships, as our consciousness shifts, the powerful learning opportunities they offer become apparent. On a psychological level, for instance, how and what we learn through our many connections and relationships in life reflect in our personality trends. In other words, our emotions, feelings, thoughts, beliefs, and behaviors, the notes of the little self, synchronize and blend to create a complex melody - a multi-dimensional song largely written by our childhood dynamics with others, originally set into motion through interactions with parents, teachers, and caregivers. Even when the interactions of our relationships drift far from our conscious minds, the images they created live on in our subconscious, influencing us moment by moment. As such, we automatically play our "melody" with each person and every circumstance in our world, re-creating events we believe make our life better, happier, more peaceful, or safer. Many times, however, our re-creations fail to yield what we intend because we don't really understand the hidden (subconscious) motivations behind them.

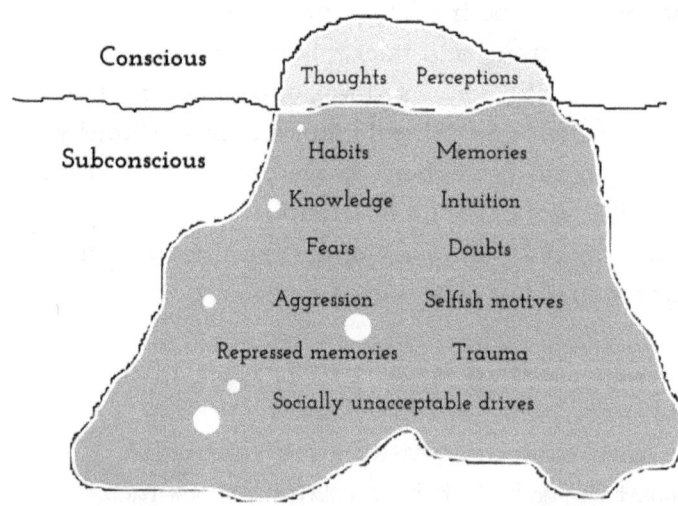

So how do we begin to understand the ways these layers of consciousness influence us? Let's begin with the diagram on the left, which depicts the workings of the conscious and subconscious mind, as the iceberg effect of Freudian psychology blends in a new way with spiritual teachings. We see from the diagram that our subconscious and conscious energies appear divided by the horizontal line that represents "water" or the breaking point between what stays in our active awareness (conscious) and that below the surface (subconscious). In alignment with spiritual teachings, the unconscious mind (absent above) instead identifies the automatic functioning of the body (breathing, heartbeat, etc.) animated by Spirit. Contrary to the psychological paradigm, our unconscious functioning, spiritually speaking, doesn't require our active participation since it embodies our physical livingness - lungs breathe, heart beats, brain functions, and blood flows innately.

Exploring this iceberg in sections, we first find that the layers closer to the surface (just above and below the water line) reflect what becomes easily accessed as thoughts, perceptions, habits, memory, and knowledge. This expanded metaphysical and spiritual model also includes intuition - the energy of "knowing without knowing how we know" - our Divinely sourced aspect that channels through our solar plexus, giving rise to our "gut feelings". (See **From Consciousness into Awareness** in **Volume III**.) The more we utilize our intuition or innate inner knowing, the more it comes to the surface for us to consciously use. And as psycho-spiritual teachings go, without the addition of intuition to this diagram, something significant appears to be missing.

The middle aspects of the iceberg, in contrast, identify our "hidden" or "less aware" consciousness where each energy or drive predominantly operates in the realm of feelings or emotions. Finally, the deepest layers of the iceberg hold hidden traumas, repressed memories, and the parts of ourselves we want to forget or deny as our shadow self or alter ego.

The collective whole of our consciousness influences all our interactions, with the lowest aspects of the iceberg (repressed memories, traumas, and undesirable drives) possessing much more potency and stealth. These frozen depths impact and color all our connections, often in ways we don't see clearly.

As we explore our relationships in correlation to the iceberg of our conscious and subconscious selves, we look at how all interactions access a vast catalog of life events - events that built our system of beliefs reflected in our subconscious and conscious mind. Looking with more detail, we identify that many of our behaviors occur at the conscious level. However, habits and defensive measures rest below the iceberg's surface along with their accompanying motivating forces. As we become aware of what impels or compels us toward acting or behaving in our particular way, we begin to get clarity on the beliefs that feed and hold our behavior in place. Thus, we develop understanding through examining the attitudes, thoughts, and emotions that created our beliefs, which inherently brings our attention to the deeper layers of our subconscious mind.

While we might notice a tendency to muscle the process of understanding ourselves regarding our more hidden layers, intense focus and struggle only impede our endeavors. Instead, through gentle witnessing and the intention to be aware, the energy of old messages and memories surface from what we long seemed to forget as thoughts, old scenes, reactions and emotional subterfuges (represented by the white bubbles in the iceberg diagram). All these naturally arise from the icy depths and burst open in our conscious mind with our intention for understanding and growth, as well as with the aid from our angels, guides, and Higher Self who support and facilitate the process. All the while, great opportunities for transformation unfold as a grand cycle of healing takes place.

We are each such a blending of personality characteristics - positive and negative, loving and hostile, peaceful and chaotic - which appear intertwined with but merely overshadow our true Self and create a unique whole. All relationships with self, Self, and others offer opportunities to learn and grow. As such, we begin unraveling a complicated network of interactions that tie the present to the past. By looking at all our relationships and the trends they unveil digging through this fertile ground, we unearth the power of our bonds and the magic they hold.

Journey I: Thoughts

Retreat to your sacred space, resting and centering.

Reflect on the chapter material, journaling your thoughts and feelings about what you read.

Re-create the iceberg model here, filling in any details that identify personal aspects generalized in the model.

Pay attention over time to the bubbles surfacing from your deeper subconscious mind. What messages or memories might you be receiving?

Journey II: Listing Relationships

Spend some time in your sacred space centering and calling in your helpers.

Using the table below, list all your significant current and past relationships with family, friends, lovers, partners, co-workers, etc. Make sure to include people from childhood forward, especially those with whom much emotional energy and/or bonding occurred.

Next to each person, list the type of relationship - mother, father, partner, friend, etc. Then write about the characteristics or qualities of the relationship and/or the person. Was it or they supportive or negligent, violent or peaceful, etc.? Is or was the person loving, kind, nurturing, hostile, punitive, etc.? (We all can be a mix of many qualities, so be sure to list them in a way most helpful to you and include all relative information.)

Now, note how you feel about the person. Do you have loving feelings and gratitude toward them or do you feel animosity, judgment, hurt, or have complaints or a mix of many feelings? What are they and why?

Name	Relationship	Characteristics	Feelings

An Intimate Journey into Self

Name	Relationship	Characteristics	Feelings

Journey III:
Relationship Clues

Return to your table/list and label people by groups with symbol and/or color code. Groups include lovers, crushes, co-workers, friends, family, etc. *Ex: For lovers put a pink heart by their name. For family put a green circle.*

Now look for key words you used to describe the person or relationship. Highlight similar qualities using the same color to show a link. *Ex: Color words meaning loving, affectionate, supportive in pink. Color hostile, angry, and aggressive words in red.*

Examine patterns within groupings and between them, writing out your observations. *Ex: Many males in my family are courageous and stoic. Ex: All my lovers have been affectionate with a strong tendency, at times, to withdraw.*

What can you observe about your behaviors in relationship to all you listed?

What are your thoughts and feelings about all you discovered?

Value Park

Your beliefs become your thoughts, your thoughts become your words, your words become your actions, your actions become your habits, your habits become your values, your values become your destiny.
— Mahatma Gandhi

Our choices, attitudes, behaviors, and deeper layers of emotional patterns reflect in many areas of our lives, especially our values. Like a beacon that illuminates our ways of being, shining a light on our values offers more opportunities for growth.

Created and shaped by several aspects of our history - ancestral beliefs, dominant past-life events, and early childhood rearing - values remain dominant and active in our adult lives whether we consciously know about them or not. Often, the ways we operate reveal our values in the automatic behaviors of day-to-day living. Many times, they are so intimately woven into our life that their importance becomes lost in our lack of self-awareness.

While our values morph and change over time as we grow and integrate lessons, core themes tend to remain, sometimes quite subconsciously. Considering this lifetime alone, for example, the critical ways for obtaining approval included doing what we were told to do, aligning with how we were expected to be, and more powerfully, what we were shown about life via our parents' rules, chores, behaviors, dress, religious practices, etc. The more approval we needed, the greater weight these expectations held.

As we consciously clarify our values, we gain more insight into how we see the world and ultimately ourselves. We often find that all the "shoulds" and "musts" (spoken and unspoken) from parents and authority figures provide a lens through which we view life's colorful kaleidoscope of experiences. This lens, compounded by the perceived values communicated through our ancestral belief system and past lives, operates as a powerful filter for all experiences as ever-changing beings on a dynamic cosmic ride.

Value Park offers another journey…one to assist in identifying personal values. The word cloud, included on the following page, helps spark ideas. Incomplete as it stands, it still provides a solid start.

Generally, readers can approach this chapter in three ways: from the mind, from the heart, or from a combination of the two. Some, for example, may be drawn to carefully think out and consider each value from a logical perspective and look at ways it rings true on a personal level. Others may just choose what feels right, what's known in the heart; others, yet, may begin with either approach and eventually include both perspectives, a blend of mind and heart. However you proceed, pay attention to your process and experience. As always, watch your thoughts, feelings, and reactions on your stroll through value park.

An Intimate Journey into Self

Wisdom Humor
Honesty Harmony
Justice Learning Balance
Kindness Fairness
Religion Adventure Community
Openness Meaningful Loyalty
Peace Curiosity Friendships Knowledge Autonomy
Growth Boldness Contribution Creativity Respect
Competency Authenticity Stability Service
Status Leadership Determination Citizenship Authority
Work Achievement Responsibility Challenge Faith
Poise Reputation Trustworthiness Fame
Recognition Spirituality Pleasure Love
Optimism Security
Fun

Beauty Self-Respect
Compassion
Influence

Happiness
Success
Freedom
Wealth

The Soul-Discovery Journalbook

Journey I: Clarifying Values

Make time in your sacred space. Spend a few moments centering and reviewing your intentions for today's journey before you begin. When ready, follow the directions below, beginning at A and moving through G. Use the word cloud as needed, while adding any other values to the list.

1.	6.
2.	7.
3.	8.
4.	9.
5.	10.

A. Make a list of your top 10 values, one to each space above.

B. Narrow the list to your top 8 by crossing off 2 values.

C. Narrow the list again to your top 5, crossing off 3 more.

D. Now eliminate 1 to have the top 4.

E. Repeat, crossing off one more to demonstrate your top 3.

F. Repeat to reveal your top 2.

G. Eliminate one.

My #1 value is _____.

Journey II: Reflections

Journal about your experience, considering the following questions:

What were your thoughts and overall attitude about the exercise?

How did you feel as you progressed?

How do you feel reflecting on your top value?

Can you see how your top value affects your life - home, work, play, relationships, etc.?

Can you identify any rules, ideas, or ways of life from your family, school, cultural practices, etc. that influenced your values? How?

You've Come a Long Way Baby...

I could tell you my adventures — beginning from this morning,
said Alice a little timidly;
but it's no use going back to yesterday, because I was a different person then.
— Lewis Carroll

You've been working hard exploring who you are, learning new aspects, discovering your pretty side, and perhaps beginning to see the side that's not so comfortable to look at. All is well, and you are just where you're meant to be!

Take a moment to acknowledge all your hard work and courage. Write or draw about what you've learned or how you've grown. Here is the space to celebrate and give yourself a big pat on the back while reflecting on the path ahead!

When you're finished, move on to **Volume II: Constant Companions**.

The Soul-Discovery Journalbook

An Intimate Journey into Self

Volume II

Constant Companions

Hope is a constant companion in this life.
It is the one thing that neither cruel nature,
God, nor other men can wrench from us.
— Dean Koontz

When you can't look on the bright side,
I will sit with you in the dark.
— C.S. Lewis

Constant Companions

You're off to a great start! Through **Volume I: A Single Step**, you navigated journaling guidelines, set intentions, created a sacred space, called on help, and hiked the many steps to begin the uncovering process. On any adventure, handy tools can guide us along the way, especially those that support our travels - items for comfort, food to nourish, a lantern when it gets dark - the important gear you began gathering in **A Single Step**. Gather again, we will.

Welcome to **Volume II: Constant Companions**. Within these pages, additional useful and practical gear facilitates your continued soul-discovery with ways to stay centered, grateful, and present in your day-to-day living. **Constant Companions** guide, teach, nurture, sustain, and light the way, moment by moment...week by week. We only need to pack with faith, remember what is offered, and allow them to ignite the magic in us.

Onward and upward!

Attitude of Gratitude

Gratitude unlocks the fullness of life. It turns what we have into enough, and more.
It turns denial into acceptance, chaos to order, confusion to clarity.
It can turn a meal into a feast, a house into a home, a stranger into a friend.

— M. Beattie

Gratitude, a powerful metaphysical and spiritual tool, is the choice to embrace what unfolds positively in our life over what facilitates negative feelings - focusing on what seems "right" instead of what appears "wrong". It stands to reason that developing an attitude of gratitude is one of the best gifts we can give ourselves.

Studies on gratitude have gained popularity in recent years, reinforcing what is already known in metaphysical teachings. Two such research projects found that individuals who journal their gratitude on a weekly basis "exercised more regularly, reported fewer physical symptoms, felt better about their lives as a whole, and were more optimistic about the upcoming week compared to those who recorded hassles or neutral life events."[6] Broadly speaking, the studies showed that gratitude strengthens physical and emotional health, relationships, and even communities.[7] In a world that seems so fraught with difficulties, injustices, and turmoil, being thankful for the kind, loving, beautiful, and pleasurable in our life heals and soothes us.

---

[6] Emmons, R. A., & McCullough, M. E. (2003). Counting blessings versus burdens: An experimental investigation of gratitude and subjective well-being in daily life. *Journal of Personality and Social Psychology, 84*(2), 377-389. American Psychological Association: Washington, DC. Retrieved from http://dx.doi.org/10.1037/0022-3514.84.2.377

[7] McCullough, M. E., Tsang, J.-A., & Emmons, R. A. (2004). Gratitude in Intermediate Affective Terrain: Links of Grateful Moods to Individual Differences and Daily Emotional Experience. *Journal of Personality and Social Psychology, 86*(2), 295-309. American Psychological Association: Washington, DC. Retrieved from http://dx.doi.org/10.1037/0022-3514.86.2.295

Like all things material and non-material, gratitude is an energy. When we feel thankful for the who and what we have in our life, we raise our vibrations higher, drawing more positive energies to us by the Law of Attraction. This law operates as the principle of "like attracts like". Simply said, being grateful, we attract more of the same positive energy. Our gratitude literally returns to us with similar vibrations as the energy we put into our world cycles around and returns to us magnified by the additional action of the Law of Cause and Effect. Thus, a gratitude practice powerfully manifests what we desire in our lives. (See **Wynebgwrthucher** in **Volume III**.)

Additionally, gratitude possesses transformative power through shifting our thoughts, emotions, and beliefs about ourselves and our world to the "good", positive, helpful, loving, etc. Changing our mind about an experience and *feeling* thankful transmutes our negative attitude because gratitude and negativity cannot co-exist in the same moment. Shifting our attention or changing our mind doesn't mean we need to stuff or ignore our negative emotions or pretend that our experiences didn't happen. Instead, gratitude offers an opportunity to find a silver lining in any dark cloud. In a world filled with many challenges, we apply gratitude to lighten our energy, mood, mindset, and heart. And as we practice it, the effects ripple out to all aspects of our life.

Let's swap, even for just a moment, our old complaints, aches, pains, disappointments, frustrations, and judgments for a fresh attitude of gratitude.

Journey: Thank you

Let's find opportunities to grow gratitude. If you're already practicing, great! If not, your journey begins here and continues interspersed throughout this book series.

After centering, take a moment to list what you are grateful for today. It can be as small as the cup of coffee or tea you had for breakfast or as powerful as the thankfulness for the love of a partner, family, or friend.

How do you feel after journaling about your gratitude?

Journey II: Gratitude challenge

Retreat to your sacred space and center. When ready, begin by rating your overall attitude and view about life on a scale of 1 - 10.

Over the next ten consecutive days, journal at least one gratitude daily.

Can you fill this page with gratitude?

On day eleven, again rate your overall attitude and view about life on a scale of 1 - 10. Did this gratitude challenge change your overall attitude, mood, or outlook compared to your beginning rating?

How did this journey shift your feelings about your life?

Journey III:
Gratitude Shifts

Begin by rating your overall attitude and view about a frustrating or challenging life situation on a scale of 1 - 10.

Journal daily for the next ten consecutive days at least one gratitude per day regarding the situation or person(s) involved. Look for small ways to be thankful about the situation or person(s).

Can you fill this page again with gratitude?

On day eleven, again rate your overall attitude and view about the situation/person(s) on a scale of 1 - 10. Reflect on how this challenge changed your overall attitude, mood, or outlook about the situation or person(s) and journal about it.

Did the situation positively change in any way, even slightly?

Breathe

For breath is life, and if you breathe well you will live long on earth.
— Sanskrit Proverb

Working with our breath, known as breathwork, finds its roots centuries ago in ancient medical and meditative practices of the East. Among the best-known forms are Vipassana meditation, Pranayama, Qigong, and Tai Chi, with Pranayama being perhaps the most familiar to Westerners. *Pranayama*, meaning control of the life force, serves as a tool for affecting both the mind and body. Used in conjunction with other tools of soul-discovery, working with breath provides many valuable outcomes. Because it can excavate strong emotions, though, breathwork done in combination with meditation, journaling, yoga, and self-development serves us best.

As mammals, our physical survival depends on taking in and exhaling air, a critical exchange with the Universe. Breath feeds our body (our cells, tissues, blood, organs, and brain) with vital oxygen and removes carbon dioxide waste. On a deeper spiritual level, to breathe is to feel and experience the worthiness of being alive. As such, breath is life, intimately symbolized by our breathing in and out, freely and fully.

Respiration, as a natural process, occurs through our body's deep belly breathing or diaphragmatic breath. An innate function that we subconsciously re-pattern as we develop, a look at typical belly breathers, infants, shows us how we begin in this world only to regress to the often tight, stress-filled way we take in life.

Looking at the mechanics of diaphragmatic breath, the muscle of the diaphragm attaches to the end of our ribs and anchors to the spine; operating naturally, it relaxes and expands. The area above our belly button and just below our ribs visibly moves outward; internally the diaphragm moves down. This allows space for the lungs to fully take in air.

When we breathe diaphragmatically, we more completely oxygenate the body, lower blood pressure, slow rapid thinking, and reduce our heart rate, bringing calmness to the mind and body. Our inherent capacity to breathe like a baby naturally lowers our stress and optimizes our body's functioning. In other words, in a world where busyness, chaos, and achievement are commonplace, we can flow more easily with life as we lessen our stress response with diaphragmatic breathing. (See Quieting Our Mind.)

On the contrary, when our diaphragm is tight, we breathe more shallowly. Our lungs fail to reach full capacity as our constricted diaphragm moves inward and upward, limiting our lung's capacity to completely fill. We remain less oxygenated and thus deprive our tissues, brain, and organs of what they need for optimum functionality.

How we breathe can tell us many things about ourselves. Shallow breathing, simply put, results from and is a sign of stress. In general, the shallower and more rapid our breathing, the more stress we are experiencing. Traumas, situational pressures, and high-stress lifestyles especially create a tight diaphragm, prohibiting healthful breathing. Commonly, we may even subconsciously hold our breath, which demonstrates repressing emotions.

Frequently, we associate stress with adulthood where busy schedules and jam-packed lives abound. Everyone, however, regardless of age, becomes affected by stress, and while small children may seem oblivious to what goes on around them, they're not. Children, by and large, are sponges and thus barometers for their environment. In fact, the younger children experience stress, the earlier their breathing becomes affected.

Fear not! The guidance to address our unhealthy breathing patterns lie within these pages. As we return to natural deep breathing, we find help in a multitude of ways. First, neutralizing our parasympathetic fight or flight response facilitates a sense of calmness. In addition, the resulting increase in oxygen diminishes pain through a release of endorphins. Toxic waste, removed through our lungs and improved lymphatic movement, aids our metabolic processes.[8] So, as we move away from breathing patterns altered by stress, trauma, or a hurried world, we can navigate life more serenely and presently.

---

[8] Benson, Herbert (1975). *The Relaxation Response*. New York, NY: HarperCollins Publishers.

The following journeys, designed to work with breath from several approaches, help illuminate our current trends, facilitate relaxation, and re-pattern the unhelpful behaviors and motor memory of shallow breathing. Get ready for a healthier, happier, and calmer you!

Breathing Prep: Go to your sacred space, bringing a comfortable, supportive chair. Sit with your back straight to give room for the diaphragm to expand. Most importantly, remember to allow space for it to move in and out in a relaxed manner. If you choose to sit on the floor, keep your chest from sinking down into your abdomen and refrain from slouching. Standing against a wall is also an option.

Journey I: Testing

Close your eyes and begin with one hand on your diaphragm (between your bellybutton and edge of your ribs) and one below your collar bones in the center of your upper chest. Just breathe normally for a few minutes.

Write your observations, considering the following questions:

Did your diaphragm relax (move out) or stay tight (pull in) when you inhale? Did you feel your upper chest expand more than or less than your belly? Did your chest expand first or your belly?

As you paid attention, did you feel that you were getting enough air or did your awareness of that change? Did you experience any emotions?

Journey II: Baseline

This journey measures your typical breath length. It will give you a baseline, a starting place so you can observe your progress.

in:

out:

Close your eyes and observe your breathing as you inhale. Begin by counting how many seconds (one hippopotamus, two hippopotami, etc.) until your lungs feel full. Do your best to not strain or push yourself beyond what feels like a typical breath. Write down how many seconds for your inhale - # in.

Now, pay attention to your exhale. Count how many seconds (one hippopotamus, two hippopotami, etc.) until your lungs are comfortably depleted of air and you are ready to breathe again. Record your exhale seconds in # out.

Remember to not stress or push your breathing. Here we are getting an idea of your typical breath length.

Journal your experience, including any observations.

Journey III: Baby's Breath

 Let's practice expanding our diaphragm to develop deep breathing, your natural belly breathing. Use the QR code on the left to listen to the recorded version of this journey at www.pathways2innerpeace.com.

Close your eyes and begin with your hands in the same positions from Journey I - one on your diaphragm at the bottom of your ribs where your tummy begins and the other on your upper chest. Start with observing your typical breathing. Keeping your hands in the same position, gently push all the air out of your lungs by exhaling until you have no more air remaining. Slowly take in a breath while allowing the diaphragm to expand in a relaxed manner. The diaphragm should feel like it's pushing your hand away from your body first, followed by your lungs expanding. Repeat.

Now we're going to expand our breathing by counting the inhale for three seconds and the exhale to four seconds. When I count to three, push all the air out of your lungs and slowly breathe in and out in alignment with the guided counting. Here we go. Exhale all the way out... Inhale...three hippopotami, two hippopotami, one hippopotamus. Pause. Exhale slowly... four hippopotami, three hippopotami, two hippopotami, one hippopotamus. Note that your exhale will be longer than your inhale by at least a second. Breathe normally again in the most comfortable manner. Let's do that again. When I count to three, push all the air out of your lungs and slowly breathe in and out in alignment with the guided counting. Here we go. Exhale all the way out... Inhale...three hippopotami, two hippopotami, one hippopotamus. Pause. Exhale slowly...four hippopotami, three hippopotami, two hippopotami, one hippopotamus. Repeat in the same fashion as many times you desire.

Allow yourself to relax and let go of your tensions as you breathe through this exercise, making the inhale and exhale as natural as possible. If you find yourself straining, just return to paying attention to your breathing with your hands in position on your diaphragm and chest. As you are able, relax the diaphragm upon inhale and allow it to naturally contract on exhale.

Move on to **Journey IV**.

Journey IV:
Baby's Breath

Write your observations regarding **Journey III**, including any notations about physical, mental, or emotional responses. Did your breathing feel any different? How do you feel in general?

Journey V:
Observing Our Breath

Observe yourself over the next week or so, keeping a notepad with you to jot down what you witness about your breathing patterns. Log what you discover.

Note any breath-holding or rapid breathing. Make sure to include when and where this occurs and what circumstances, situations, and people were around you when your breathing changed.

What emotions came before or along with your breath-holding or rapid breathing?

Move on to **Journey VI** to address these challenges and your accompanying breathing response.

As you practice, be sure to make note of changes regarding your breath, emotions, thoughts, etc. that come to your awareness. Be sure to give yourself the time and space to practice gently and non-judgmentally. Should you find that your breathing is shallow, practicing **Journey III** will help in multiple ways. Do your best to be patient with yourself.

Journey VI:
Positive Practice

Center in your sacred space as you ready yourself for this journey.

To practice diaphragmatic breathing, it's also helpful to identify the circumstances where breathing can be used to navigate the situation more calmly. Let's begin by making a list on the right of ten stress-filled situations where healthier breathing can aid you.
Ex: Stressful meeting.

This is a brainstorm list so do your best to just list and not evaluate, yet.

Now, on a scale of 1 - 10 (on the dotted lines to the left of each number), rate the stressors listed, 10 being most stressful.

My Ten Stress-filled Situations

- - - - 1.

- - - - 2.

- - - - 3.

- - - - 4.

- - - - 5.

- - - - 6.

- - - - 7.

- - - - 8.

- - - - 9.

- - - - 10.

**Journey VII:
Reflections**

Journal observations about your stress list and its rankings in **Journey VI**.

Consider the following: Which situations dominate your list in intensity? Is there a common pattern or trend in your list or ranking?

Looking at your **Journey VI** list, write out one or two predominant emotions on each of the ten points.

Is there a common emotion across all or several events?

What trend(s) do you notice now?

How do you feel about what you discovered?

Journey VIII: More Practice

Go to your quiet space and center. Choose one stressor from **Journey VI**. In your mind's eye, re-create the situation, using your imagination to connect with all the stressful pieces of it. How you feel as you re-create this? How would you rate your stress on a 1 - 10 scale, 10 being the most stressful?

Now, use deep breathing to re-center and calm yourself. Breathe slowly and deeply, allowing the stress to melt away with each breath. Become one with your breath, joining with it and allowing every cell of your body to naturally move with your inhale and exhale.

Now draw your attention back to the images about the situation in your mind's eye. How would you rate the situation now? Did the rating change? Did your thoughts or feelings about this situation change?

Journal about your experience. How did deep breathing help you navigate your stressful reaction?

**Journey IX:
Real Time**

Use deep breathing to navigate your stressor in real time, repeating the process you learned in **Journey VIII**.

When situations arise, apply deep breathing. Allow your thoughts and feelings to pass through you while deep breathing, assisting you in being a more centered you.

Journal your experience.

Create a plan for using deep breathing to assist you as you grow and learn. Write it out here.

Keep up the good work!

Wise Baby Vision

If your eyes are opened, you'll see the things worth seeing.
— Rumi

The chapters in **Volume I** - exploring senses, relationship ties, habits, values, and dreams - gave us a glimpse into how we see the world through invisible lenses that unknowingly rest precariously between our self and what appears outside of us. These ghostly spectacles truly color our perceptions (as a metaphorical relative of the proverbial rose-colored glasses) and create an internal image that continuously filters our vision. Our physical state, mood, and current mindset add even more layers of impact. All these pieces coalesce into a unique whole, creating a general attitude we carry about life. To investigate, we can ask ourselves, "Am I one who views the world positively and my life with happiness, openness, and peace, or do I look through a scratched and darkened lens where life is heavy, frightening, and burdensome?" This question can help us become aware of the way we "see" or experience the world, giving us a clearer picture of whether we view our glass as half-full or half-empty.

Regardless of our overarching attitude, moment by moment, many opportunities may serve to shift our perception, helping us gain new understanding, worry less, be more positive, and discover answers to difficult questions; or we may find the reverse order where shedding, gaining understanding, being positive, and finding answers change our perceptions and how we view life. Whether we tend to ignore what requires our attention by staying task-oriented and logical (which disregards our feelings), or worry about every little situation that crosses our path, this chapter offers another set of mindfulness tools that prompt new behaviors for a more centered, present, and joyful life.

Mindfulness - the practice of maintaining a non-judgmental state of heightened or complete awareness of one's internal and external experiences on a moment-to-moment basis - calls us to new vision. In becoming mindful, we "see" the world with fresh eyes - shedding labels and judgments while bringing novelty to common or recurring experiences - opening the door to other possibilities or solutions.

One such way to develop this practice of changing perceptions occurs through beginner's eye or wise baby vision (as I like to call it). Wise baby vision shifts our "sight" by looking at everything in a whole new way. We remove as many labels, judgments, or preconceived notions that tell us we already we know all there is to know about it, employing the wisdom of our Higher Self in tandem with the innocence of a baby. A simple example of exploring this may best be shown by one of my students who found that after wearing a watch for over ten years, wise baby vision illuminated many details that escaped his attention.

Wise baby vision calls us to be more present by paying attention to little things in life, especially the easily accessible and taken-for-granted gifts like a beautiful sunset, delicate flowers in our lawn, or the smell of fresh-baked bread. This mindfulness-based tool generates appreciation of all we overlook as unacknowledged blessings or forgotten daily miracles. Its continued application creates an open view, helping us expand new perceptions to increasingly challenging circumstances.

As we apply wise baby vision spiritually, we develop sight beyond our physical eyes and witness people and situations with the heart or heart-mind - a loving and centered, yet discerning look from deep within our compassionate Self. Our consciousness expands, our vibration rises, and through increased loving-kindness and forgiveness, we grow by feeling our connection to the world around us, seeing the Divinity in all things.

These are not Me
these eyes that see,
ears that hear,
tongue that tastes,
skin that feels.
It is a vehicle that I have chosen
to navigate this world and crawl
across the grassy fields
to find my way back Home.

Oh, this dull head of mine.
How it tries to trick me!
My eyes see danger, hardship, and challenges.
It tries to fool my heart,
who cares not to listen,
playing and rejoicing
in all that is loving.

I long for life's sweet fruit
to fill this belly.
The hunger is deeper than flesh,
a longing for a resting place
that cradles heart and soul and mind.
A crystalline light,
radiating gentle warmth
that shines away all
so, eyes and ears and flesh forget.

– Adriene Nicastro 2015

Journey I: Trends

Spend time in your sacred space and center.

Reflect on the chapter. What are your thoughts and feelings about the material?

Are you aware of a general trend in your thinking and feeling? In other words, are you a glass half-full or glass half-empty type of person?

How do you think your overall approach to life influences your day-to-day experiences?

Journey II: Beginning Baby Vision

Find a simple cooking or egg timer, or a digital one on your computer or phone. Choose an object that is simple but familiar to you - a strawberry, a ring, a penny, etc. Take the timer and object to your sacred space. Put them aside while you close your eyes and take a few slow, deep breaths and center.

Now, set your timer for at least 5 minutes. This encourages focus on the exercise without the distraction of watching a clock.

Place your object in front of you on a cleared tabletop or space. Imagine for a moment that you are a baby, seeing your object for the very first time. Connect with the feeling that this object is completely new to you…never seen before. Carefully observe it in all angles by moving it to different positions. Allow all you witness to come to your awareness. Continue this exercise until the timer rings, or longer if desired.

Move on to **Journey III**.

Journey III: Reflections

Journal your experience with **Journey II**.

Consider the following questions: What did you notice about the object? What new observations did you make? What did you like or enjoy? Dislike?

How did it feel to witness this object with wise baby vision? Did you notice many other thoughts or feelings during the exercise? Were they related or not?

What might this journey communicate about how you experience familiar people, places, or things?

Can you list other situations where wise baby vision may provide a new perspective or understanding?

Could wise baby vision help with how you tend to see the world, a general trend you identified in **Journey I**?

Quieting Our Mind

Small rodents hide in my head,
constantly spinning on tiny wheels,
creating circuses.

They spin words that link in long, braided strings,
little children holding hands,
playing games.

I want them to be still,
but they spin all the faster, creating constant chatter,
like small, noisy blackbirds on a wire.

And in this twirling web of never-ending wandering,
scrambling,
somehow, I emerge with a clear thought.
Often not my own,
it comes from Somewhere Else,
and feeds my soul.

— Adriene Nicastro 2015

Our mind moves endlessly, never resting, always creating, evaluating, and commenting. Sometimes we welcome this busy hive in the flurry of daily activities to help us complete tasks; at other times it overwhelms, confines, and confuses us. If trained, like taming a wild horse, we become the master of our mind and it serves us in many ways.

In contemplating the "what" and "where" of our mental energy, most would point to their own brain, but constraining the mind to some skeletal cage prohibits us from reaching beyond that solitary, earth-based consciousness into the expansiveness of our being. While at times we all feel locked in a thought-puddle known only to ourselves and separate from everything around us, in its totality, our mind is a vast sea, more immense and connected than we can imagine.

Our personal mental energy as a whole is reflected in our mental body, which cannot be contained in our physical form but is intimately connected with it. (See **From Consciousness into Awareness** in **Volume III**.) Our mental body projects the workings of our mind, a multi-level consciousness, which is in Union with Source at higher vibrations. Because we are surrounded by pure thought, this energy exists in tandem with the mental energy of what we individually and collectively create. We mold pure thought as creators and thus manifest our life by the manner in which we use it.

To understand the levels of mind, we can separate it into two distinct but interconnected arenas - concrete or reasoning mind and abstract mind. The practical, contemplating, figuring mind is known spiritually as concrete mind - thought generally associated with our left brain. A metaphorical beehive of activity, this mind constantly plans, calculates, figures, deciphers, unravels, and processes, even when we sleep. In addition, it's intimate link with our five senses keeps us tapped into and inadvertently feeling contained by our physical world.

Because our concrete mind naturally constrains our thinking to what is logical, rational, and practical, as we move to more creative, intuitive, free thought (what we typically associate with right-brain processes), we transition out of concrete mind's influence and into vast possibilities of abstract mind. Here we can receive answers that reasoning faculties cannot accept, as well as ideas and inspirations of brand-new technologies, cures, and inventions. Through abstract mind we reach into knowing our limitless nature, our expansiveness of being - abstract mind in Union with Universal Power or Source.

On the material level, our glandular neurology serves as the physical conduit to experiencing and opening to a consciousness beyond our concrete mind and thus limited thinking. Specifically, our pituitary gland in conjunction with our pineal gland unites us with the abstract mind. Through these glands' influence we become attuned to our Higher Self and linked to Intelligent Force or Source, expanding our consciousness beyond this small world.

> Know you what a pituitary gland is? ... It is a little ductless gland that is in your brain. It opens and fills your brain with energy, electricity. It awakens in you, cells that make you aware. It has great power. You have a pineal gland...this is at the base of your skull and it brings the awakening of the pituitary into your spinal column...[9]

Great benefits lie in going past the busyness of concrete thinking to access the wholeness of mind in a more conscious way, intentionally awakening our connection to the Universe and Self. This requires movement on our part, an intentional shift from "doing" to "being". Meditation facilitates this forward movement.

There are many approaches to meditation that we can choose from based on our current beliefs, evolution, and state of being. Broadly speaking, all serve as a means for facilitating wellness and stress reduction. Moving meditation, for example, offers a simple, easily reproducible task that provides the activity for concrete mind to stay helpfully engaged while allowing for relaxation and peacefulness. Even sedentary, repetitive activities where motion is limited to the hands provide our rodent-infested thinking just enough of a job to elicit true relaxation by what is known as the Relaxation Response. We can create this phenomenon - identified by Dr. Herbert Benson, founder of the Mind-body Medical Institute of Massachusetts General Hospital of Boston - through simple physical activities, breathing exercises, clearing the mind, and meditation,[10] though Eastern spiritual practitioners long knew about these inherent benefits. (See **Breathe**.)

True relaxation lowers our body system responses elevated by stress, including heart rate, blood pressure, cortisol level, adrenaline output, blood sugar, cholesterol, and brain activity. It also improves our oxygen production and lowers the psychological symptoms of agitation, anxiety, and sadness. Even though individuals often resort to behaviors thought to facilitate relaxation like surfing the internet or watching TV, entertainment such as this does not produce the Relaxation Response. In other words, *entertainment does not create true relaxation*. So, our favorite show may feed our longing to be a couch

---

[9] Donovan, Rev. Penny (2017). *I AM GABRIEL: Selected Lessons from an Archangel, Book 2, 1988*. Albany, NY: Sacred Garden Fellowship.
[10] Benson, Herbert (1975). *The Relaxation Response*. New York, NY: HarperCollins Publishers.

potato (which we all love from time to time), but it undeniably lacks the mental, physical, or psychological benefits that create true relaxation and stress reduction.

Below are examples of typical activities that activate the Relaxation Response:

Meditation	Walking	Skiing	Drawing	Cleaning
Nature time	Running	Dancing	Painting	Gardening
Yoga	Biking	Hiking	Coloring	Knitting

Additionally, when we are emotionally overloaded, filled with anxiety, or burning up with anger, movement provides the release of energy to help cultivate an internal state of peace. More physically active meditations, for example, also help us transition to a quiet, sitting meditation as we master staying present only to the task at hand. The newly formed habits of staying present and letting go of thoughts moves us beyond the distractions of concrete mind, laying the groundwork for the detachment necessary to quiet our thinking without the aid of movement.

Touching into the deeper meaning of meditation, we arrive at a spiritual practice. Moving past our five senses, emotions, and thinking into stillness, we access the presence of our Higher Self...our God Self.

> The doorway to knowing God is the door through which you step when you meditate. I cannot emphasize enough to you the importance of daily meditation or communion with the Divine, for it is only in that way will you leave behind you those things which hold you down, limit you, and cause you pain.[11]

To consciously reach into our Divinity through meditation, we first withdraw attention from our sense-driven nature and its continuous stream of information about the body and external world. Next, we allow all emotions to fall away or dissolve, going past whatever surfaces or removing our energy from them. Then, we drop all attachment to our hamster wheel of thoughts, moving beyond their influence. Our concrete mind's chatter may still seem present in the background as subtle noise even when we disengage from active thinking. But, as we remove our energy from engaging in any distraction, including our concrete mind's antics, we instead find ourselves *not in* our thoughts, emotions, or sensations. The gradually diminishing effect of our internal noise can be seen as the difference between *being* in a parade versus *watching* one, where we

---

[11] Donovan, Rev. Penny (2013). *Introduction to Practical Spirituality: Select Lessons from an Archangel.* Albany, NY: Sacred Garden Fellowship.

eventually move beyond all of it into a deep state of being, touching into the small, still Voice within us.

Many years ago when first meditating, I wrestled with my thoughts too often to count. The grocery list, a recent conversation, worries of the day, week, or month served as common themes. Then struggles with a growling tummy or stiff muscles added to the mix. Practicing letting go - to not engage the reminders or the desire to control my environment - came through a gentle re-centering and dropping of thoughts and attention to physical sensations, slowly enabling me to disengage from concrete mind. Now, though I may witness activity in the background much like hearing a radio off in the distance, the soft static of its presence doesn't distract me as before. Sometimes, however, when I feel too busy for sitting, meditation comes through nature walks or gardening to give my reasoning, pickle-headed brain something worthwhile to chew on, like staying on the forest path or digging surreptitiously past slumbering earthworms.

The practice of letting go of our thoughts and sensations, moving past them and remaining unattached, takes intention, focus, and surrender. This chapter is aptly named **Quieting Our Mind**, as many find releasing themselves from the influence of mental spinning most challenging, yet also most rewarding. Quieting our mind on all levels often requires time and patience. Remember, our concrete mind functions even as we practice letting go of our lists, physical sensations, and personal dialogue. After all, we've spent a lifetime developing and encouraging this kind of thinking. Shifting our mental summersaults requires more than a mere few weeks, so be tolerant, loving, and gentle with yourself. Again, this part of soul-discovery unfolds more so as preparation for a marathon than a sprint.

Our personal circus can really challenge us in meditation, as well as in everyday life. Here we are all in good company as a community of little wheel-bound rodents. Know that you can travel beyond all this mental babble and open to the wisdom, guidance, and peace of your Higher Self. The more time you spend clearing the path through quieting the mind, as well as detaching from emotions and the five senses, the more opportunities unfold to access the gifts of inner guidance.

With dedication, we find an invaluable gift by stepping into the flow of Divine Presence through meditation as we quiet all our distractions within and without; the knowingness, Unity, love, and acceptance of God becomes a conscious awareness and we heal. Let's move beyond our restrained and confined consciousness into the limitlessness of our Divine Self, where stillness lies and connects us to a cosmic soup perfectly seasoned with wisdom and peace.

Journey I: Moving Meditation

Chose a comfortable, simple exercise or activity to use for quieting the mind. Should you need ideas, return to the list in the chapter. Below are some important general pointers to consider:

- Be sure that the activity produces no struggle. "How-to" need not be a distraction, so choose something within your knowledge base and comfort level.
- Make sure you are in good physical health if you choose a more strenuous physical activity. Also, make certain outdoor paths are safe and well lit. Let's not add safety distractions to the list.
- Start with 15 minutes and increase over time.
- Focus only on the present moment.
- Let go of all thoughts. Focus only on what you are doing and the simplicity of the activity or the beauty of nature presented on your journey.
- Whenever your thoughts drift to conversations, lists, to do's, situations, etc., bring yourself back to free movement, observing the activity or environment non-judgmentally.
- Let go of all judgments of how you are doing. Trust that all is well.

At the end of your meditation, journal about your experience.

Additional Notes:

The Soul-Discovery Journalbook

Journey II: Sitting in Stillness

To listen to the recoded version of this journey, use the QR code that takes you to www.pathways2innerpeace.com. If unable to access the recording, find a trusted friend to read this meditation to you. Before you begin, familiarize yourself with the four suggested techniques for dropping thoughts, emotions, or sensations listed as **Options 1 - 4** on the following page. Choose one option per meditation time, allowing yourself room to experiment with each over the next several meditations. The recorded version incorporates one option at a time.

Retreat to your sacred space, giving time for centering. Make sure your core muscles are supported. Close your eyes and breathe in and out slowly.

In your mind, imagine a sturdy box with a strong lid and an inlaid, thick iron lock. Look down into your hand; a key for it rests in your palm. Lift the heavy lid and feel the spacious, velvety interior. Here is a space to place all your worries, to do's, lists, discomforts, errands...
anything that might distract your peace. One by one, place these inside for safekeeping. When all distractions are inside, close the lid and lock the box with the key. Place the key in your pocket.

Bringing all attention to your breathing, take another slow, deep breath. As you rest, distractions may surface as images, internal chatter, categorization of or attention to sensations, previous conversations, or imagined events.

Insert option from the next page here...

Continue the meditation for as long as you are able, increasing the length over time.

Option 1:
When you hear noises and feel body sensations, gently acknowledge them without following or attaching to what you observe. For example, say to yourself, "I feel hungry," or "I feel tension in my shoulders," or "I hear dogs barking," then drop the thought.

Option 2:
Imagine each thought, emotion, or sensation as a ball that appears in your hand. Imagine the ball dropping to the ground and rolling away until it disappears. Repeat this with each thought, emotion, or physical distraction like noise or body sensations.

Option 3:
Allow thoughts to pass by as marchers in a parade or as clouds drifting by. Allow all distractions within and without to just flow past as you gently witness them.

Option 4:
As internal or external distractions come to your awareness, completely remove all attention from them. Totally disengage from any thought, emotion, or body sensation, gently releasing any focus on them.

Journey III: Journal

Journal about **Journey II**, reflecting on your experience.

What thoughts, emotions, and sensations did you notice?

Were any sensations, thoughts, or emotions harder than others to let go of?

What was easiest about this journey? Hardest?

How did you feel at the end of your meditation?

What did you observe as you experimented with each option? Is there one that felt more resonant than the others? Why?

Journey IV:
Video Homework

Research the TED Talk by Jill Bolte Taylor, Ph.D., called *My Stroke of Insight*, and watch the video.

Journal your thoughts and feelings about the video.

How can you apply what you learned in this chapter to what Dr. Taylor discusses?

Journey V: Meditation Practice

Set aside time in your sacred space to practice quieting your mind through meditation in whatever way feels most congruent.

Write about your experiences practicing and consider the following questions: When might this practice be best to do on a more regular basis?

What type of practice do you desire to have for quieting the mind and meditation? Moving, sitting, or both? Why?

Do you have a desire for communing with your Higher Self through meditation?

Journal your experiences with stillness and feeling the presence of your true Self through meditation.

Thankfulness Tree

Gratitude is not only the greatest of virtues,
but the parent of all others.
— Cicero

Manifesting what we perceive as positive is intimately bound with gratitude. Bringing "good" into our life requires being thankful - thankful for ALL we already have - valuing and believing that whatever we desire merely waits for us, temporarily hidden from our awareness.

Commonly, we look out into the world and ask if not plead for what feels missing, calling to things. We also might long for good health, loving relationships, compassion from others, well behaved children, or a rewarding occupation, to name a few. So often we want someone to provide these for us without considering what we might offer to others or the Universe.

Having positivity in our life includes being an example of what we desire from others. It's the energy of bringing "good" by being "good", embodied in teachings like "Love thy neighbor as thyself." (See **Our Energy** in **Volume III**.) So, whatever we want to manifest more of, be thankful for it, imagining that it's already in our hands and remember…we must BE to the world what we desire. Be loving, respectful, patient, compassionate, generous, peaceful, and joyful. As we honor all the positive and uplifting in others and thank them for it, we can in turn be it to ourselves, offering it back to the world.

Journey I: Generator

Below is a "thankfulness generator". Completing the statements will grow your gratitude.

I am grateful for ...

    people in my life (past/present) who are...

    the things I have including...

    beauty in nature like...

    my loving pets, present and past, including...

    opportunities the Universe has provided including...

    teachers I've found along the way that taught me...

    the wonders of my body which are...

    my amazing mind that can...

    all the talents I have been given, such as...

    difficult situations where I have learned...

    spirituality and/or religious practices that have given me...

    other...

Journey II:
Generator Reflections

Journal what you uncovered using the thankfulness generator from the previous page.

How do you feel when you embrace these gifts?

Journal about your experience.

In being what you desire, what could you offer more of to others or yourself? What behaviors or attitudes could you change to be what you desire?

Journey III: Thank you!

Your thankfulness tree awaits below! The beauty and fullness of this tree depends on your awareness of the gifts you have been given. Each day draw at least one leaf for something you are grateful for no matter how small. Add a background and strong earth around the roots to keep your tree well grounded. As you continue to adorn your tree, watch how much love you grow in your life!

The Ego

There is a great battle of two wolves inside us. One is evil.
It is anger, jealousy, greed, resentment, lies, inferiority and ego.
The other is good. It is joy, peace, love, hope humility, kindness,
empathy, compassion, and truth. The wolf that wins is the one you feed.
— *Native American Proverb*

The word and concept of "ego" echoes through our modern times. In the Western culture, the term frequently becomes inserted in everyday conversations to identify how we think of ourselves and others. References to this common meaning include egomaniac, egotistical, and egocentric labeling, which negatively categorize our human tendencies toward self-aggrandizement, inflating our personal worth well beyond others through conceit and arrogance.

According to the Merriam-Webster Dictionary, ego is the opinion that we have about ourselves; however, the term's old Latin roots reach back to 1714 as a metaphysical identification of "I". In 1932, the father of psychoanalysis, Sigmund Freud, introduced an altogether different view of ego as the part of the personality that experiences and reacts to the world, mediating between the pleasure-seeking, pain-avoidant demands of our id and the conscious, guilt-ridden social drives of the superego. It essentially operates as a regulator, a decision maker between the "rules" of life and what we want. As such, we might welcome the interventions of Freud's ego, thinking it will guide us down a mediated road between rigid rule-following and total debauchery.

These pages offer another approach to the ego, one that explores the concept from a spiritual context. In this framework, our ego is seen an aspect of who we think or believe we are - the little self that includes the rule-bound, the gratification-motivated, critical, immature, hyper-responsible, emotional, and shrewd aspects all rolled into one. While the distinction between our commonplace understanding and the spiritual may seem relatively thin, the difference lies in what appears as a mere opinion or attitude versus who we think we are in totality - the very vision of the little self that attempts to separate us from our Divinity.

To understand this spiritually-based ego, we must revisit a long-ago time when monsters dominated our earth, easily taking advantage of our physical form's vulnerabilities. In this landscape, our bodies stood unmatched against animals sporting big teeth, long claws, and brute strength; tall cliffs and deep swamps posed other threats. Because of these earth-based dangers, we created an ego for protection and survival to keep us from danger by sounding an alarm. Instead of living moment by moment in Union with our Divinity for guidance and navigation, we created the ego to steer for us. It issued warnings, making sure that predatory jaws didn't turn us into lunch, we didn't plummet to our physical death, or we avoided playing "victim" to any number of life-threatening scenarios. As a result, we invested so much energy into this energetic personal security system that we forgot how to operate without it.

Flash forward and we witness how the ego still treats every perceived danger as if some big, toothy beast were snapping at our heels. Common stressors today like traffic jams, insults, weather, deadlines, and mistakes (to name a few) generate a survival response identical to prehistoric dangers; our ego makes no differentiation between threats of old and what we see as threats to our pride, confidence, image, and career success. Moment by moment, our ego may jump into defensive action cloaked as judgment, criticism, blame, hostility, or jealousy. Any negative state of mind or emotion, in fact, holds ego's fear-based brand, acting to "protect" us from perceived dangers. At other times when our ego appears to cease fire on others, the arrows and daggers intended to defend from outside forces can instead stealthily turn tail and attack us as self-criticism. Simply said, any type of judgment, criticism, or blaming of ourselves or others is the work of the ego, and it will use anything and everything from thirty seconds ago to thirty lifetimes ago (keenly reaching into our soul memory) to convince us that we are in dangerous territory, alone in this world, and especially lacking the help of Source.

My dog, Zannah, offers a good example of ego in action...more specifically her quirky behavior. How I wish you knew her! Early on, she proved to be a very sweet handful - escaping through our legs as we exited our home, barking at everything and nothing, getting trapped in tick-filled, brambly patches on our wooded walks, trying to sleep on my head in the middle of the night, and using carpets like grass if it was too cold or wet outside. If she led the way on outings, Lord knows where we might go. The distracting tricks, scattered thinking, alarmist reactions to everything and nothing, and entanglement in the briar patch of our imagination…these are the tactics of the ego.

Please don't misunderstand. Our feelings, emotions, thoughts, and experiences are not to be denied. Rejecting our personal climate is a recipe for misery. All our experiences, in fact, provide rich lessons. How we feel or think merely calls us to pay attention in the here and now and to own our part in any interaction or reaction. Looking within to be aware, authentic, and personally responsible provides opportunities to identify the themes of our life via *all* interactions so we can shine through our true Self.

The following lists common ego reactions, though we may uncover many variations and additions based on our personal experiences. Our ego is operating when we engage in:

- blaming others or ourselves;
- judging others or ourselves;
- excluding others or ourselves;
- believing in the superiority of a culture, race, gender, sexuality, religion, career, ethnicity, etc.;
- accusing others or ourselves;
- negative or positive labeling that criticizes or inflates;
- complaining or gossiping;
- demanding recognition;
- demanding attention;
- needing to assert our opinion;
- needing to make an impression;
- needing to be right;
- making others/ourselves wrong as a character flaw;

- having aggressive or hostile reactions;
- being a martyr;
- having jealous reactions;
- whining/complaining about our life;
- staying in a victim role;
- feeling insecure, inadequate, or like a failure;
- rescuing others capable of action; and
- focusing on concerns about appearance - physical, status, possessions, career, etc.

Quite a list, eh? Do you feel like someone just looked in your underwear drawer? Shining a light on how often we become distracted, overcome, or tricked by the ego's subversive influence opens the way to truly dealing with it.

So, how do we remove power from the ego? Yep, you guessed it...the famous "o" word - observation, combining our exploration with non-judgment. The simple exercise of "Well, look at that," or non-judgmental observation allows us to witness what we are experiencing instead of being immersed and consumed by thoughts, emotions, and situations. Removing all evaluations as good or bad, we adopt a neutral attitude when paying attention to our internal climate and behaviors. Non-judgmental observation immediately dispels the energy and the strong hold of our ego, removing us from its grasp.

Next, as we become adept at recognizing our ego in action, we can ask, "What am I feeling?" allowing our emotions to come into full view. We can also uncover, "What thoughts contributed to that feeling?" Allowing ourselves to go deeper to expose ego's derelict attitudes or actions brings the questions, "What's under this?" and "What am I afraid of?" to the fore. This helps us take charge of ourselves, own our emotions, and uncover what may be operating beneath our conscious awareness. Continued non-judgment becomes imperative here, as the more we discover, the greater the chance for negative assessments about ourselves, further entrenching the operation of ego.

After full consideration of our internal climate, we can consider other possible reasons for people's attitudes and behavior when ego finds fault or blame toward all we encounter throughout our day. Exploring simple reasons for how people act instead of personalizing their behaviors helps us shift any perceived antagonistic reactions and stops us from making assumptions that lead to feeling attacked. Realizing that people are people - easily affected by their own ego as we are of ours - provides the space to be more loving and accepting and recognize that they may be merely having a challenging day or period in their life. Additionally, we may be presented with an opportunity to speak up, set a boundary, or identify how the situation requires change. And let's not forget, ego reactions can always point to areas in our life that call for growth and healing.

Finally, after learning to observe our ego in action and diffusing its control, we acquire the skills to employ it with useful tasks. Giving our ego a job to do keeps it busy in a more productive way than collecting situations grounded in worry, competition, or conflict; we can mentally send it off to count butterflies or monitor when the mailman arrives, occupying it like a bored child.

As we move forward, know that our ego merely activates fear in its various and sundry forms, ultimately to perpetuate the mindset of separation - separation from our true Self. Because we gave and continue to give it power, it will generate ways to convince us how much we should listen to its call. When it has us believing in "us vs. them", or that we're unlovable, or that God is too busy playing golf to help us, it keeps us from remembering who we really are, Children of the Divine - ever protected, ever cared for, and infinitely loved.

Journey I: Ego Themes

Spend time centering in your sacred space, giving room to contemplate your thoughts and feelings about the chapter material.

Consider the common ego themes listed in the chapter. Journal about which resonate with you and list ego reactions currently in your life.

What situations trigger your ego reactions? Why do you think/feel ego was triggered?

Be sure to write about your whole experience with all you discovered.

Journey II:
Your Ego Net

Let's put observation into action throughout your day. Spend time with your thoughts, emotions, conversations, situations, events, etc.

Stop at least two times during the day and get out your "ego net". Catch yourself and observe any negative emotional state or thinking toward others or yourself using the "Well, look at that" attitude of non-judgment.

Use the list to help identify the ego theme in place.

Write about what you observed and your experience in the process.

Have your observations of ego shifted your thoughts or feelings about others or yourself? How?

Continue to practice using your "ego net", growing in recognizing its influence. Log your progress as you evolve.

Journey III: Questioning Fear

Retreat to your sacred space to center and meditate.

Reflect on using non-judgmental observation, journaling your progress.

Now, let's move on to deeper exploration. Take a recent ego reaction that is fresh in your memory. Name the behavior, your thoughts, and feelings.

Contemplate the question, "What am I afraid of?"

Allow all the possible fears to come into your consciousness. Write them down, adding any reflections.

Can you embrace these fears knowing they are transient? What might help you move beyond them? Are these fears indicating a need to voice your feelings, let go of something, or set a boundary?

Journey IV: Depersonalizing

Retreat to your sacred space to center and meditate.

Contemplate a recent ego reaction toward others and journal about it.

Now depersonalize the situation related to your ego reaction by considering other possibilities for the behaviors of others? Brainstorm alternate perspectives and journal about them.

Ex: Someone cut me off on the highway today and I got very angry thinking the person was a jerk. Other possibilities: Maybe they were rushing to the hospital because someone in their family was injured; maybe they are emergency care workers rushing to help.

Did depersonalizing help you release any of your ego thoughts? Did these alternate views change your feelings and thoughts about the other person(s)?

Put your depersonalization into practice in real time? Observe, question your reaction, depersonalize.

Journal about your progress.

Spiritual Chutzpah

Happiness requires courage, stamina, persistence, fortitude, perseverance, bravery, boldness, valor, vigor, concentration, solidity, substance, backbone, grit, guts, moxie, nerve, pluck, resilience, spunk, tenacity, tolerance, will power, chutzpah, and a good thesaurus.

— Peter McWilliams

As our little personality self distracts us with gripping mental logic, a bruised heart, or survival pangs that claw their way free from soul memory, chutzpah offers the audacity to fearlessly live from our true Self. Chutzpah is the very spark that ignites our internal fire to stand in our power, to speak an unpopular truth, or to exercise our rights and leave behind emotional, social, political, racial, religious, sexual, or gender-based imprisonment.

Etymology traces our bold friend, chutzpah, to the ancient language of Aramaic as *hu spa*, and footprints to Yiddish roots unearth the word *khutsp*, meaning gall, brazen, nerve, or incredible guts. The generational view of this term, especially within the Jewish culture, chastises those who may use their boldness to step on or over others. In recent years, however, chutzpah has marched into a position of favor that speaks to savvy and courage. Now, our current culture sees it as a positive attribute, something required to navigate difficult situations and a challenging world.

We must remember that in exercising chutzpah, what is most acceptable to one may be offensive to others or vice versa. Here lie the challenges of chutzpah as the very sandpaper against the tender skin of family, community, cultural, racial, or religious norms. So, while the spirit of chutzpah within these pages may include actions and mindsets that stand against the fray, this author intends to do no harm by any means. What we bring to the fore, instead, underscores the freedom and fortitude to be who we are without infringing on others' rights, using our power, not force.

Chutzpah weaves its way into our very nature as spiritual power - to see beyond appearances, to practice non-judgment, to be authentic even when it may be unpopular, and to be loving in the most challenging of circumstances. At its very heart, there rests a deep and abiding desire...the desire to transcend all labels, groupings, and devices that separate us, inherently denying our equal and unique nature.

The birthright to live our life as a Child of a loving Creator with freedom from oppression, exercising expression in a loving way, not only asks for spiritual chutzpah, it begs for it. We might take a stand by removing ourselves from any related conflict to embrace our truth, accepting ourselves and others, and saying "no" to situations and people who intimidate, violate, or otherwise appear to act in unloving, fear-based ways. Then we truly rise out of the confines of our own minds, past the rigid rules, regulations, or righteousness imposed by our experiences or ancestral beliefs, past the societal norms that gag and bind our inner creativity and inherent diversity, beyond the individuals who attempt to denigrate our skin color, sexual orientation, or gender expressions. Yes, we must be audacious, calling on the god of chutzpah to speak our truth and live it! Owning our Divinity with authenticity, integrity, and strength is the very chutzpah exemplified by Rosa Parks, Martin Luther King Jr., Jesus of Nazareth, Mary Magdalene, Joan of Arc, Jackie Robinson, Mother Theresa, Oskar Schindler, Jane Goodall, and Harvey Milk, to name a few.

Indeed, the very work encouraged in these pages requires courage, strength, vulnerability, and authenticity - the brothers and sisters of chutzpah. And while siblings like vulnerability and chutzpah may seem diametrically opposed, they do not occupy separate space. Instead, we watch them joined arm in arm, marching forward as sacred rebels on the same path, inspiring, supporting, and empowering us as seemingly two different but co-dependent forces, each necessary to navigate the journey. At one point or another in our lives, we all will be challenged and urged forward in ways that beckon chutzpah to move in and take up residency.

One particular experience has become a testament to my own spiritual chutzpah. All during childhood, my Catholic upbringing presented more challenges than comfort. At the time, I was in sixth grade getting ready for the Catholic ceremony of confirmation. Part of the ritual was to take a confirmation name, which could include a new first name, while retaining our given surname. Weeks before confirmation, my mother received a call from the priest who informed her that I was forbidden to use my adoptive name. Because she had been previously married and refused to pay the money to acquire an annulment, my legally adopted name from my stepfather was denied in the eyes of the church; rules dictated the use my birth surname, the last name of my mother's ex-husband, incorrectly recognized as my birth father. A past filled with alcohol-fueled violence and troubling memories became the last thing I wanted associated with a ceremony of passage.

My mother took this fated call and her frustration echoed through the whole house as a tearful argument, addressing what she saw as unfairness. Quietly, I made my way to the kitchen to retrieve books from my religious education classes and walked out of the house. Somehow, I knew what I was about to do, and it didn't require too much forethought, or so it seemed.

The church, a few short blocks from my home, stood as a heavy, windowless, abstract building; it's asymmetrical roofline and lack of warmth represented a cosmic joke of sorts - nothing about it looked welcoming, loving, or church-like. Knocking on the rectory door, I patiently waited as the assistant priest, a gentle and kind soul, arrived in the doorway, his face painted with surprise and curiosity. (He was, by the way, the one and only positive influence in my entire church experience.)

With books in hand, I extended my arms, returning them like a bag of poisoned apples that clearly said, "No thank you, I'll pass."

"I quit," I said, my offering representing resignation from an institution that felt much like an outgrown pair of jeans - tight, confining, and outdated.

"What do you mean, Adriene?" asked the assistant priest in his soft, deep voice that now demonstrated an air of shock.

"I quit the church. I don't want anything to do with it anymore. I'm not using that name, so I'm done," I said, offering a staccato answer - swift, to the point, and matter-of-fact as I turned to walk down the rectory steps.

The priest's astonishment and confusion hung behind me like a dark cloud, but I had nothing more to say, nor could I look back to see the disappointment on the only face I cared about in that cold, stone building.

When I arrived back home, my mother asked if I visited the church. Shocked at how fast "bad" news traveled, I hesitantly inquired, "Why?" I knew she must have received a call from someone telling on me, the insolent, audacious girl.

"I got a call from the Monsignor," my mother reported.

Here it comes, I thought. *Big trouble now...*

"He said you can use whatever name you want," replied my mother, wearing a twisted smile that meant she was pleased.

I stood there swallowed up by an internal silence; there was nothing more to say. I had no intention of playing games or winning any battles. I just didn't want any part of a ceremony that didn't honor how I saw myself. A name relegated to the past had no business in my future; appeasing the establishment felt incongruent. What I saw as a male-dominated institution with limited vision clearly communicated more concern about old rules than my personal plight, punishing a rebellious mother and her child caught in the cross-fire. Plain and simple, I chose to sacrifice ceremony out of principle, honoring what was right for me. In truth, my twelve-year-old self grounded her spiritual chutzpah. She was more courageous than I ever thought.

There is an energy within each of us, a sacred rebel who urges us to live our Divinity, to accept and access the creative force within us, and to be that Truth. Living in alignment with this innate aspect of our being in this world often takes spiritual chutzpah - the dedication, focus, intent, and desire to live in Oneness with all and All and the authenticity and fortitude to stand strong, honoring and being honored for who we are.

Go forth sacred rebel...you are beautiful!

Journey I: Discovering Chutzpah

Retreat to your sacred space, spending time to relax and center.

Journal about your thoughts and feelings regarding the chapter. What did you experience reading this?

Can you remember examples from books, movies, or real-life that demonstrate chutzpah?

Reflect on experiences in your life when you had chutzpah, journaling what you uncover.

Journey II:
Spiritual Chutzpah

Retreat to your sacred space, spending time to relax and center. Ask your Divine helpers for guidance on this journey assisting you toward your highest and best.

Journal about situations in your life that currently require chutzpah?

Can you use any examples or experiences that you wrote about in **Journey I** to assist you in accessing the energy or expression of chutzpah?

How might spiritual chutzpah help you navigate any current challenges?

Can you set forth some action steps to assist in using this energy to meet your challenges and transform them?

Journey III: Reflections

Return to your sacred space, spending time to center and meditate. Call your helpers for guidance on this journey.

Reflect on the action steps using spiritual chutzpah to meet any life challenges.

What action steps did you use that demonstrated your chutzpah?

Journal about your experience using spiritual chutzpah.

Journey IV: Sharing Chutzpah

Share your experience using spiritual chutzpah with a trusted friend to ground and honor it.

Journal about your experience sharing.

How does it feel to own your power?

Laughter is the Best Medicine

Humor is an antidote to all ills.

— *Patch Adams*

Laughter echoes the halls of many healing places, especially the Gesundheit Institute. Popularized by the famous clown of a doctor, Patch Adams, MD, goofing around serves as a vital healing modality. Remembering that last good belly laugh, we too can feel the powerful and transformative nature of humor.

Among the many outcomes of humor, we discover its beautiful benefits - combating fear, changing our perspective, lightening our mood, and shifting any heavy energy currently in our life. Finding humor or allowing laughter to comfort us may be just the reassurance we need, a way to get through the most difficult of times. Physiologically, humor relaxes us and eases tension as it lowers our autonomic nervous system activity, allowing the heart to slow. On a cellular level, it lowers pain through a release of endorphins. As Robin Dunbar, evolutionary psychologist at Harvard, explains, "simple muscular exertions involved in producing the familiar ha, ha, ha," he said, "trigger an increase in endorphins, the brain chemicals known for their feel-good effect." He theorizes that among the many benefits of laughing, the social bonding that occurs through shared humor functions as the evolutionary glue that brings and keeps groups together.[12]

Finding humor is not difficult to do. It's all around us in the laughter and play of children, the silliness of comedies, the frisky banter between animals, and the giggles of a shared joke among friends. So, what keeps us from reveling in its joy? Sometimes it's

---

[12] Gorman, James (2011). Scientists Hint at Why Laughter Feels So Good. *Science*. Retrieved from http://www.nytimes.com/2011/09/14/science/14laughter.html

our heavy heart or the seriousness of a situation. Perhaps we feel so anxious or sad that humor feels foreign. Embracing laughter, humor, and playfulness, however, when it's most needed might seem difficult, bogged down in our heavy hearts and minds, but as we begin our ascent out of darkness, a good case of the giggles or even a gentle smile offers much needed relief. It lifts our spirits, elevates our mood, and offers hope to life's challenges. And when we can laugh or find some humor in the most difficult of situations, we can know that healing is afoot.

Let's get a good belly laugh rolling, find joy in our world, and revel in the gift of humor.

Journey I:
Laughter Generator

It's time to do some research. Take a trip to the library and/or go online and make a list of laughter resources. Consider joke books, comedic movies, cartoons, and comic strips.

Choose one of your "laughter generators" and enjoy!

Journal your experience with this journey.

How did the "laughter generator" change your mood?

Journey II:
Humor Healing

Journal about any current bad mood, illness, or difficult situation calling for humor healing.

Choose a "laughter generator" from your research in **Journey I**.

Now use your "laughter generator".

Journal your experience.

How did laughter help offer healing in your current situation?

How could humor serve you on your continued journey of healing and soul-discovery?

Here and Now

You must live in the present, launch yourself on every wave,
find your eternity in each moment.
Fools stand on their island opportunities and look toward another land.
There is no other land, there is no other life but this.
— Henry David Thoreau

There is only now. The past is gone and the future, yet to come. Each moment unfolds anew and presents many opportunities. This is the nature of being in the here and now, another valuable and practical mindfulness tool for soul-discovery.

Experiencing a constant stream of thoughts and feelings, we choose where our attitude lies moment by moment as surely as the clock ticks. Will we come from a place of centeredness, peacefulness, lightness, and wisdom or become weighted down with a heaviness in our heart and mind?

In truth, our choice in the now is simple, but not always easy. Staying completely present is an ongoing process that often seems dependent on ignoring the past or forgetting the future. Instead, present moment engagement makes us a full participant, one breath at a time, in whatever or wherever we focus our mind and heart, our thoughts and feelings.

For many, the concept of here and now feels elusive and slippery, calling for a more tangible understanding to the practice of staying present. While each person's actual experience of the present moment (here and now) remains highly individual, the following example wraps our understanding of it into a metaphor on life.

Imagine a peach. As it sits on our table, the peach carries with it a history; all it encountered as sun, rain, its life on the farm, and the journey to our home represents its past. In contrast, when cut open, the peach reveals its future; one perfect seed that bursts with unexpressed potential. Experiencing the peach, we rest in the now. Smelling, feeling, and tasting - the fragrant scent, juicy flesh, and fuzzy skin that brushes against our teeth and tongue in one delicious bite - creates our moment-by-moment symphony of sensations. While the peach's past and future influence it as a part of the whole, only the unfoldment of our accompanying sensory experiences happens in the now. Eating the peach, our thoughts and emotions can travel to the past, its history. We may wonder how it came to us in such perfection or why bruises cover the soft exterior. Or we might remember picking the peach at the store, the selection of just that one. We can even dream about its future; will it make a tasty pie, grow a wonderful tree with fruit, or merely compost in the garden? But *all we have is the here and now* and in this present moment we experience the sweet gift of rich, juicy, goodness as it unfolds one bite at a time.

With an understanding of the here and now through the peach metaphor, our experiences in life find new context. However, the question remains…will we engage the here and now fully or divert our attention elsewhere? Past and future seem real and hold potency *through our attention to them*, but our history and each passing moment can only be re-lived by directing our thoughts and feelings backwards to a time that's gone and lingers in memories. The future, experienced in our imagination, projects our thoughts and feelings ahead of us by looking forward in anticipation. Thus, our present moment or here and now experiences can be contaminated if our energy stays stuck in the past or worries about our future, pulling us to a consciousness that thwarts our growth. That's not to say we never reconsider, reflect, or plan; it's not an all-or-nothing premise. When we engage in either past or future energy, we can intentionally and consciously employ present-moment mindfulness and the attitude of personal development so that our reflections, contemplations, manifesting, or planning occur to help us learn, evolve, and truly live life. As such, we engage with everything and everyone in "real time" as our experience unfolds before us and we create our lives consciously. Even when we dip into the past or consider our future, we can learn from where we've been to employ new behaviors and mindsets moving forward so that any reactions and responses to what surfaces can offer rich soil to help us grow.

Practicing the here and now, we again pay attention to our internal climate, noticing thoughts, emotions, and imaginings as the non-judgmental observer. From witnessing, we become informed of the typical trends of how we spend each moment. Are we generally a positive thinker or are we prone to pessimism? Are we ruminating on past relationships and previous conversations, imagining "what if's" and worries on a regular basis, or can we go with the flow, let go of perceived mistakes, forgive, and trust?

Becoming more and more present, practicing mindfulness through being in the now, our world truly opens. As our focus and intent shifts to a conscious presence, we can create in an authentic way and become aware of all our attitudes - the ones that create joy and those that perpetuate anger or sorrow. Like taming a wild horse, staying in the here and now requires us to actively guide our inner climate, providing our thoughts, emotions, and attitudes a space to roam on a landscape with healthy boundaries while facilitating a fullness in life and living.

Journey I: Peach Presence

Purchase a piece of ripe fruit or your favorite "live" food for this journey. Take your food with the utensils necessary for eating it to your sacred space.

After centering, slowly approach your food, first exploring its exterior. Touch it with your fingers and experience the texture and smell of it.

Now, keeping your mind present in the task, taste your food. Chew slowly. How does it taste? How does it feel on your lips, tongue, and teeth? Focus just on the food and what your senses are providing for your enjoyment.

Shift your attention to swallowing. How does it feel going down your throat and into your belly?

Journal about your whole experience.

Could you employ this mindful eating to every meal? What do you think you'll discover? Why?

Journey II:
Well, Look at That

Set aside some time in your sacred space for reflection. Non-judgmentally observe the state of your thoughts, emotions, or attitudes right now.

As best as you are able, adopt a "Well, look at that" mindset to facilitate non-judgment.

Journal about your observations.

Consider the following questions: Are you mentally replaying situations? What thoughts and emotions do those situations evoke? Are they in the past or are you imagining new situations and how you might handle them based on old experiences?

How do you feel about your observations? Are there any patterns to your thoughts, emotions, or attitudes?

Journey III: Life Practice

Take your practice of being in the now into your everyday life, using it during work, social time with friends, home life, and other settings.

Can you catch yourself dipping into the past or reaching into the future in a non-helpful, ruminating, or worrying fashion? Use the "Well, look at that" attitude to help you observe non-judgmentally.

What patterns do you still notice in your attitudes, thoughts, or emotions that you uncovered in **Journeys I** or **II** of this chapter?

Choose to break the pattern by consciously changing your mind or focusing differently; any new choice alters the pattern. Journal your experiences.

Practice staying present and note your progress as you develop this mindfulness tool.

Mandala

The flower's perfume has no form, but it pervades space.
Likewise, through a spiral of mandalas formless reality is known.
— *Saraha*

A kaleidoscope of color, a stained-glass masterpiece, sacred shapes in a temple. Across many settings, mandalas display their beauty. From the North Rose window of Chartres Cathedral to the thangka paintings of Buddhist deities, even Mother Nature generously shares her most famous mandala, the snowflake.

Known mostly to Eastern religious practices, recent trends have presented the splendor of mandalas to the mainstream. Encompassing a variety of images that span the traditional symbolism of gods/goddesses and idols, the universal language of nature's blooms, and the geometric designs inspired by sacred geometry, mandalas are rich with history in temples, worship, and art. Woven throughout cultures and religions like Hindu, Buddhist, and Jainist traditions, as well as other spiritual practices like meditation, these powerful, sacred symbols maintain various purposes. Generally, mandalas serve to impel the contemplator toward the realization of the spiritual force within themselves. Collectively, they speak to wholeness - the wholeness of life, life as a cycle, and the all-encompassing nature of the cosmos.

In more traditional practices, mandalas serve as a means for gentle contemplation and going within, while others may use them as a focal point in meditation. Current popular uses include creating or decorating these patterns in a return to childhood play, recognizing the restorative and nurturing value in the simple process of coloring. Because simple activities have an inherent quality of keeping our reasoning mind busy, our physical, mental, and emotional consciousness relaxes and finds repose. (See **Quieting Our Mind**.) Additionally, by allowing our artistic flow, we tap into our innate Divine energy, which is always creative and nurturing on all levels.

Any mandala can be used for gentle focus by examining all the colors and details to stay present in the moment. (See **Here and Now**.) Since objects, phrases, prayers, and mantras can help us practice being here and now, these tools facilitate a quieting of the mind. Providing a means for gentle focus, the mandala offers a visual mantra, which helps to exclude other thoughts during meditation, bypassing our reasoning mind's intrusions.

Amidst writing this book series, I discovered the gifts of mandalas. For me, the magic resulted from drawing my own. While absent in the perfect symmetry of computer-designed creations or that of the ancient mandala masters (or the very talented), the perfectly imperfect possesses a charm all its own. With each mark of the pen, I learned to transform mistakes and mismarks into a shape not originally intended but altered to fit into the whole. Reflective of an important life lesson - moving beyond our own bloopers to create beauty - it served as a valuable experience in my tendency toward perfectionism.

So, whether mandalas provide gentle focus, relaxation, and a creative outlet or facilitate a spiritual awakening to connect us with a greater cosmic consciousness, this journey is each of ours to make. May it generously offer its gifts and provide wonderful surprises along the way.

Journey I: Color Me

Gather your favorite art materials and move to your sacred space. Close your eyes and take a few minutes to center yourself, taking slow, deep breaths.

When ready, open your eyes and observe the detail in the mandala, allowing your mind to simply focus on the form. Begin coloring, staying present only to the activity. When your mind wanders, return it to the present moment of the activity - the shapes, colors, your coloring, etc. Continue to return from your mental wandering to the activity, allowing the flow of the exercise to carry you while enjoying the simple act of creating a design uniquely yours.

Journey II:
Mandala Creation

Create your own mandala. Consider using phrases, prayers, words, or poems that are meaningful, inspiring, or encouraging to you as part of your drawing.

As you create, allow the inspiration to come to you; flowing with it, stay present to the activity.

Journey III: Mandala Reflections

Journal your observations and experiences with **Journeys I** and **II**. Consider the following: Did you notice any emotions? Thought trends? Tendencies or compulsions?

How relaxing or stress-reducing were each of the journeys?

Now use one of your completed mandalas for meditation. Place the finished piece in front of you at a comfortable distance. As you look at the mandala, allow it to go out of focus, keeping your eyes on the piece as the edges fade or blur. Just permit this to happen as your mind stays present with the shape and colors, dropping all other intrusions.

Journal about your experience.

Which did you find more relaxing, coloring or using a mandala as a focus object for meditation? Why?

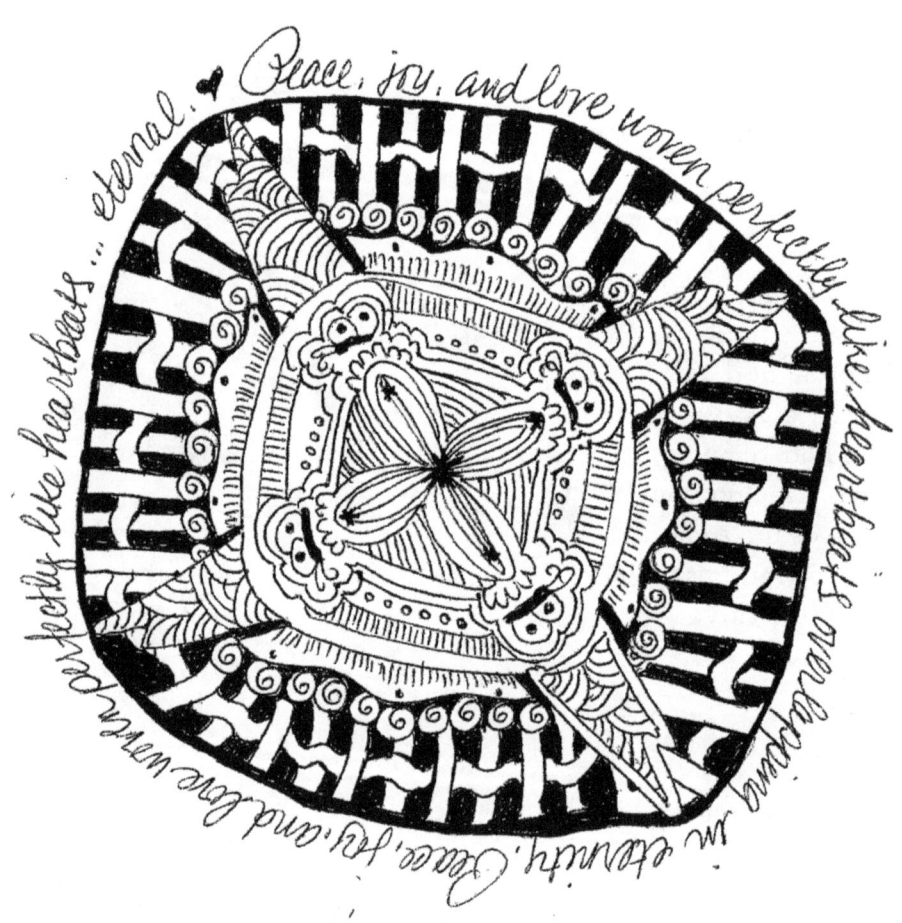

Mindfulness and Gratitude

...because all things have contributed to your advancement, you should include all things in your gratitude.

— Ralph Waldo Emerson

Wedding bells ring, celebrating the powerful marriage between two perfectly co-dependent practices - mindfulness and gratitude. Mindfulness (conscious attention to our life events, situations, thoughts, and feelings) reaches a tender hand to gratitude, igniting our awareness of all the positive in our life. What can we truly be thankful for if we don't first notice it?

As our mind highlights the vital players and things in our life, we must remember that the practice of gratitude is much more than an intellectual exercise. Through mindfulness, we first become consciously attuned to what is present in *all* our life in order to grow a thankful mindset. And as our thoughts sprout wings with the power of feeling, gratitude delivers its gifts.

When our heart fills with the warm glow of happy, joyful, peaceful, and loving treasures, we bask in the energy of thankfulness. Again, being present to the experience of appreciating the who and what in our life honors the holy matrimony of these fated lovers. And in this perfect union of the mind and heart, we grow, and our Self is revealed.

The Soul-Discovery Journalbook

Journey I: Heart-opening Gratitude Meditation

 To listen to this journey in a recorded version, click the QR code to the left which takes you to the OM page of www.pathways2innerpeace.com. This guided meditation, meant to connect you with the feeling of gratitude, is detailed below. Here we practice mindfulness, being thankful, and embracing the gift of love.

Set aside time in your quiet or sacred space. When ready, close your eyes. Breathe deeply to center and relax into a sense of peacefulness. Ask for guidance to open your mind and heart. Rest in the knowingness that as you ask, it is given.

Allow your awareness to reveal someone to be thankful for today. This may be a pet, friend, family member, or work mate.

Now, imagine this someone present in front of you in your mind's eye. Briefly look at them, witnessing them in your familiar way. Focus closely on their face, especially into their eyes. Now direct attention to your feelings and connect with this someone heart to heart. Allow your heart to open to theirs. Imagine this connection as loving energy, a pink light that grows and grows and grows. This love-light fills your heart and radiates out through your whole body, gently and sweetly wrapping itself all around you. As it expands, the pink reaches out to the other and touches into their heart and flows all around them, too.

Now, express gratitude and love:

"From my heart to your heart, I connect with you in love and gratitude. Thank you for your gifts of _____ (name what you love about them or how they are precious to you).
Thank you. I love you. Thank you. I love you. Thank you."

Allow the feeling of love and gratitude to remain with you, resting deep within your heart and filling your whole being.

When ready, take deep breath and open your eyes.

Move on to **Journey II**.

Journey II: Heart to Heart

As you spend some time in your sacred space, reflect on the following: What has been your experience and practice of gratitude prior to **Journey I**?

Journal your experience with the guided meditation in **Journey I**, considering the following: What thoughts and feelings surfaced in the guided meditation as you became aware of gratitude?

What was your experience with joining heart to heart? How did it feel? Could you connect more deeply with the feeling of being thankful than other similar chapter journeys?

How is this journey different from other journeys practicing gratitude?

How and when might you use this practice in your life?

Journey III: Gratitude Transformation

Spend some time in your sacred space to relax and rejuvenate. Reflect on relationships in your life that could use a boost of loving energy. Journal about these relationships and the ways loving energy may transform them.

Now choose one of the relationships as a focus, calling to mind the person involved. Returning to the **Heart-Opening Gratitude Meditation** of **Journey I**, we again practice a heart-to-heart connection. Find a positive quality they possess to aid in your process of feeling gratitude in more difficult circumstances. If you are challenged and discover resistance or negative feelings about them, ask for help. Below is one example of asking for Divine assistance:

> *Dear God/Divine Source/All-That-Is, I truly want to heal this relationship with _____ (name the person). I find myself feeling unable to be thankful toward them right now and cannot see any reasons to be grateful for their place in my life, but I know that You do. I ask that You be loving and thankful for me, through me, and I pray that Your loving hand be upon us both as we grow. Thank you.*

Practice this meditation and prayer as you are drawn. The more that you do this with willingness, sincerity, and love, the more healing and loving energy you send the person, and therefore your relationship with them.

Journal your experience with this connection journey. Did your feelings toward this person change? How?

Pay attention to how your relationship changes over time and journal about the shifts. Be sure to include how your attitude toward them changes, too.

Additional notes:

Creating Affirmations

*I've found that there is always some beauty left —
in nature, sunshine, freedom, in yourself; these can all help you.*
— Anne Frank

Affirmations are powerful tools for our personal and spiritual growth. Most commonly, we know them as positive statements of intent designed to change negative patterns of belief and behavior. These proclamations help us shift old, limiting habits into living declarations of a "new way", the most potent of which speaks to an inner consciousness aligned with our Higher Self.

What imbues affirmations with such power? First and foremost, our belief in them. In other words, the more strongly we feel our affirmations and *know* their power, the more potent they are. Remember, our thoughts alone possess little potency, as without emotion or feeling, they hold no staying power. So, affirmations that we *truly feel*, embracing and believing their power, are the ones that affect us and the world through us, whether they are positively or negatively framed. Secondly, words have power; as we use them with intention regarding our life and our being, the more compelling they are. (See **Our Energy** and **The World Sings with You** in **Volume III**.)

Generally speaking, affirmations feed our subconscious mind and reinforce "our truths" through the influence of what we declare moment by moment, drawing to us energies that we exude and own. And while we can take our Divine energy to create whatever we like, we often unknowingly or carelessly speak, think, and act. Remember, as held by the Law of Attraction, like energy attracts like energy, so whatever we affirm collects a similar vibration that returns to us more intensely than what we originally put into the Universe. (See **Wynebgwrthucher** in **Volume III**.) Whatever we affirm and put into our world becomes the bliss or the proverbial poop, cast before us to revel in or to precariously navigate. Again, another choice on our path of consciously managing our energy.

All the work in soul-discovery thus far, paying attention to our inner climate, has revealed many assertions of what we believe about ourselves and our world, as they essentially name and thus reinforce our ownership of the sensations, qualities, and values that we embrace. Statements about ourselves using directly expressed or implied declarations starting with "I am…" hold the most power. In fact, no combination of words is more potent than "I am…", which activates the very power of our inner Divinity. Because "I am…" taps directly into our creative ability through Self, it commands our belief into reality.

So, how do we create and affirm consciously for our highest and best? Becoming aware of our subconscious, as well as our conscious careless ramblings, is the first step. These are the statements we so casually toss about throughout our day like, "I'm tired," "I'm sick," "I'm fat," or "I'm stupid." These "accidental" affirmations may surface when we are not feeling our best on any level. Even our subtle self-chastising, mumbling "stupid" or "idiot" implies "I am" ownership of judgments against ourselves. Additionally, complaining about our world or what's in it or "practicing" thoughts that affirm events we fear are the unintentional and subconscious affirmations that create self-fulfilling prophecies. Swearing at ourselves holds similar negative qualities, illuminating the reason it's called cursing or the intentional sending of unloving energy to others.

Paying attention with non-judgmental observation, helps us become increasingly aware of what we affirm, opening the space and opportunity for re-patterning. Eliminating "don't", "can't", or other love-lacking word-trends frames our affirmations positively and affectionately in the present moment, aiding our movement forward. Affirming in the now is also important since stating in a future tense keeps the energy locked in a time perpetually ahead of us. If our intention is to create what we affirm, we only need remember that everything is ever-present, though not yet in our conscious awareness or physically manifested because of the lag in materializing from the higher planes to the slower vibrations of the corporeal world.

Remember, once we become cognizant of how we communicate, the habit of unhelpful affirmations may still magnetically draw us to old ways. Creating new affirmations to practice assists us in our endeavors to relinquish archaic patterns and manifest in more loving and life-affirming ways.

Below are examples of affirmations to assist in a positive practice:

- I am loving, powerful, and joyful. Everything I do, say, think, and feel today is through my Divine Self.
- This body feels tired, but I am OK, or This body feels sick, but I am OK.
- My car works perfectly, effortlessly, and efficiently as a symbol of how freely I move through life.
- I am filled with the love of the Divine, Who guides me every step of my path.
- All goodness comes to me through my Divine Nature. I am abundant, loving, and joyful.
- Though I am sad and disappointed, I am OK. This too shall pass.
- I gratefully pass this money as an energy to pay the bills that sustain this home and affirm that the energy returns to me as financial abundance in perfect order.
- I am infinitely abundant, rich in Spirit, love, peace, and joy.
- I am creative, filled with the innate, Spirit-driven power of my Higher Self.

By now you may be thinking, "I don't believe these positive affirmations. I am really overweight or cranky or poor or sick." Important point. Trying to create a new belief over an existing negative one, one that we consciously or subconsciously buy into hook, line, and sinker, won't work. Personal beliefs form the foundation upon which all affirmations are created. Their power is in what we feel. So, whatever we proclaim must be felt to have any power. When our affirmations feel disingenuous as if we're reaching or striving for positive outcomes, we only shoot ourselves in the foot. And we can't fake an affirmation by playing a mental game with ourselves and crossing our fingers for different results. We do need to own where we are, be honest with ourselves about how we feel, and then explore how we can shift our negative mindset and self-talk. As we come to terms with the attitudes about ourselves, we can aspire to a more healthful lifestyle, body, or mindset without kicking ourselves in the shins. To grow for our highest good, we hold a vision of our desires, one at time and with the feeling that they are already present, even though they may seem a long way off from our "goal". As we affirm the change, we seek by connecting in mind and heart with the "new", we shift the energy to owning and being. Always, our Higher Self supports our evolution, transforming and loving us through our challenges. (See **Faith in Ladybugs** in **Volume III** and **the Power of Belief** in **Volume V**.)

As we make the space to rest in the light of Self, connecting to our Divine Nature, we build our life consciously with faith and trust. By aligning with this loving, joyful, peaceful Self - ever-present, always helpful, and eternally ours - we come to know from the inside out that...

We are beauty. We are peace. We are truth. We are love. We are light.

Journey I:
Affirmation Survey

Set aside some time in your quiet space to center and contemplate.

Consider "I am" affirmations that you currently use in your daily life. Think about times you've witnessed the little voice in your head that says, "I'm fat," or "I'm exhausted," or "I'm happy."

Journal about all you discover.

Now spend a few days observing your thoughts, emotions, feelings, situations, and interactions. Write about what you experienced when intentional or accidental affirmations surfaced. Were they loving or unloving?

Write about your observations with all you uncovered.

How do you feel about your discoveries?

The Soul-Discovery Journalbook

Journey II: Reframing Affirmations

Write out the affirmations below that you uncovered in **Journey I** that are imbued with negative, unloving energy. Reframe them in your own words to loving ones.

Negative Affirmation	Reframed Affirmation
Ex: I'm fat.	I feel uncomfortable with this body's weight. I take in only what I need for total health. I am OK.

Journey III: Reflections

Journal your experience with **Journey II**.

Consider the following:

How do you feel about changing these affirmations? Can you embrace the shift and feel it?

Journal about which affirmations seemed the most difficult to shift toward positive, loving thoughts and feelings. Why were they difficult to shift?

How could these affirmations point to limiting beliefs that call for more soul-discovery, support, or acceptance to release?

Practice using your new, loving affirmations. Journal about your experiences and progress.

Have these loving affirmations helped you? How?

Additional Notes:

Journey IV:
New Vision Meditation

Set aside time in your sacred space, meditating to relax and calm your mind.

Choose a reframed affirmation from **Journey II**. Close your eyes and say this affirmation aloud or in your mind, feeling the connection to what it means to you.

In your mind's eye, imagine a vision of what this affirmation declares. If perfect health, see your body perfectly healthy and vibrant. If affirming an efficient, well-working car, then envision driving in a car that gets from A to B in perfect order.

Feel whatever you are affirming as you paint the image in your mind, connecting with the abundant, generous, loving Universe that provides.

Journey about your meditation experience. Can you feel the Universe providing? Why or why not? Can you hold the image of what you desire as it manifests?

Only Love is Real

Love understands all languages.

— Romanian proverb

Within each of us is a Divine Center, our Higher Self. Our Self, as compared to our little self (ego, personality), is loving, peaceful, and joyful. Filled with compassion, it "sees" with the "eyes" of Spirit, which look beyond the appearances perceived by the little self. Envisioning a bigger picture, our Higher Self witnesses and revels in the gifts of all situations, even those we experience as challenging. "Something valuable, loving, and growth-producing rests here," says our Self, even when we are unaware of what that is. Most undoubtedly, our Self chooses love every time because it is love.

How is this possible? our reasoning mind might think. The heartache from a recent relationship was very real…the car accident six years ago, the nightmare trip with family, the fight with our boss last week. I am by no means saying that our life's events didn't happen or that the pain we experienced or still feel is/was a figment of our imagination. We certainly need to be authentic about where our consciousness lies and the experiences in our life. Perhaps most importantly is to know that immersed in our ego-based personality, we experience pain and difficulties because our Self rests vibrationally well beyond that idea of who we think we are. What the Higher Self offers us is a life raft, the realization that our time here and all our challenges are transient. The pain of our little self, then, can be seen as tool for us to learn through.

So, what is eternal, lasting, and real? Only love. Only love, however it emerges, helps us rise from the ashes of our transient difficulties to transform painful situations. Moreover, that suffering or difficulty can offer a blaring contrast to illuminate the love that seems so hidden, concealed behind a wall of anger, sadness, misunderstanding, etc.

Individually and collectively, we are love, created in and by love, and stand as a representative of it in the flesh. Love whispers from the very core of our being, while our ego, on the other hand, appears as a shadow - one that seems to block out the potent internal sun of our Divine Love. Ego is not our true Self - never - though its convincing clamor can make us think otherwise. Even when our mask or false face (of the ego) appears to dominate our consciousness, squeezing our heart and clouding our mind, this hollow ghost's haunting presence isn't a signal that our True Nature just up and left; our Higher Self can't disappear, leave, or be diminished. Under the influence of ego, our inner light merely appears missing or blocked - temporarily obscured by a "cloudy day", an apparition of the negativity we so believe in. Remember, no clouds can ever destroy the sun. And so, all experiences, situations, and interactions with ourselves or others simply offer a choice to call forth love or to allow our unloving reaction and ego-based fear to surface and provide another opportunity for growth.

> The mind will speak of love and yet hold the heart prisoner to its new rules, new laws, and still say "this is right" and "this is wrong." It will speak of love and not see its intolerance or judgment. It will speak of love to be helpful and with all sincerity, and yet the very logic that it uses, though new, wounds the heart of the most tender, of those most called to love and its sweetness. "I am wrong to feel the way I do" the tender-hearted says to herself and, convinced that another knows what she does not, covers-over her tenderness with protection.
> — A Course of Love, C:I.3

By now, each of you may be thinking, "Well that just sounds so unrealistically positive." I understand. Coming from love can feel fake (and challenging) when we're angry, disappointed, or frightened. This isn't about wearing a veneer of candy-coated sweetness over a seething hotbed of negativity. Again, it's not about pretending to be positive when we want to scream or cry or destroy something. Choosing love doesn't come through ignoring how we feel. That would be steeped in denial or just plainly untruthful. In other words, we don't pretend to be happy when we're not. Equally important, we become mindful of dwelling in our daily miseries.

Choosing love, to this author, means knowing that anything not from love is only a contorted version of the pure love energy from Source, the wellspring of our nurturing, creative power. Fear is love adulterated by our ego, influencing us through personality trends and soul memory. We cannot arrive in a place to consistently choose love by trying to be someone we are not. Choosing love means loving ourselves enough to accept where we are at any given moment, whether we like how that looks or not. It means being purely authentic, as well as recognizing where the ego wants to take us.

Then we can see any non-loving state as temporary, a surfacing defensive pattern predicated on past experiences, an old T-shirt of outdated personality clothing that we can change.

Unerringly, our Self urges us to grow through all experiences - to walk through them and be present so we become aware of new choices. New choices allow us to change our thinking or release the pain and move through whatever holds us back from love.

What about being with those who are not ready to accept love or those who may not value what we offer? This is where the Self comes into play again, this time through wisdom. Beyond the judgment of the ego-based, little self that would identify those individuals as "bad", the Self guides our sight and offers the discernment to come from Truth. As such, Self helps us "see" an absence of readiness for love, resistance to love, or relational one-sidedness as a lack of self-love. (See **Leaving Our Swamp of Judgment** in **Volume V**.) We may then be guided to communicate our feelings more clearly or to honor, nurture, and value ourselves differently as we navigate those experiences. We may even be urged to step away from such situations or relationships, especially when they don't serve our highest good, most particularly the relationships that become stunted or stagnant by another's refusal to grow. Though our little self may initially feel hurt, abandoned, or shunned, Self moves us beyond the energy of ego-based judgment. And as we heal, thoughts previously steeped in negativity become replaced with love and compassion.

Life offers many, many opportunities to see from the eyes of love. Our mere intention to grow and learn about love brings situations to our attention. One of my most memorable experiences came from an otherwise ordinary trip to the grocery store. An afternoon many years ago, I stood in line waiting for my turn to check out. As much as I tried to not be drawn into another's family drama, the noise of a distressed child mirrored by her shouting parent echoed unnervingly, bouncing across the hard linoleum floor. Peering over the aisle divider, I witnessed this young girl crying loudly, having been harshly corrected and berated by her parent. The mother seemed outraged; the girl heartbroken. As an empath, children crying often presented difficulty for me. That's not to say that children shouldn't be corrected, but loud, critical reprimands in public are shaming, embarrassing, and ineffective as parenting tools. Often, I imagine how the screaming parent operates at home if they're so comfortable screaming in public. As a fellow parent, I find these types of situations painful to witness, easily slipping into irritation and condemnation, mixed with a desire to rescue the child.

Before I jumped straight down the rabbit hole of judgment and heroic feats, I centered myself and raised my consciousness. Envisioning the mother and her child in light, I asked to see them both with the eyes of love - the mother calm and nurturing, the child loved and cooperative. A sense of peace washed over me as I continued to send loving thoughts to them. Very shortly, the little girl stopped crying, her energy evening out and calming. The mother became caring and supportive. As I rounded the checkout aisle and passed by, my eyes met the child with warmth; as I connected with the mother, a feeling of love and compassion passed between us. I believe that seeing mother and daughter with love helped call forth their loving energy, which radiated from them both and echoed in their demeanor. The message became loud and clear...never underestimate the power of love. (See **Let Your Love-Light Shine** in **Volume III**.)

So, look back over the valley, fellow travelers. You've traveled far. Many opportunities to choose love have crossed your path, many more lie ahead. Remember that any cloudy day is only temporary; clouds pass by and your Sun is always with you. Look through the eyes of love and bask in your inner light.

Journey I: Love vs. Fear

Retreat to your sacred space to center, breathing deeply and slowly.

Journal your initial thoughts and feelings about this chapter.

Next, contemplate recent reactions to a situation, event, or person and your choice for love or fear. This could be an internal interaction with yourself as you witness how you feel about your life, or a seemingly external one as an interaction with someone or something.

Journal what you observe.

Consider the following questions: What influenced your choice for love or fear? How could you choose differently? What would you need to change or let go of to choose love? How do you feel faced with your choice?

Journey II: Meeting Our Higher Self

 This is a journey to meet your Higher Self. For a recorded version, use the QR code to the left that takes you to www.pathways2innerpeace.com. If you have no access to the internet, ask a trusted friend to help you by reading the following to you at a comfortable pace.

Set aside some time in your sacred space. As you rest comfortably, close your eyes and take three slow, deep breaths.

Imagine yourself in an all-white space. Here you are completely safe and comfortable. Everywhere you look, it's as if you've stepped into a cloud. Light streams in from all around you, making the space bright, nurturing, and soothing.

Allow this space to transform into a large meadow. Lush green grasses cover the hills and expanse all around you. A field dotted with wildflowers of all shapes and colors blooms in your mind's eye. As you look across the grass, a beautiful hot air balloon sits on the other side of this meadow. You instantly know it's waiting for you and you make your way toward it.

Now you stand before this colorful ride. The rich brown, woven carrier is ready for you to climb into, it's door open and welcoming. As you step inside, you look up into the balloon and feel the heat that continuously fills the vibrant inflated top. This hot air balloon begins its ascent, traveling away from the ground. As it rises into the blue, cloudless sky, the meadow below becomes smaller and smaller. You can see across hills, mountains, and towns. It continues to climb, and your body feels lighter and lighter and lighter, like you are joined in harmony with the balloon, buoyant and free. Continuing your assent, look down to see the vast distance from Earth; you are safely above it, perfectly protected.

The earth begins to shrink in your view as you go higher and higher. Looking all around you, a cosmic field filled with stars is your playground. Though you are far from Earth, you still feel connected to her as you look out into the Universe. And in your other view, the Milky Way, the Big Dipper, and the Little Dipper all seem to wink at you. As you look to each constellation, you feel a connection to them, too. In fact, you feel that connection to everything around you - that intimate link, deep within your heart. You and the stars…born of the same magical energy.

Gazing into the depths of space, a light in the near distance comes to your attention. You can't take your eyes from it. Magnetically, it pulls you with the beauty it holds. Closer and closer it comes, growing as a traveling column of light. Closer and closer, it now rests immediately before you, this bright white sparkling light. You realize that this light is the shape of a person - the size, shape, and feel of you. In your heart, you can feel a deep connection. It is You, your Higher Self, your Divine Light. It wraps its luminous arms around you…holding you…as you hear it whisper, "I love you." You know instantly that you and your Higher Self are never apart, were never apart, and could never be separated. You allow yourself to be held, resting in the feeling of total and complete love, knowing that you and your Higher Self are One.

Slowly allow yourself to return to the room with this feeling of Unity and Oneness, joined with your Higher Self. Open your eyes when ready.

Move on to **Journey III** to journal your reflections.

Journey III: Reflections

Journal about your experience with **Journey II**.

How did you feel connecting with your Higher Self?

Can you feel the difference between being in your personality or ego-self as compared with your Higher Self?

Journal about the differences between being with your ego-self (little self) vs. Higher Self.

Your Inside Circle

Who looks outside dreams. Who looks inside, awakes.

— Carl Jung

You've been working hard exploring who you are, learning new, forgetting the old, building an inside circle of friends for your continued journey. What first appeared outside became an opportunity to awaken the constant companions within you from a long and deep slumber. Take a moment to acknowledge and celebrate all your work, dedication, and courage. Write or draw about how you've grown through and with the tools operating as internal friends, guides, and helpers introduced by **Constant Companions**. Which companions shall you choose to accompany you on your continued soul-discovery?

Volume III: Metaphysical Musings awaits. When you're finished move on to your next adventure!

The Soul-Discovery Journalbook

An Intimate Journey into Self

Volume III

Metaphysical Musings

You know what the issue is with this world?
Everyone wants a magical solution for their problems,
and everyone refuses to believe in magic.

— C.S. Lewis

Metaphysical Musings

In the recesses of our subconscious memory lies a remembrance of something greater than our small world. It calls to a consciousness, a vastness, an awareness of life and Life. This memory moves us beyond the confines of the physical to tap into that which infuses everything through an intimate bond with us and the world.

Metaphysical Musings looks at the world from a higher perspective through spiritual law, levels of energy, and our invisible universe. Within these pages, we explore basic metaphysical principles, reaching into the nature of all things and beyond our objective experiences into the limitlessness of our being. These chapters offer new ways to understand ourselves and the world, guiding all to navigate life from a majestic peak, beyond the mundane.

Our Energy

*If you want to find the secrets of the universe,
think in terms of energy, frequency, and vibration.*
— *Nicola Tesla*

We enter from Spirit into this world coming from a weightless freedom to a dense and heavy body. When we arrive here as infants, our connection to Source and all others across the veil remains strong, even as we transition into a new realm - new to another body but very familiar to us across lifetimes. In other words, we have incarnated many, many times, which lies beyond our conscious remembrance yet remains deep within the recesses of our subconscious mind through soul memory.

Until about the age of three, we easily communicate with angels, spirits, guides, and passed loved ones, though many of us forget. As we grow, earth life increasingly governs our active memories and pushes our connection to the spirit world further and further from our conscious mind. In addition, small children learn quickly that communicating with ghosts and other entities frightens parents, appears fantastical, or becomes judged by the mainstream as unhealthy. All the while, new dimensions for exploration and learning through this fleshy vehicle on the physical plane progressively dominate our consciousness, so we quickly forget we are Spirit living an earthly life.

Learning through our earth life repeatedly make us feel bound to our physical world, as if it is the only place that's real; however, so much exists beyond what we commonly accept as "life" and the body we identify as ourselves. Instead, our hard-wired, neurological navigational system has us groping in the dark, thinking we are awake when there is so much to discover beyond the awareness of a world that is but a shadow of the vastness that rests at our fingertips.

The Soul-Discovery Journalbook

Many desire to expand into a consciousness that moves beyond this limiting physical nature. To do this, we can begin to use everything around us to expand our mind, cultivating and grooming our senses to serve us and not the other way around. (The process we began in **Volume I**.) All that's required as we continue is a willingness to be open to the infinite possibilities of Life beyond life and the echoing reminders of our purpose here. And in our willingness, we begin to release limiting beliefs to ultimately facilitate our unlearning of old paradigms, especially those that keep us stuck in our earthly thinking. Only then can we meld with the hidden remembrances of Truth - the Truth of our being, life between lives, and the very livingness of all things.

In order to release our old ways of thinking and transition into new learning, which enables an understanding of our world and ourselves beyond the body, we begin with a different look at the very foundation and structure of everything around us. Witnessing the familiar constitution of our world, we find a collection of solid, liquid, and gaseous matter that we have identified and labeled based on our experience with them through our five senses. Reaching into science for greater understanding, Newtonian mechanics, for instance, describes the nature of interacting objects through force and matter; think of the proverbial apple falling from a tree onto our head. Ouch! If, however, we advance to quantum physics, our world becomes defined quite differently. Quantum physics holds that we only *experience* an object as solid. In other words, our five senses deceive us, and the feeling of hardness or solidity occurs from electromagnetic forces of atoms against atoms - atoms of the object against atoms of the body. This counter-intuitive paradigm demonstrates that the constitution of any object on an atomic level is 98% space - air, void, nada. Appearance doesn't equal reality. In fact, this amazing construction of everything around us aids our understanding of the world of form *and* well beyond it by drawing us to instead explore everything as energy.

Everything is energy. Yes, EVERYTHING. In truth, there is nothing we can conceive of that is not energy. If this seems totally foreign, unfathomable, or crazy, just imagine explaining a radio to someone from the 1600's or a cell phone to someone from the 1800's. Such commonplace contraptions would be science fiction to those living centuries ago.

As we now look at everything as energy, we may wonder how this applies to our world and all that is seen, as well as unseen. Simply said, what differentiates solid, objective, tangible matter from all other energy is merely a rate of vibration. Currently, science offers ways to measure some of the higher vibrations in our world; brain waves, heartbeats, and microwaves, for example, can be measured and witnessed through our advanced technology but not objectively seen with our physical eyes.

Higher vibrations of energy without solid form "live" invisibly beyond the body's vision unless a person is highly psychic. We may witness *the effect* of this energy, but unless we've developed our abilities or can naturally read energies, we typically can't see it. Take wind, for instance. Even something as powerful as wind is invisible. Only the result of its demonstrated power is observable - coolness on our face, blown leaves, or a downed tree.

What happens when we apply this idea of invisible energy to humans and other living things? If we remain bound to what mainstream education teaches, we may believe that this realm is a nothing, a fantasy - all our silly conjuring swirling in powerless made-up whips, right? Think again...

When we open our consciousness to a different idea about matter, moving beyond our five senses to the "substance" of thoughts, emotions, imaginings, dreams, and life past our three-dimensional world, our comprehension of energy expands far beyond bodies and form. Remember, our heart and brain alone emanate measurable energies, and so does each cell. We are a living, vibrating, pulsating light, expressed through a fleshy meat-locker filled with tender and tough cuts of feelings, emotions, thoughts, intuition, and knowingness. And while we think that this body holds these subtle energies, our energy as a collective whole is much greater than what the naked eye witnesses. All of what we see and experience, our many layers, coalesce into an energy field - an electric, magnetic, and unique body of vibrating energy.

Everything, inanimate or animate, has an energy field - a field of electromagnetic energy known as an aura. This means humans, animals, plants, minerals, as well as anything made (which would hold the energy of its original material combined with that of its creator) possess an aura. As humans, for example, our aura is a manifestation of our personal, spiritual energy field that radiates out from us into our world. It is projected as a collection of vibrations from multiple levels of our consciousness - our physical body, our etheric body (the energetic bridge to our mental and emotional bodies), emotions and feelings from our emotional body, thoughts from our mental body, and beliefs from our soul memory. (See **From Consciousness into Awareness**.)

To understand what our aura looks like, we can envision energy from Spirit coming to us, entering our body by traveling through a kind of channel and expanding out around us by encircling our body like a donut. This personal energy field extends into our world, interacting with everything and everyone; it "feels" it's way, much like the antenna of a snail senses its surroundings. Each time we experience input through our five senses or have a thought or feeling, that energy is expressed in our aura. All current experiences present themselves in our energy field along with all past experiences that we hold continued interest in, especially unresolved struggles or issues. Everyone, in fact, whom we meet leaves a small footprint in our aura as a tiny piece of their energy. (See **Wynebgwrthucher**.)

Individuals must be very psychic to see auras with the physical eyes, especially to witness the various, dynamic hues and subtleties, but all of us can see a portion of the aura with some guidance. We explore this simple practice through **Journeys I** and **II** in this chapter.

Our new understanding of energy offers much to discover as ways to "see" the world through different eyes. Knowing the power of our energy, especially the impact of our thoughts and feelings on our life and the life of others, is an integral part of soul-discovery and our personal evolution. As we begin to realize and accept the parts of us typically invisible but ever-present, we arrive at the knowledge that we are more than our body. Expanding our awareness and embracing our spiritual Self helps us remember that we are ever guided and loved as a unique, yet collective part of the vast Cosmic Consciousness - energy never separated from the Whole.

Journey I: Reflections on Energy

Retreat to your sacred space to center and meditate. When ready, reflect on this chapter about energy. How do you feel about the material? Does it align with what you've been taught about energy?

What do you find most challenging about what you read? Why?

Is there anything intriguing or comforting about the information? Disconcerting? Why?

Journey II:
Basic Aura Reading

Ask a friend to dress in a dark shirt and stand with their back against a light-colored wall in natural lighting, but not in bright sunlight. Place a sticker or piece of colored tape on the wall about three inches from the angle where the person's head and shoulders meet.

As the observer, stand about six feet away. Now look at the person but keep the sticker as your focal point. As you continue your gaze, soften your focus by not blinking or moving your eyes. Staying on the sticker, your eyes will relax and the person will appear "fuzzed out" (unfocused).

As your eyes un-focus, a thin halo will appear around the person. You may even notice different colors, but commonly a bluish-gray layer comes into sight close to their form – their etheric body.

Journal your experience and consider: How do you feel witnessing this energy? Can you imagine how your aura puts you in contact with everything in your world?

Journey III: Tree Aura

Experiencing the aura of other living things facilitates our connection to life as an intricate, continuously communicating web. The auras of trees in spring become particularly active as they ready themselves for a new growing season.

Begin with a tree-top. If the season is colder, observe a fir, as they remain more active through winter. Again, focus past the tree, allowing for branches to be in your field of vision indirectly. Look for squiggles of energy directly above the tree.

Describe and/or draw what you see. Do you notice any color? Do you notice any movement to the tree's energy? How do you feel witnessing this amazing display of life in action? How might this living energy connect to you, the Universe, and other living things?

Practice aura reading with other plants, people, and pets to hone your vision. Record your observations.

Beautiful World

The best and most beautiful things in the world cannot be seen or even touched — they must be felt with the heart.
— *Helen Keller*

Child of the most loving Divine Light, you were created in unspeakable love and infinite beauty. Look with your heart at this cosmic sea as it magically sparkles with life all around you…

…in the gift of a crimson and lavender painted sky placed before you, a beautiful treasure and reminder of Life's simple pleasures;

…in the pure, angelic laugh of a small child expressing unbounded joy;

…in the bursting forth of a bright green seedling from its protected enclosure, reaching into the world with all its Divinity;

…in the adoration of one cuddling, furry four-footed curled upon your lap; and,

…in the treasures which roll forth from the frothy waves, sharing color, texture, and rhythmic sounds of an emerald, watery home.

The more we can appreciate beauty, the more it grows our own inner beauty through love of our world, a world that we are intimately connected to and bound with. As we experience connection to everything around us, our awareness blooms as Union with Divine Source, the wonderful Cosmic Consciousness. Child of God, you are Beauty, One with all of Life.

Journey I: Find

Take a walk in nature, allowing all that surrounds you to draw your attention.

Select one nature object to focus on. Spend a few moments looking at the uniqueness and detail of this living wonder.

Now look at this object using what you learned in **Journey I** of **Wise Baby Vision** in **Volume II**.

What do you see that you never noticed before? Draw or take a photograph of your object, placing it here.

Journal about your observations and experiences.

Journey II: Oneness

Spend time in your sacred space with your nature object, its image, or a drawing of it from **Journey I**. This is a living being, unique and different on the surface yet created from the same Cosmic energy as you. Through that energy, you both are intimately connected with all of life.

Open your heart and unite with your nature object. Use your own words or your version of the following to open to your connection:

"Heart to heart, soul to soul, Spirit to Spirit, I connect in Oneness with _____ (nature item) through the love, joy, and peace that is Universal Power."

Write and/or draw about your experience.

The World Sings with You

The human being holds a universe within,
filled with overlapping frequencies,
and the result is a symphony of cosmic proportions.
— Masaru Emoto

From the songs of nature to the music of the tune makers, the magic of sound inspires, entertains, and encourages us to express. It gives voice to the Universe and sings the melodies of the soul.

Among the amazing properties of sound is resonance, which occurs when one object pulsating at a natural frequency compels a second object into vibrational motion. We can understand resonance most easily through musical instruments. Let's imagine for a moment two violins side by side. Pluck the D string on just one violin and the D string on the other vibrates in unison at the very same pitch. This occurs with no contact to the accompanying violin. The frequency of vibration of one instrument calls forth the same vibration of its partner - musical resonance in action.

Resonance, while observable with string instruments, is not relegated to the musical realm and operates with emotions as well. Recall, as we discussed in **Our Energy**, that each person's aura holds their personal vibrations of the present and past - physical states/illness, beliefs, thoughts, emotions, and experiences. Because our aura is so magnetic, it attracts energies according to the universal Law of Attraction. In addition, when we spend time with others, we unknowingly resonate to them and them to us; as our auras touch into one another, we vibrate to similar energies much like the two violins. Therefore, anyone and everyone, individually or as a group, can influence us, just as we can them…emotional resonance.

So, what does emotional resonance look like on an average day? Let's say, for example, that we are in a happy mood. La, la, la, la, la…life is good. Then, we walk into a group of people where reddened, angry faces turn to meet our gaze. Whether the tension present is obvious to us or we remain oblivious to it, this atmosphere can easily pull us down from a positive mood into the dominant energy of the group where we wind up feeling angry, irritated, frustrated, and/or overwhelmed. In other words, emotional resonance occurs between the group's energy and other heavy energies in our aura from unresolved situations of the past and/or leftover emotional experiences from earlier in the day.

On the other side of the spectrum, however, let's say we instead attend a celebration - wedding, birthday, graduation party - where people joyfully embrace each other's company and join in admiration of the celebrant(s). Typically, the dominant energy tends to be happy, uplifting, and festive. Arriving in a good mood, we resonate with the happiness, sharing the light energy of the group. If in a negative mood, we can allow the energy of the celebration to lift us up as it calls to other happy life events and similar vibrations.

As we reflect on how emotional resonance and energy impacts us personally, situations may come to mind where everyday interactions and encounters with life seem to affect us more than what appears to be "normal." Individuals more sensitive to energies, otherwise known as empaths, feel strong impressions and energetic effects from other people, animals, places, or objects. These individuals often:

- feel another's mood and may experience it as their own;
- become impacted or overwhelmed by another's energy;
- find that watching bloody, violent, or conflict-laden movies, shows, and news feels overwhelming, heart-wrenching, or unbearable;
- sense another's body pain or discomfort and may experience it as their own;
- feel moved to help and/or provide healing to others;
- become "rescuers" because other people's pain (mental, emotional, physical) feels like their own (See **Transforming Drama** in **Volume V**);
- find another's crying very difficult to witness and may be easily moved to tears;
- experience vivid dreams filled with graphic, multi-sensory details;

- repeatedly replay the day's events in their minds and relive scenes from life, movies, or book dramas in dreams, especially any experiences that impact them emotionally;
- have difficulty setting boundaries (see **The Final Frontier** in **Volume IV**);
- feel more comfortable in black (cloaking) or white (shielding and neutral) clothing as they subconsciously attempt to manage the overwhelming nature of people, crowds, or highly populated areas;
- feel physically drained or a general malaise when around groups;
- know about people, events, etc. without knowing how they know;
- may see or feel the energy of angels, guides, and those passed-over; and
- can sense the energy of a house, room, or location but may not be able to identify the cause or source of what they feel.

Energy is all around us and is who we are on all levels. It's part of our world and all situations. Our attitudes, mindsets, beliefs, and physical health compound this energetic impact. As a result, our overall mood may be mildly, moderately, or profoundly affected depending on our own internal state. When we know how energy works, however, we can employ measures to better navigate its influence, taking charge of the emotional and energetic resonance instead of it controlling us.

As we uncover the nature of our energy and how resonance affects us, tools on the path of soul-discovery help us tune into our personal energy, allowing us to manage it consciously. In this chapter's journeys, we first reflect on our overall energetic awareness, becoming familiar with how the world affects us. Then we can use a simple technique of grounding to smooth and stabilize our energy, which lowers stress, keeps us present, and makes us fully engaged in our body. Subsequent chapters explore auric protection. (See **Wynebgwrthucher**.) Finally, through many other chapters, we continue to shed the limiting beliefs that we hold in our energy field. This clears away the debris that collects the energies that don't serve us. And so, our soul-discovery continues to richly unfold.

Becoming increasingly attuned to our world, we develop awareness of the unseen forces within us and around us, all that we are intimately and profoundly connected to. The world sings with you and you with it…resonance as a grand, cosmic symphony. What tune will you carry? The choice is yours. Choose wisely.

Journey I: Reflections

Center and meditate in your sacred space. Journal your reflections about the chapter. Did it provide new understanding about you and your world? How?

Now ask for guidance to uncover and understand people and situations that influence your energy (thoughts, mood, attitude, etc.).

Journal on times when the mood of others affected you. Describe what you felt or sensed and how you became influenced by emotional resonance.

Consider the following: Can you identify people you desire to be around or not and why? Can you identify what emotional moods of others you find most difficult/easiest to deal with and why?

How and in what situations would you like to shift your emotional energy?

**Journey II:
Empathic Reflections**

Center and meditate in your sacred space.

Identify which characteristics of empaths fit you and list them here. Journal your thoughts and feelings about this. Is it a new discovery or clarification of something you've always known but could not describe?

Can you identify the unique ways these play out in your life?

How might understanding your empathic nature help you walk the path of soul-discovery?

Note: **Wynebgwrthucher** and other chapters in this volume and beyond aid those who identify as empaths.

Journey III: Grounding

Through this journey, we explore grounding via earthing, etheric roots, and physical grounding measures. Grounding enables our energy to be fully engaged with the body in a way that helps us be present and centered to bring our spiritual energy more fully into our physical form.

Begin by journaling about your current physical, mental, and emotional climate.

Now choose one of the grounding activities listed below. Experiment with each of them and journal your experience. Be sure to sample them all, noting how each affects you.

1. Walk on natural terrain in bare feet to do earthing, drawing on the energy of our Sacred Mother. Walking on grass or sand are the most common practices of earthing.

2. Grounding through the five senses you can:
    a. rub your feet;
    b. have someone rub your feet;
    c. think about your favorite foods or smells;
    d. eat food that you enjoy and feels nurturing like root vegetables (mashed potatoes, roasted carrots, stewed beets), comfort foods (pasta, whole grain breads, homemade soup), chocolate, and hot, herbal tea.

3. Revisit the Centering meditation from **Setting the Stage** in **Volume I** and practice growing your etheric roots deep into Mother Earth.

Notes:

From Consciousness into Awareness

I am a spark from the Infinite.
I am not flesh and bones. I am light.
— *Paramahansa Yogananda*

We are many, many layers of energy. What we experience through the body, however, is but a small fraction of our wholeness because of the slow and heavy nature of our physical form. As we open our consciousness to move beyond thinking associated with the earth and our experiences here as the totality of who we are, we step into the vastness of all things and come to know ourselves as something more than this fleshy encasement.

The broad spectrum of our energies paints a wide swath; at one end, a pure corporeal nature reflects our consciousness at its lowest point. In the middle, there are many levels of consciousness that change and refine through our evolution. At the other end, we awaken our awareness, touching into the experience of Self and our Divine Nature. All exist regardless of how much we understand about this seemingly great mystery.

Exploring this spectrum, otherwise known as us, greater understanding comes by dividing it into vibratory rates of five interconnected "bodies" - physical, etheric, emotional, mental, and spiritual. And while our study begins with the physical, a place we tend to view ourselves from, we are first a spiritual being, and all manifestations of the other bodies follow that eternal truth as "lesser" vibratory rates. In addition, while these energies appear to be compartmentalized or separate, they intermingle and work from Spirit "downward", slowing in frequency while moving and descending in purity.

Before exploring our bodies, understanding the terms Spirit, soul, and soul memory is necessary. While our initial glance seems very esoteric and mysterious, any current confusion becomes compounded because many spiritual and metaphysical writings use the terms Spirit and soul interchangeably, though they vastly differ. To differentiate, we use a metaphor on the topic.

Let's say that a massive storybook representing each person sits on a shelf in a great library - a library of electromagnetic energy, a vast field called the Akashic Records. Our personal storybook, commonly known as our soul, is our individualized part of the Akashic Records (the library). Much like any book holds information, our soul is a record inasmuch as it actively records. Within its pages lies our entire history from the time of our creation through our potential future. As such, this living energy functions as an ongoing, active "biography" of sorts that contains both fiction and non-fiction. This unusual literary blend holds the memories (soul memory) of our life's grand adventures through many, many lifetimes as a collection fed by two sources:

1. Our Spirit (non-fiction) that writes the chapters filled with the Truth of our being and the remembrance of our perfection as Children of Source; It sees beyond the eyes of the ego and personality with love, abiding as a part of Source.

2. Our little self (fiction-based, collective personality energies dominated by ego) that pens the perceptions of ourselves and our world, commonly through fear.

We have one Spirit and one soul with several personalities. These personalities incarnate over and over again with one shared ego as we learn and grow to raise our vibration and return Home.

Returning to the five bodies, we begin with what's most familiar - our physical body, the vehicle of this earth plane and the most transient aspect of our consciousness. We see our body as "who we are" and the "place" we experience everything - all senses, all thought, all feeling, all emotion - as if those experiences are us, too. In truth, however, our denser physical form serves as a landing pad, influenced by our subtle bodies (spiritual, mental, and emotional) as their vibrations register in our nervous system.

Our etheric body, the next more refined level above our three-dimension form, serves as an exact replica of the physical and as a conduit for our non-physical energies by way of energy centers called chakras. The etheric acts solely as a bridge from our spiritual, mental, and emotional bodies to our physical body, as the direction of energy flows from higher to lower vibrations.

Next is our emotional body, a range of the energies of feelings and emotions - a spectrum of states from the pure feelings of joy, love, and peace to the more rapid yet coarser emotional energies of lust, anger, frustration, and anxiety, as well as the lower, heavy vibrations of lethargy, sadness, and despair. (See **Wynebgwrthucher**.) While uncommon in other writings, this book series differentiates emotions from feelings. Important for soul-discovery, this distinction lies in the source of emotions, which emanate from our emotional body at a lower frequency. Feelings, in contrast, come from the highest aspect of the emotional body as Feeling Nature fed by Source through our Self (our individualized aspect of Source connected to the whole of our Spirit and Source/God). Our Feeling Nature infuses us with the love of Source, the wellspring of our true feelings. While all energy emanates purely from Source, we can contaminate that purity using our free will through ego and personality trends, making us express in a way that seems lesser than the light that we are. So, when we allow the highest aspects of love from Feeling Nature to be influenced by the ego, our feelings change appearance into various and sundry emotions of fear that we experience as jealousy, rage, frustration, anger, grief, contempt, hostility, and more. As powerful creators, we manipulate the energy by our intentions and/or how we use it.

Next, we come to our mental body, a spectrum of vibrational energy that intermingles with the higher aspects of the emotional body. Like the emotional body, the mental body consists of an energetic range spanning from concrete mind to abstract mind. As discussed in **Quieting Our Mind** in **Volume II**, our concrete mind operates as the slower energies of logical, planning, figuring thoughts, helpful to the practical tasks of the day - paying bills and operating in earth-based chores. Abstract mind, in contrast, is the energy of pure knowingness and awareness fed by our Higher Self in tune with Source. Because concrete mind acts separately from any sense of Unity, confined by this mind's consciousness, our connection to the infinite whole (the Mind of Source) remains a mental construct or becomes denied. Connected to abstract mind, however, as an individualized aspect of this glorious wholeness, we know our connection (awareness), we witness all from Truth, and can access all wisdom - one Mind with God and all living things.

Finally, we come to the Truth of our being, our Higher Self or Spirit represented in our spiritual body. As the Child of the Divine, we remain eternally connected with the totality that is Source through our Spirit, the perfection and wholeness of our Divinity. We are a vast collective, entities experiencing their own life adventures but intimately linked in the limitlessness of Divine energy. As such, we are each an aspect of Source and Source is a part of us. Lovingly held in the nurturing brine of creation that is God, there is nowhere we can go that is absent from Him/Her/It. Nowhere.

As we step back to witness all of our layers, we begin to see the range of consciousness to awareness represented through the vast array of our energetic bodies. But what does this have to do with life and our movement through it? Is there value in differentiating between consciousness and awareness?

Simply put, having the clarity to identify whether we are operating from lower, personality-based vibrations, the purity of our spiritual center, or a place between that moves us higher in our understanding offers an opportunity to learn about ourselves and others. Growing in consciousness, we may still react, eventually coming to know that a more loving way exists. Soul-discovery and a desire to grow continues to bring us to a state where we can ultimately go beyond the ego's gravity.

When we move beyond consciousness, even in its higher vibrations, we can step into awareness. Through awareness, we *know* our perfect Union with Source, resting in Oneness moment by moment as we elevate our mind and heart to be in Unity.

Our personality, however, would have us think otherwise in its constant navigation through ego-based intrusions, believing in separation, judgment, and other states opposite of Unity. Fortunately, we all possess a counterpoint of balance on this great scale of life…the influence of our Higher Self and Spirit. "They" unerringly lead us to discover our Truth, help us change our perceptions through a shift in consciousness, and feed our soul memory a remembrance of Home and our Divine inheritance. This spiritual lucidity comes from practice, an intentional pause to consciously witness how we may be operating.

Identifying whether we are experiencing feelings (Feeling Nature) or emotions (lower emotional body), knowingness (higher mind) or mental grinding (concrete mind), informs us of the path on which we travel so we can align with our highest vibration and shed the mistruths that keep us locked in our own prison. And when our earthly world requires action through the tasks of day-to-day living, we can unlearn our old ways and proceed from a place within us in peace, joy, and love, even if that's just scrubbing our floor.

To simplify, there is only love or fear, knowingness or doubt. Aspects of love are feelings of unconditional love, compassion, joy, and peace. Fear (driven by ego) is the umbrella that covers all other emotions of our little self. Knowingness, in the diluted form we tend to experience, comes as moments of intuition - the feeling that we just *know* something but typically not why or how. Love and knowingness are the very core of our being in its Truth. All other vibrations beyond love and knowingness we manufacture as a lower energy, a manipulation of our Divinity, as our purity becomes twisted through the influence of ego. Remember, the very essence of ego is fear, which attempts to keep us from knowing who we are in Truth. It loves to use our soul memory of painful events to taint new experiences and deter us from growing. Without conjuring fear in all its various and sundry forms, the ego is jobless.

So, it's up to us. Remember, Spirit feeds us Truth and soul memory remembers Truth and our blockages. All knowingness and feelings present a remembrance of our True Nature, while other thoughts and emotions offer opportunities to explore and release what no longer serves us - the lessons which help us grow. Stripping away and rising above our lower vibrations unveils our Divinity so we can shine our Light in the world.

Journey I: Reflections

Spend some quiet time in your sacred space reflecting on this chapter. What are your thoughts regarding the information? How do you feel about the lesson provided?

To aid your understanding of this lesson, look to **Resources** for more information.

Can you begin to differentiate when you are coming from a higher vibration versus a lower one in your personal responses and reactions?

Can you go deeper and identify feelings versus emotions? Concrete mind thoughts or intuition? Journal your observations.

Journal about times when your instinct or intuition kicked in and you knew something beyond the evidence of your five senses.

Journey II: Practicing Higher Vision

 Let's connect with your Higher Self. For a recorded version, use the QR code that takes you to www.pathways2innerpeace.com. If you have no access to the internet, ask a trusted friend to read this journey to you at a comfortable pace.

Set aside some time in your sacred space. As you rest comfortably, close your eyes and take three slow, deep breaths. Ask that you be aligned on all levels of your being. Know that as you ask, it is done.

Imagine yourself in an all-white space. Here you are completely safe and comfortable. Everywhere you look, it's as if you've stepped into a cloud. Light streams in from all around you, making the space bright, buoyant, nurturing, and soothing.

Now allow this space to transform into a large meadow. Lush green grasses cover the area as a field dotted with wildflowers of all shapes and colors forms in your mind's eye. Make your way across the field, taking in your surroundings. As you walk through the grass and flowers, people from your life join you. Look out over this group, taking note of who is present. Then, take one or more steps forward toward the crowd. You have a feeling that there is some work for you to do with them. They are here so you may witness a replay of a challenging interaction or event. Immediately, you see yourself in a past situation with someone from the crowd as if you are replaying a movie. The scene unfolds with all the interactions, behaviors, and dialogue. Take a moment to witness this event in your mind's eye.

How do you feel about this memory? About the people involved? About yourself?

Can you witness any ego reactions?

Next, drawing your attention to the center of you and look down at your body. A bright light glows near and around your heart, a warm pink-white like a candle. It begins to grow as an orb and gets brighter and brighter. The feeling of its presence is a sense of peace, joy, and gentle loving. You know immediately this is your Higher Self. This light, your pure Divine center of love, emerges from you, remaining attached to your form by a strand, a bright silver cord.

All your awareness remains in this ball of light as your Higher Self, which goes up and up and up into the sky above the people like a bird. You travel high enough to be well above any difficulty or challenge, only seeing specks and dots below. Here your higher vision rests, the clear "sight" of the lessons and the Truth beyond what the little self could only see with the eyes of the body.

Affirm, "I know now with the eyes of my Higher Self about this memory or these people."" How do you feel with this new vision? Embrace your greater understanding, love, and compassion for yourself and/or others.

When ready, return from this higher perspective to your body, bringing the orb of light back to the core of you by following the silver cord. The love, compassion, and understanding of your Higher Self stays with you, a feeling that remains united with you.

Is there anything you'd like to say now to the people still playing out this memory with you?

Thank all those who participated with you and when you are ready, return to the all-white space. Bring your awareness back to your hands and feet, taking a nice deep breath before opening your eyes to return to the room.

Move on to **Journey III** to journal your reflections.

Journey III: Reflections

Journal about your experiences with **Journey II**, writing out the questions from the meditation. How did you feel about the memory seen through the body, the little self? About the people involved? About yourself?

As your consciousness became joined with your Higher Self, what about the memory did your Higher Self know? How did you feel with this new vision? Did you have greater understanding and compassion for yourself and/or others? How did your feelings or energy of the memory change?

As your Higher Self rejoined with your body, what did you say to the people in your memory? Did you bring the love, compassion, and understanding of your Higher Self with you or did you feel your personality or ego trying to interfere?

Continue to practice connecting with your Self, journaling your progress.

We Are So Loved

For he will command his Angels concerning you,
to keep you in all your ways.
— Psalm 91:11 King James Bible

It is He Who calls down blessing on you, as do His angels,
to bring you out of the darkness into the light.
— 33:43 Qur'an

Faithfully and lovingly, we are guided, protected, taught, encouraged, and nurtured… moment by moment, day by day. Our Divine helpers love us deeply and remain ever-present, spreading their love from birth to our final transition, as we grow during our time across the veil, and all the spaces between. As we learned in **We Are Guided**, each Helper, imbued with their own purpose, supports, inspires, and advises us in their own unique ways. These include assistance with life's more difficult tasks - loving reassurance when we feel down, guidance in seeing the Truth of any situation no matter how it looks, support to grow, and/or aid with the simplest of jobs or activities.

Our Divine helpers include an array of entities who include passed-over loved ones, spirit guides, and angels. Loved ones who have crossed into the realm of spirit provide their assistance to let us know of life beyond our perception of death, to urge our release of misunderstandings and misguided beliefs, and to help move us forward on our path. All they offer is influenced by their consciousness and their own evolvement. In other words, the personal belief system each carries into the afterlife from their most recent incarnation, combined with what they learn after physical death, determines the help they offer. Paying attention to their personality and level of awareness as we knew them when "living" (in the flesh) often informs the kind of help they provide from the spirit realm.

Guides are entities who previously incarnated on the earth plane. We draw them to us depending on our energy, which changes as we grow. That is to say, we attract our guides based on the path we travel and where our consciousness and evolvement lies, so their consciousness is reflective of our own. Because of our guide's earth experiences, they understand our undertakings here and may be better suited to our present lessons as we engage in our purely earth-based life. For example, should we need assistance finding a parking space, we would ask a guide of parking. For help with writing, we would attract a guide knowledgeable in essay creation or journalism according to the task. Often our guides (and we have many throughout our lifetime) come from a previous incarnation of ourselves, a past-life aspect who helps us on our journey in specific ways because of their understanding and knowledge of our lessons.

Angels are different than guides. Broadly speaking, they are individualized vibrations of pure Divine Energy who never forget or become misaligned with Source. The more common accounts of angel sightings, witnessing a human-like, winged figure, merely come from our desire to witness them in an acceptable form. Many angels solely exist in higher realms beyond personal contact with humans and other life forms. There they direct the energies of Divine Essence, serving as the perfect memory of the Universe and all within it; others tend to the very livingness of universes within universes, holding the energy of life with the utmost devotion. In contrast to guides, angels *never* live out an earth existence. They can, however, occupy animal or human form for a short period to carry out particular tasks or duties to help people on their journey, typically in emergencies

Every living creation - humans, animals, plants, and the mineral world - has angels to watch over them. We rest in the company of hundreds of thousands of angels. That is to say, as humans we *each* have 443,000 angels; at least a hundred or more are with us at any given time and two guarding us while we sleep. Our personal angels assist us with small, daily tasks like choosing our clothes for work or putting on make-up. In the same fashion, our guardian angels offer protection and guidance throughout our day like safeguarding us while we drive or travel. Some angels, known as devas or earth spirits, also protect and care for our animals, minerals, and plants. Others, yet, inspire our spiritual evolvement and help us learn or teach. There are literally angels for *every aspect* of our life. They bring us little songs, whisper in our ears, urge us lovingly to grow, help us understand lessons and new information, hold the vibrations of healing and love, and remind us of the Truth of our very being...all for our highest good and *never* against our own will. The one thing they cannot do for us, however, is release our limiting beliefs or errors in perception. That, my friends, is up to us! (See **Into the Butterfly**.)

I feel very fortunate to look back and witness past angelic help. One of many examples includes their assistance before a devastating but life-altering car accident in my twenties. Over and over in my mind (which is how angels communicate...with a thought that seems our own but is not), the thought, *Put on your seatbelt,* came as an insistent and repetitive reminder for a full half-hour before a head-on crash with an eighteen-foot moving van that ran a red light. I never wore a seatbelt...was never taught to...and so these angelic whisperings (that appeared as mental ramblings) were so obvious but misunderstood as idle chatter. How I wish I had listened.

I want to impress upon each and every reader the magnitude of angelic love and guidance. So, at the risk of sounding like a crazed sports fan, I offer some insight and understanding using a relatively traditional setting.

Let's imagine, for a moment, a sports stadium. Consider as a reference point that the top ten baseball stadiums in the world by size range from 41,000 to 56,000 seats. Dodger Stadium in Los Angeles stands at the top of the list, holding 56,000 screaming baseball fans. Our local Penn State University football stadium, Beaver Stadium, is the second largest of its kind in the U.S. and holds bragging rights as the third largest in the world, hosting 106,572 fans. For those readers not familiar with attending a game, take a little trip online for some perspective. Searching scenes from any of these stadiums should offer a glimpse.

Massive, right? Do you get the feel of swimming in a sea of excited sports fans, being surrounded by thousands of people? Now, let's apply that to our angelic consortium. Beaver Stadium, with 106,572 seats, holds fewer than one quarter of the angels available for help, guidance, protection, and the like. In other words, we have four, filled Beaver Stadiums of angels at our disposal at any time. Or take Dodger Stadium with 56,000 seats; it would take nearly nine of them to hold all our angelic help. Do you have an idea now of how much support rests at our fingertips? Why we ever feel alone is beyond me, though I understand it more than I'd like to admit.

How can we begin to understand the variation, yet specificity of angels in our world and beyond? We explore them by angelic dominions, recognizing their purpose and vibration. Every angel was created to possess a great devotion in the same way that we each have a unique calling in life. Each is responsible for their own task according to their respective realm. In the higher realms of the Seraphim, Cherubim, Thrones, and Dominions, angels exist and carry out their responsibilities well above our earth plane vibration, never coming into form nor having direct contact with us. (See **Dominions of Angels** table.) For this book series, however, we focus only on angels directly interactive with the earth. These include the Virtues, or the Angels of Miracles, who bring to us sudden healing or actions we perceive as miracles; the Powers, or Angels of Planetary Changes, who work with the evolutionary process of the earth plane; devas or earth spirits, the angelic forms who interact with plants, animals, mineral life, and weather; the Principalities, or the Angels of Spiritual Pathways, who inspire all life to become more and grow in awakening of Self; and the seven archangels: Michael, Gabriel, Ariel, Metatron, Zadkiel, Raphael, and Uriel. Each archangel has many angels under their direction to act on their behalf and assist them in carrying out their tasks. For example, the Angels of Protection work with Archangel Michael, the Warrior Angel, who serves to destroy our error perceptions about ourselves and our world. When we desire immediate assistance to aid our safety energetically (and physically), call on Archangel Michael and his Angels of Protection to guard from negative energies from within and without.[13] (See **Dominions of Angels** and **The Seven Archangels** tables.)

Listed on the following pages is a simplified overview of the complex angelic world. For more detailed understanding, please refer to the books listed in **Resources**.

Asking for help from our Divine companions is a simple exercise of reaching out our hearts and minds to accept what they offer. Along the way, remember to thank them through loving words, acknowledging their generosity, guidance, and adoration. They love assisting us and rejoice when they witness our growth and alignment with our True Nature. Our Divine helpers want nothing more than to call us to the Home that lives in our hearts.

---

[13] Donovan, Rev. Penny (2017) *Angels, Spirit Guides & Other Beings: Selected Lessons from Archangel Gabriel.* Albany, NY: Sacred Garden Fellowship.

Dominions of Angels [14]

Seraphim	Angels of the First Cause	Attend to birth of Divine Essence into Spirit, also known as "life".
Cherubim	Angels of the perfect memory of All	Serve as perfect record keepers and the perfect memory of God; the "eternalness" of the Divinity of life.
Thrones	Angels of keeping the flame of life	Hold steady the essence of all life so there never is death.
Dominions	Angels of keeping and maintaining the action, interference, behavior, and gifts of other angels	Determine all angel duties except Archangels, Seraphim, Cherubim, and Thrones; they don't interact with humankind from Dominions through Seraphim; contain many levels of angelic division.
Virtues	Angels of Miracles	Bring humankind any healing or acts that express beyond limited beliefs; angelic awareness or interaction with humankind begins at this vibration.
Powers	Angels of Planetary Changes	Protect, care, and work with changes to earth's plant life, animals, minerals, and weather; include earth spirits, devas, fairies, and gnomes.
Principalities	Angels of Spiritual Pathways	Inspire all life to grow and evolve; clear the path of higher entities for growth; guide world leaders and government officials.

---

[14] Donovan, Rev. Penny (2017). *Angels, Spirit Guides & Other Beings: Selected Lessons from Archangel Gabriel.* Albany, NY: Sacred Garden Fellowship.

The Seven Archangels [15]

Archangel Michael	Warrior Angel	Provides protection from anything negative, especially what we create; helps us slay our error perceptions.
Archangel Gabriel	Angel of the Annunciation; Spirit of Truth	Teaches Truth as the message bearer; urges us to pray, meditate, and know more; helps us to learn and grow.
Archangel Raphael	Angel of Healing	Brings healing on all levels - mental, emotional, etheric, and physical - to anyone desiring healing or delivering healing to others.
Archangel Uriel	Angel of Repentance	Makes us aware of feelings of regret and a desire to be more; helps those who desire to change their ways.
Archangel Zadkiel	Angel of Joyous Mercy and Benevolence	Helps those who are merciless; works with those who deal with forgiveness; brings laughter.
Archangel Metatron	Angel of Spiritual Sustenance	Clears our path when we desire to grow.
Archangel Ariel	Angel of Emotions	Heals sorrows of all life; uses water to heal; works with other angels, especially Michael, Raphael, and Gabriel; assists with droughts or too much water.

---

[15] Donovan, Rev. Penny (2017). *Angels, Spirit Guides & Other Beings: Selected Lessons from Archangel Gabriel.* Albany, NY: Sacred Garden Fellowship.

Journey: Pay Attention

Set aside time in your sacred space, centering and meditating.

Revisit your personal invitation for help in **We Are Guided** in **Volume I**. Make a list of current life situations or personal experiences where you could ask your Divine helpers for guidance. Consider starting small, like with help finding a lost item.

As you practice asking for help in your daily life, pay attention to the clues that your Divine helpers leave along the way - songs on the radio, melodies in your head, resurfacing memories, and random messages given on your path through various sources like passages in books, words from another person, etc.

Journal about your ongoing experiences asking for and receiving guidance, blessings, understanding, and help with tasks, projects, and personal growth.

There Is Order

Geometry will draw the soul towards truth,
and create the spirit of philosophy.
— *Plato*

For centuries, humans have studied their surroundings to understand the world, looking for patterns to the why's and how's of life. Sacred geometry, called the language of nature, serves as one such explanation, pointing to the deeper meaning of our existence as more than an arbitrary occurrence. Sacred geometry follows a formula called the Golden Ratio, also known as the Golden Section or Divine Portion. The mathematical basis of this formula, Phi (Φ = 1.618033…), remained unnamed until the 1900's, though demonstrated in science and nature multifold. The Golden Ratio has been applied to architecture, nature, beauty, the stock market, art, and the cosmos, to name a few.

Ancients linked to use of the sacred formula in their work or writings include Plato, Phidias, and Euclid. Others directly credit Leonardo Fibonacci, who uncovered a specific mathematical progression. With three-dimensional precision, the Golden Ratio appears in a myriad of places in nature where self-generating patterns manifest like the gentle spiral of a nautilus shell or the sequence of leaf patterns as they twist around a branch. (See image.)

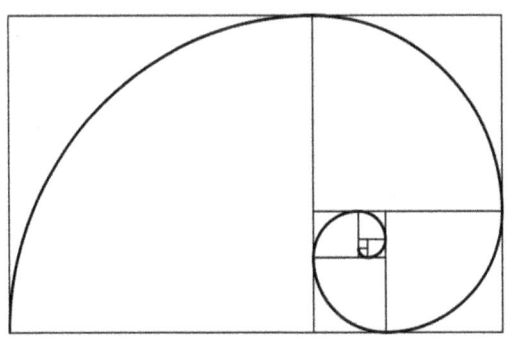

Whether you explore the Golden Ratio or Phi mathematically, esthetically, or philosophically, its history and use span millennia. From the Renaissance artists of the 1500's who used the ratio to bring balance to their work to the philosophers expounding on its deeper significance as a sign of Universal Intelligence, a whole world exists to explore on the topic of sacred geometry.

Today, let's use sacred geometry to open our awareness to the perfection in nature. As we intend to find its presence, we witness Divine patterns all around us in pinecones, succulents, sunflowers, snowflakes, and the spiral of a set of winding stairs re-created by man to mimic cosmic gifts.

Investigate and see what your world reveals. Nature is a wonder with treasures waiting for all to receive.

Journey I: Reflections on Sacred Geometry

Spend some time in your sacred space centering and meditating.

Reflect on the chapter material. Journal your thoughts and feelings.

Consider the following: How do you feel about sacred geometry? What does it mean to you? Why?

What does sacred geometry communicate to you about an intelligent force or Source?

Journey II: Discovering Sacred Geometry

Spend some time outside today, opening your awareness to the presence of the world's amazing display of sacred geometry. If bad weather keeps you inside, use the produce section in your local grocery store, a greenhouse, or flower shop.

Once your living sacred geometry object is discovered, use **Wise Baby Vision** from **Volume II** to observe what you see. Allow the flow of the pattern to relax your mind.

Write down any observations about your experiences.

Allow your newfound awareness to help you stay present and spend a whole day observing sacred geometry.

Journal your experience.

Moon Moods

*Let the waters settle and you will see
the moon and stars mirrored in your own being.*
— *Rumi*

Humans have long held a fascination with the moon historically, astrologically, astronomically, and poetically. As myth and legend of long ago intertwined to weave wild tales of unexplained behavior and unusual experiences, suspicious fingers pointed to the moon, blaming the celestial siren as a cause of epilepsy and madness otherwise known as lunacy. Modern testimonies add to the mix with reports of increased births, traffic accidents, rambunctious behavior, and hospitalizations under the influence of lunar energy at her fullest. While the moon merely seems like a giant rock orbiting the earth - lonely, glowing, and rhythmically touring her cosmic path - to those studying the metaphysical, astrological, or spiritual teachings, she is a metaphor and an influence on our highest evolution…our journey Home.

Many individuals with personal experiences regarding moon energy assert that she influences us on many levels, specifically our moods, behavior, and bodies. One attempt to explain this effect on humans looks to the influence of the moon on water - driving the tides and affecting the seascape that covers over 75% of the earth. Coincidentally (or not), the constitution of the human body contains an equally high percentage of water, ranging from 50 - 78% depending on age, gender, and body composition. This theory, though not definitively proven, pokes at the possible physical impact of our moon.

Sifting through scientific research on lunar influences yields little significant results. Many researchers, in fact, dismiss the moon's impact altogether; however, a recent study from a professor and director for Chronobiology at the University of Basel, Switzerland demonstrates our celestial friend's influence on sleep.

> We found that around full moon, electroencephalogram (EEG) delta activity during NREM sleep, an indicator of deep sleep, decreased by 30%, time to fall asleep increased by 5 min, and EEG-assessed total sleep duration was reduced by 20 min. These changes were associated with a decrease in subjective sleep quality and diminished endogenous melatonin levels. This is the first reliable evidence that a lunar rhythm can modulate sleep structure in humans when measured under the highly controlled conditions of a circadian laboratory study protocol without time cues.[16]

Unfortunately, this study offers little insight into the array of influences attributed to the moon and her cycles. While many dismiss any claims of lunar impact as old wives' tales or urban legends, my personal experience has shown otherwise. Conversations with metaphysical practitioners, law enforcement, hospital staff, and crisis workers have corroborated these beliefs. Tracking my own experiences with heightened emotions, intrusive thoughts, and old memories that probe my consciousness for release, I uncovered the power of lunar energies. The great value in exploring this energy and its role in soul-discovery is how **Moon Moods** came to be.

While we know that current science lacks the physical tools to demonstrate complete understanding of lunar energy, metaphysics and astrology fortuitously shed light on the subject. First, we turn to metaphysics to understand the nature of this celestial body in terms of energy - the moon representing feminine energy. Feminine energy does not mean gender, much like we are conditioned to believe. Metaphysically speaking, feminine energy nurtures and sustains, giving masculine energy (drive and action) its direction and purpose. Feminine energy holds ideas and thoughts in incubation for a period of gestation until they can be birthed or manifested into form. As an example, my feminine energy held and nurtured the idea of this book series while my action and drive moved its ongoing creation forward until it became a reality.

We all possess female energy regardless of our gender. Yes, men and women hold masculine and feminine energy in varying proportions, though biologically women hold more female energy because of their body. Because of hormonal constitutions largely demonstrated via breast development and a menstrual cycle, young girls and women

---

[4] Cajochen, Christian et al. (2013). *Evidence that the Lunar Cycle Influences Human Sleep*: Current Biology, Volume 23, Issue 15, p1485-1488. Amsterdam, Netherlands: Elsevier. Referenced at https://doi.org/10.1016/j.cub.2013.06.029.

more dominantly express feminine energy. This happens regardless of other mental or emotional vibrations demonstrated by being a tomboy, a delicate flower, straight, bi-sexual, or gay.

We can explore moon moods through astrology, the ancient study of planetary influences on earthly existence. Looking through this lens, the moon's energetic effect on humans speaks to a magnetic game of attractions and repulsions, a veritable push and pull during specific points of the lunar cycle. In alignment with spiritual or metaphysical teachings, we again see the moon as the embodiment of female energy, in addition to other planets like Venus, Neptune, and Pluto. Moon reflects our emotional selves as humans or animals. More specifically, she speaks to the whole of our conscious and subconscious emotions and feelings.

Lunar energy affects everyone differently; the amount and intensity of her influence depends on each person's planetary line-up, a natal celestial map informing the details of our spiritual birth plan. Regarding gender, the moon generally impacts women more so than men, depending on where she (moon) is in her cycle of thirty days. And yes, there's no doubt of the mirroring to a women's menstrual monthly clock. While common knowledge says that women have their period near the full moon, I suspect that factors such as the use of birth control pills and being out of touch with our natural environment alters this considerably. That said, we all operate cyclically, but women physically demonstrate what runs more quietly in men.

The images below illustrate and name moon phases as eight distinct stages, labeling the celestial object's movement from partially illuminated to fully illuminated and back to blackness as it travels along its monthly orbit.

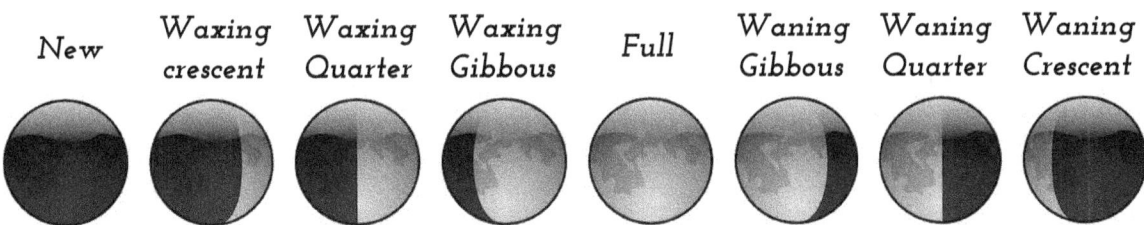

Examining the four primary phases of the moon's cycle, we find waxing, waning, full, and new. Waxing phases identify changes in the moon's lighting toward full illumination or full moon, while waning phases identify the changes toward her return to darkness or new moon. Crescent, quarter, and gibbous further categorize the changing proportions of lighting, much in the same way that full indicates complete illumination and new is absent of all light.

While astronomy (the study of objects and matter outside the earth's atmosphere) dictates that a new lunar cycle begins in a period marked by the absence of light or new moon, astrology instead utilizes our relationship to moon energy for personal development by beginning with the movement from waxing to new (waxing phases → full → waning phases → new). The celestial momentum embedded within the lunar cycle offers significant help in our soul-discovery, impelling us toward shedding thoughts, emotions, beliefs, or situations that do not serve our highest good. Broadly speaking, we gain understanding from examining the moon's phases as a balance of light and dark; whatever we are walking through or working on in our personal development metaphorically surfaces into our consciousness or comes into the light to be seen and subsequently shed or transformed. In other words, as the light of the moon emerges in the waxing phase, we can grow in awareness of our current learning opportunities by simply paying attention to our thoughts, emotions, beliefs, situations, and life events. What is the Universe *shedding light on in us* that may appear outside of us (in our life)? What are we directly experiencing as we observe emotions surface into our awareness?

From my own experience, moon is a potent motivator. It's typical energetic influence presses me to change, causing a steady and mounting increase in my mental and emotional states from mildly unpleasant to extremely uncomfortable. Sometimes it compels me so intensely to deal with my garbage that I feel like tube of toothpaste under pressure – being squeezed to release the particular negative forces once and for all.

To summarize what may feel complicated at first glance, we refer to the table on the following page, which outlines the influences of moon's energies during her major phases. As each quarter (quarter waxing, full, quarter waning, and new) marks significant transition points from light to dark or dark to light, the impetus for growth as realizations, regrouping, re-decisions, or changes is strongest. And as we move into the new moon, we can rest in the "darkness" allowing what we have learned to integrate. Like seeds that need darkness to germinate, in the new moon's absence of light we generate new ideas and possibilities.

Moon's Influencing Energies

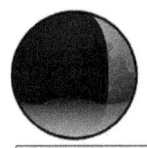 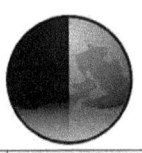 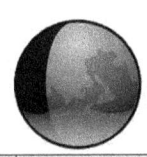   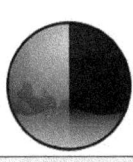 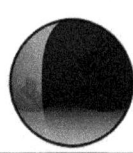 

Waxing Crescent	Quarter waxing	Waxing Gibbous	Full	Waning Gibbous	Quarter waning	Waning Crescent	New
First emergence of an opportunity to grow. Restlessness emerges because of what is being presented. Increased appetite and water weight begin.	Time for realizations, ah ha's, regrouping, re-decision, and change of course. Restlessness may peak.	Restlessness continues because of what is being presented. Appetite continues to increase.	Fullest expression of the lesson or opportunity we are walking through. Frequently female period coincides here.	Impetus for resolution, consolidation, reflection, and/or releasing what came to fullest at full moon. Weight loss begins.	Time for realizations, ah ha's, regrouping time, re-decision, and a change of course. Restlessness may peak	Impetus for resolution, consolidation, reflection, releasing of what came to its fullest at full moon. Weight loss continues.	Repose period to assimilate what was learned. Symbolizes a new beginning. May not be formed yet but is generating.

The journeys for this chapter bring many opportunities for discovery. On the following pages, three tables provide organized space to log general notations and trends while navigating the lunar phases. The accompanying blank pages provide the space for detailed reflections to illuminate all opportunities for transformation. Remember, be particularly mindful of experiences, situations, and reactions during each of the quarters throughout your tracking. Over the course of a month, a pattern will be revealed but may not be apparent until three or more months can be observed.

To read about ongoing monthly astrological information or for a deeper look into your personal planetary map, visit Margaret Lassiter's blog at www.astrohealing.net. Many thanks to her for guidance in constructing this chapter.

The moon constantly changes, yet she is steady in that change in her path from one new moon to the next. We follow a similar cyclical pattern. When we become aware of what this celestial goddess shows us, it provides rich fertilizer for growth. Using our own proverbial poop for soul-discovery helps us sow the multi-colored seeds of life's lessons into beautiful flowers.

Journey I: Moon Moods

After resting and meditating in your sacred space, journal your thoughts, feelings, and reactions to this chapter.

Consider: What do you think you'll find as you explore? What do you hope to uncover or what questions might you desire to answer about yourself or your life?

Journey II: Charting Progress

The following tables encourage you to log the day of the month, mood, physical state, sleep quality, and moon phase. Start your **Moon Moods** tables *any day* of the month. Trends will reveal themselves regardless of when you begin your log; so, note all details until the end of the month, then return to the 1st on the same table to complete the rest of the lunar cycle for table one.

Using the table: Mark the **Mood** column with your dominant emotions or feelings for the day. Also, rate the intensity of your feelings using a 1 - 10 scale with 10 as most intense. For the **Physical** column, mark your overall physical well-being on a scale of 1 - 10 with 10 as feeling your best. Note any symptoms. Females in menstruating years can mark the cycle's start date with a red star or circle. Be sure to note sleep quality in the **Sleep** column, like wakefulness, restlessness, etc. This can also be rated using a 1 - 10 scale with 10 as your best sleep. Use the internet or a moon calendar to fill in the **Moon** column, noting the exact phase of the moon with a drawing or label.

Journal any additional observations regarding your thoughts, feelings, and emotions, adding situations and other experiences during the four quarters (quarter waxing, full, quarter waning, and new). Use the **Moon's Influencing Energies** to assist you in identifying what to pay attention to, as well as how the moon is influencing your internal and external world. Don't forget to date any journal entries.

An Intimate Journey into Self

Date	Mood	Physical	Sleep	Moon
1				
2				
3				
4				
5				
6				
7				
8				
9				
10				
11				
12				
13				
14				
15				
16				
17				
18				
19				
20				
21				
22				
23				
24				
25				
26				
27				
28				
29				
30				
31				

Notes:

An Intimate Journey into Self

Date	Mood	Physical	Sleep	Moon
1				
2				
3				
4				
5				
6				
7				
8				
9				
10				
11				
12				
13				
14				
15				
16				
17				
18				
19				
20				
21				
22				
23				
24				
25				
26				
27				
28				
29				
30				
31				

Notes:

An Intimate Journey into Self

Date	Mood	Physical	Sleep	Moon
1				
2				
3				
4				
5				
6				
7				
8				
9				
10				
11				
12				
13				
14				
15				
16				
17				
18				
19				
20				
21				
22				
23				
24				
25				
26				
27				
28				
29				
30				
31				

Notes:

Journey III:
Discovering Trends

Spend some time in your sacred space, centering and asking your Divine helpers for guidance.

Having the opportunity to observe your moon moods, what did you uncover?

Consider the following: Was there a theme or pattern in any one of the moon's cycles regarding your moods and/or physical symptoms? Across three months?

What situations or experiences revealed themselves and when?

What did you discover in your ah-ha moments or realizations about what the moon helped shine the light on in your life?

Did any theme reveal itself in your moon moods consistent with other chapter journeys thus far?

The Soul-Discovery Journalbook

Additional notes:

In the Heart of the Jungle

Every animal is a gateway to the phenomenal world of the human spirit. What most fail to realize though is that what they think about animals reflects the way they think of themselves.

— Ted Andrews

High on a branch that looks down to the forest below, a sleek panther the color of midnight rests silently among the rich emerald tree-tops. This potent female archetype of independence, determination, grace, and inner sight is but one of the many totems from our natural world. Animals, birds, insects, reptiles, and fish hold powerful metaphysical symbolism that help us identify lessons in a way that circumvents opposition from our subconscious mind.

As humans, we tend to think of ourselves as sophisticated entities, sitting smugly and aristocratically on top of the food chain. Fundamentally, however, we are all still animals and this aspect lives on in us, rich with information. Through vivid metaphors, those from the animal kingdom can guide, advise, and remind us of our innate nature as we examine each creature by its specific traits, behaviors, and instincts through what is known as Animal Medicine. Representing ego trends, personality, or aspects of our shadow self, as well as higher truths, they offer valuable insights on our path of soul-discovery.

Because every animal represents different aspects of who we are as humans, our conscious associations and reactions to the creatures in our life tell us a story, too. Attraction, affection, fear, repulsion, irritation, and anxiety toward any creature's presence (in real-time, movies, books, meditation, or dreams) become commentary on how we view the many pieces of self and Self. So, openly examining how we feel about any animal provides us with opportunities to better understand ourselves, helping us learn and grow.

Much like investigating archetypes, the discoveries of creatures in our life can also help us decipher life lessons signified by struggles, relationship strife, self-judgment, and stagnation on our path, to name a few. In addition, our interest in Animal Medicine provides another set of symbols for our guides and angels to use for communicating with us.

Where do we begin to draw on the benefits of Animal Medicine? Our mere intent for guidance from terrestrial creatures joined with our attention to whomever enters our world is all that's required. As we clarify and set our desire, who and what appears may amaze and inspire, as well as tell a beautiful, mystical tale that illuminates the benefits of changing directions, eliminating old patterns, and/or looking at how we feel about our shadow side and our Self. As we intend to allow the power of totem animals into our life, every bird, insect, mammal, reptile, and fish that appears can send a message to help us travel our path of spiritual evolution. Careful consideration of those seeming to stand out, acting unordinary, or begging for notice can often tell the most impactful stories; sometimes they seem more important or dramatic because we finally notice them on what may have been a long mission to finally get us to stop and heed their presence.

Reflecting on the study of totem animals and their help in my life brings memories of graduate school over twenty-five years ago. At the time, my training included working with a talented art therapist, who taught me the value of symbolism. Through the years, my understanding of metaphor and symbology grew. In the present, the recurring totem helpers on my path continue their guidance. When I needed to slow down and step into stillness, a praying mantis graced my office window for nearly a week. Through mysterious insistence, she appeared repeatedly, demonstrating her identity with a patch of scarred wing. Turkey vultures, hawks, and eagles taught me to observe, employ vision higher, trust my leadership, and honor inner strength. Perhaps most memorable was an etheric coyote who stealthfully peered from the weeds in the early morning hours, marking a workshop's beginning; he heralded a time to be mindful of innate intelligence, as well as the pull of ego or the great "trickster". He announced the hidden themes of this particular event - to move beyond ego's influence and release the mask of personality - long before we knew them. Intuitively witnessing others' totem animals and my own continues to infuse my professional and personal work with new insights as current lessons and ways to move forward find voice.

Sometimes we desire to discover totem animals by more direct investigation instead of waiting for the Universe to deliver them to us. This calls for the use of animal tarot or guided meditation. Use of either helps us to open to the gifts of these methods.

Each creature in this great world plays a part in the vast web of life as another individualized aspect of Source birthed through the cradle of corporeal life we know as Mother Earth. May you find many furry, scaly, thick-skinned, and feathered cousins along your path to inspire, inform, guide, and support your journey in soul-discovery.

The Soul-Discovery Journalbook

Journey I: Totem Meditation

 Follow the guided meditation below to discover your animal totem. Use the QR Code on the left for the recorded version of this meditation on www.pathways2innerpeace.com or consider asking a friend to read it to you as you journey within.

Retreat to your sacred space. Spend a few moments centering, setting your intent for clarity and understanding. Ask your Divine helpers to join you and guide you on your journey toward your highest good.

Close your eyes and focus on the space just between your eyes on the bridge of your nose. Relax into this space, breathing deeply and slowly. Now allow the darkness behind your eyelids to transform into an all-white space. You are surrounded by white, fluffy, energy; all you see around you is soft and safe, a nurturing space that feels as if you have just walked into a cloud.

In your mind's eye, the white transforms and a rich green forest lies before you. At your feet a narrow dirt path travels between large trees of all shapes and sizes. Lush green ferns and foliage line both sides of a dirt path. Though it appears that you are completely alone, you know that you are safe and cared for.

As you look around this velvety emerald landscape, all the life here seems to bow in greeting. The trees nod to you. Brightly colored flowers stretch closer for you to enjoy their fragrant essence. Bushes, ferns, and tall thin grasses sway a warm hello. Here you are welcome…always.

Follow the worn forest path, walking forward and listening to the sounds all around you - the wind brushing over the leaves, the small animals scurrying in the underbrush, the birds announcing your arrival. The sun streams through the tree-tops, lighting each leaf and branch; the warm rays make their way to the forest floor as speckled bright yellow dots.

Just ahead, you hear water gurgling and burping as it flows over rocks. Walk toward the sound; you find a stream that crosses your path. Across this water rests a rustic wooden bridge. You step across board by worn board to the center of the bridge and look over the edge at the water as it dances on the rocky stream bed, making its way into the forest, nourishing everything on its travels.

Shift your awareness now to the trees and grasses in the distance; you feel eyes, a deep gaze hidden by the greenery. Something rustles. As you turn toward the noise, your totem shows itself to you. Know it is here to bring understanding and guidance for your highest and best. You look at it, examining its shape, color, and demeanor. As you witness your visitor, pay attention to your thoughts and emotions. What do you feel and think about this creature?

Thank your totem for its help. As you offer gratitude, it nods in recognition and leaves. Watching it disappear, you feel something else is hiding, watching you again. You know it's in the shadows. You cannot see anything but can feel its presence. Ask for whatever is hiding to reveal itself. Out of the darkness, a new creature emerges; this is your second totem. You look at it, examining its shape, color, and demeanor. As you witness your second visitor, pay attention to your thoughts and emotions. What do you feel and think about this creature? Thank it for delivering its healing message and watch as it nods in response and quickly disappears into the shadows.

Look out over your surroundings one last time before continuing on the path. A feeling of gratitude and clarity washes over you, knowing that you have entered another world of discovery. Continue on your way, crossing over the water to the other side. You've navigated the bridge of revelation, readying yourself with fresh knowledge. Somehow the trees look brighter, leaves fuller, and flowers more colorful. As you look ahead on the path, you spot a fallen log, perfect for a rest. Walk to the log and feel how nurtured and full of new possibilities you are. As you sit, take a deep breath, allowing yourself to rest. Your journey has finished for now. Allow the image of the forest to fade, returning to the white space, cleansed and refreshed. Take a nice deep breath and slowly return your awareness to feeling your chair, your body, and your sacred space. Open your eyes when ready.

Move on to **Journey II**.

Journey II:
Totem Investigation

Journal what you experienced through your guided meditation.

What was the first creature to show itself? Journal how you thought and felt about it. Also note how it appeared, it's demeanor, attitude, stance, etc.

What was your second creature? This one reveals a deeper and more hidden aspect of yourself. Journal what you thought and felt about it? Note again how it appeared, it's demeanor, attitude, stance, etc.

Now investigate your totem creatures. Suggested resources include books by Ted Andrews. Websites that contain animal spirit guide information sourced to him may also be helpful.

Journal the meanings and messages for each creature that appeared.

Journey III: Totem Reflections

This journey is meant to elicit deeper study of your totem messages and what they reveal.

Consider the following: How do you feel about the symbolism and messages revealed from your research?

How does each creature's symbolism surface in your thoughts, emotions, situations, or events currently in your life or even in your past?

How do any messages from what you discovered apply to what you are learning in your life currently as a life lesson?

How can you use this information to help you grow?

Are there any action steps that would benefit you in relation to this new information?

Wynebgwrthucher

☙∴

...Un waith ydiw calon wych
* tharian o waith eurych.*

...a fine heart is of the same manufacture
as a shield made by a goldsmith.
— Gutto'r Glyn[17]

A strong and courageous knight rides across a rocky plain clad in armor, sword and shield at his side. Known for his bravery and a famed sword called Excalibur, this royal hero of medieval English landscapes travels the pages of ancient literature. While many remember King Arthur Pendragon and his famed sword, less familiar weapons fade in memory to avid readers and followers of the tales. One such weapon is the king's shield - a mouthful of Welch called *Wynebgwrthucher*.

While legends such as King Arthur remain ambiguous as fantasy or history, one detail remains certain; the titles and names of medieval times held special meaning because ancients knew the power of words. Returning to the King's shield, *Wynebgwrthucher*, we discover a deeper meaning.

> *Wynebgwrthucher* /win-e-big-rith-ush-er/ - night gainsayer; night opposer.

Metaphorically, this decorated form served as protective guardian of chivalry, morality, truth, and justice, shielding the prophetic king from negative forces as an opposer of ill

---

[17] Joe, Jimmy (1999). *Timeless Myths*. Retrieved in https://www.timelessmyths.com/.

will and darkness. Aptly titled, this chapter is dedicated to a shield of another nature, equally potent and protective in the metaphysical realm.

Beyond any far-off thoughts of clashing armor and iron, modern day understanding of protection often brings to mind physical weapons. More commonly though, in our present-day interactions, is our use of emotional protection through the self-created psychological shields known as defense mechanisms - subconscious behavioral barriers to perceived dangers. These self-created shields - the hidden relics of childhood that remain operational long after we leave our youth - operate less effectively than we realize, but nonetheless can seem to protect us from perceived threats.

Metaphysical protection or shielding holds similarities to our understanding of both the psychological and the forged metal shields of the Medieval past. In addition, it's more powerful, lighter to pack, and surprisingly effective. As we vibrationally elevate shielding to a spiritual level, its protective nature emerges from the power of loving, life-affirming thinking and feeling combined with an energetic buffer built in our mind, aided by our Divine helpers, and cemented by our belief - belief in ourselves, the Universe, and a loving Creator. This chapter, dedicated to each reader's personal *Wynebgwrthucher*, reveals the what, when, where, why, and how of energetic spiritual protection.

To begin our lesson, we return to our previous information on energy. Recall from **Our Energy** that everything is energy.

> Concerning matter, we have been all wrong. What we have called matter is really energy, whose vibration has been lowered as to be perceptible to the senses. There is no matter. There is only light and sound.
> — Albert Einstein

Energy is what we are - Spirit energy animating a body, a vibration slowed significantly to create what we see and feel as solid matter. Universal Energy or God energy, which is everywhere and in everything, generously flows to us and through us, providing whatever we need to carry out this great adventure on Earth or elsewhere.

Energy, in and of itself, is neither good nor bad. *Energy is.* Our *intent* determines the nature of any energy; thought creates as we mold mental energy by our emotions and feelings. Emotional energy joins with thought to give our mental energy direction and purpose. How we use energy makes it positive or negative, loving or unloving. The energy used to heal, comfort, and soothe is the same energy used to injure, attack, and destroy. Our intentions create very different outcomes depending on how we shape our personal spiritual energy and release it in our world.

Energy has specific "qualities" depending on how our intent influences it. If our intent comes from hostile, angry, jealous, competitive, and/or vengeful emotions, the energy becomes heavy, sticky, and negative. But if our intent is loving, compassionate, and/or generous, it results in smooth and slippery positive energy. To simplify, we can look at energetic manifestations on a continuum from most heavy and sticky to slippery and smooth, demonstrated by the following:

Heavy, sticky -- *Slippery, smooth*

depression	jealousy	conditional love	unconditional love
lethargy	anger	lust	joy, happiness
grief	busyness	favoritism	compassion, peace

Energy also follows spiritual laws - The Law of Attraction and The Law of Cause and Effect (and several others beyond the scope of this discussion). Whether we believe in them or not, everyone remains bound by and held accountable to them. As discussed before, the Law of Attraction holds that like attracts like. Energies of like vibration magnetically collect - negative attracts negative (sticky, heavy energies collect sticky, heavy energies) and positive attracts positive. The Law of Cause and Effect holds that what goes around comes around. Whatever we put out toward others or in our world comes "back home to roost."

Applying these concepts of energy to better understand the world and ourselves, we turn our attention to personal energy. Remember in **Our Energy** we discussed our personal spiritual energy field or the aura. This field is created by a combination of our pure Spirit energy AND what we contribute to the field through interaction with "our world" (as the who, what, and where of our personal universe) through our inner climate (beliefs, reactions, attitudes, thoughts, emotions, and feelings). Our aura contains these multiple levels of our being - spiritual, mental, emotional, and physical states - as an energetic representation of the personal use of our creative power. (See **From Consciousness into Awareness**.)

Because our aura is so magnetic, it naturally samples and experiences all the energies it encounters as it literally "touches" our immediate and extended environment. Following the Law of Attraction (LA), our aura collects additional energies that resonate with what it already holds. (See **The World Sings with You**.) Additionally, because of the Law of

Cause and Effect (LCE), whatever we put out toward others not only collects similar energies (LA) but also cycles around and returns to us stronger and more powerful because of what becomes collected on its cycle (LCE). For example, if we are in an angry mood, the angry energy we put into the world by our negative attitude goes out from us and cycles around, gathering similar vibrations on its journey like a little Velcro ball collects fuzz; what returns to us is more potently negative than when we "sent it". This is why when we "get up on the wrong side of the bed" per se, more of the same easily follows as similar energies are collected. Before we know what hit us, one foot is in the toilet and we feel like the Universe just leaned on flush. Likewise, if we are in a happy mood, little blessings arrive throughout or day as compliments or small gifts - people open doors, act friendly, or tell us we look nice. All experiences are a living projection of the wonderful creators that we are...Universal Law in action.

We all project our energy into the world, impacting ourselves and others; thus, auric management and protection serves as an important and valuable tool. Additionally, when we're more profoundly affected by energies and easily wear others' mental and emotional climates, auric protection offers significant relief, transforming our daily experiences and helping us stay centered in our own self rather than being buffeted by energetic contamination. Furthermore, workers in the care fields (doctor, nurse, massage therapist, mental health practitioner, etc.) and empaths benefit greatly from shielding and cleansing, which help manage the impact and effect of being in close proximity with others.

Spiritual energetic protection became a vital part of my daily practice several years ago, though in retrospect I wish I knew it sooner. I learned quite late in life, in fact, that being a psychic sponge was not a universal trait; not everyone could feel what I felt or know the things I knew. Feeling sick from trips to the grocery store, wearing the moods of clients, knowing what individuals were going through without them saying, and feeling the pain or illness of my children were just a few occurrences of my daily life. Years passed before the level of my understanding caught up to the intensity of those empathic connections.

One very intense experience that happened in my teens served as a significant data point and more extreme example of psychic absorption. Without notice or reason, I found myself bombarded by repeating impulses to jump out of a window. I was not depressed, anxious, or suicidal. The only thought was to jump. It wasn't until years later, learning about my constitution as a psychic sponge, that the mystery came to conclusion. A friend, battling with depression and suicidal thoughts, wore the heavy energy of their struggles. Being highly energy sensitive made me susceptible to absorbing their energy as my own. Without any understanding of auric protection, all I could do was confusingly experience what this besieged soul went through every day. This, among other events, served as a valuable lesson on protection and managing my energy.

Protecting or shielding our aura from energies we experience has several key aspects. First, we learn and practice fortifying our energy field to remain buffered from the impact of others by building a protective barrier with our mind, created out of love, and formed of light and other etheric materials. Second, we *watch* our thoughts and emotions. Watching our reactions and judgments informs us of the old hurt, lack of compassion, or blame we still carry. Shedding the energies (thoughts, emotions, and beliefs) that attract similar heavy, sticky energies to us by observing our attitudes, healing our pain, and releasing old beliefs alters what we project into the world and manages what we attract. Third, we employ our Divine helpers to assist us with shielding. Specifically, we can call on the Angels of Protection to protect us from negative energies, especially as part of our shielding practice. Any time, in fact, we feel bombarded by energies or unsafe in our environment, we can enlist their help. And lastly, we can regularly cleanse our aura to remove the energies we've collected along our day from interactions with others and our world. Because the Universe immediately responds to a vacuum, anything we remove must be replaced with life-affirming, loving energies to fill the open space with the positive vibrations we desire.

Equally important in protecting our aura is the understanding of auric damage. Intense emotional states - rage, despair, profound grief - cause tears or holes in our aura as explosive expression of emotions literally rip the energetic "fabric" of the aura or puncture holes in it. As a result, we become susceptible to other negative, unloving energies that allow "psychic dirt" inside it. Chronic fatigue, intense tiredness, and frequent nightmares are signs of such damage, calling for repair and healing. Additionally, any auric weakness and damage leaves us more vulnerable to individuals who can unknowingly or intentionally drain our energy. If any encounter with someone leaves us immediately feeling tired or drained, a "psychic leech" is in our midst, offering another excellent opportunity to practice protection, cleansing, and healing our aura.

One of the most dominant energetic influences in our environment created by psychic contamination occurs as the energy of a person or people projects into any work space, community area, or residence; because the quality of energy abides, it remains where individual(s) express it until cleansed. When, for example, a fight with our spouse generates angry energy (as all fights to do), the negativity stays in the rooms in which the argument occurred. Without clearing the energy, if at any later point in time we walk through that "fight cloud", we can experience it as an instant shift in our own mood, thoughts, or attitude. If our internal climate is already swimming in negativity or we're struggling with our day (because we're human, after all), we become more susceptible to the energy, which will attach to our aura (LA). Additionally, because any structure or dwelling holds energy, homes, buildings, and offices follow the same laws; the walls, furniture, and objects also absorb and hold the collective energy of the occupants. Metal, in particular, retains energy more than wood or plastic. Because metal is relatively unresponsive to cleansing, for instance, as we do healing work, furniture made from it is best avoided. Also, the more negative interactions and attitudes of the inhabitants and visitors, the greater the accumulated heaviness of the space - think hospitals, psychiatric clinics, police stations, violent homes, etc. So, paying attention to sudden mood shifts, attitude changes, and/or feelings of unease may indicate a need for cleansing to remove psychic contamination. And perhaps most importantly, if we are empathic or energy sensitive, cleansing our spaces frequently proves to be beneficial.

As we learn to manage our personal energy cleansing our spaces - home, apartment, offices - becomes a vital part of our practice. Cleansing or removing of heavy, ill-serving energies occurs when we intend to remove any vibration that is not for our highest and best. Again, replacing the open "space" that remains with love and light, understanding and compassion, forgiveness and truth, completes the process.

It's important to remember that most people are unaware of the energy they project into the world. Anyone with anger, revenge, and (conscious or subconscious) intent to do harm sends out psychic barbs whose double-ended daggers stay hooked in the sender's aura. When our vibration is light - thoughts uplifting and feelings loving - any attack from others slides off us like water rolling down a slate roof. Energetic protection enhances and consciously enforces shielding as we navigate a physical plane where these experiences serve as valuable lessons, remembering in truth that our eternal Spirit is always safe.

So, whether we are currently aware or not of how energy affects us, paying attention to our experiences, exploring our personal history with unexplained events, and reviewing the list of empathic traits in **The World Sings with You** can offer clarity. Taking charge of our attitudes as we develop spiritually and personally actively puts us in charge of our aura and thus, our life. The journeys for this chapter walk through the steps to learn and practice auric protection. May each of you navigate and enjoy the next part of your adventure while truly relishing this huge interstellar soup spiced with magical and amazing psychic ingredients. With new tools in hand, may you find peace, knowing that protection is ever-present and available.

Journey I: Basic Auric Shield

Sit quietly to center yourself in your sacred space for a few moments, breathing slowly to relax and cultivate a sense of inner peace.

In your mind's eye, imagine you are in a space that is all white. Everything is clean, billowy, and bright, like you just stepped into a cloud. As you look down in your mind's eye, you see your body. Around you is the glow of your aura - a living, magical energy radiating from you. Knowing that your aura retracts in response to your focus and will, pull it closer to you until it is between 6 - 12 inches from your physical form.

Looking up, you now see a vibrant white light coming down from above you and when it reaches near the top of your head, it pours over your body, bathing your form in energy. This living light sparkles and shimmers as it creates a powerful protective egg around the outside of your aura. Make sure to envision the light all around every part of your body, including behind you and under your feet.

Practice using this protection before you encounter people and especially prior to leaving your home for the day. Renew your shield whenever you feel the need, knowing the protection lasts as long as you desire according to your belief and intent.

Journal your experience with creating your auric shield. How do you feel without and with it?

Additional notes:

Journey II: Special Effects

Sit quietly to center yourself in your sacred space for a few moments, resting silently to relax and remove yourself from the energies of the day. Read through this journey to familiarize yourself with its steps before walking through it in your mind's eye.

Begin by repeating the guided imagery in **Journey I**.

Now let's add two more steps. After pulling in your aura, practice using layers of one or more of the following vibrations of light. Depending on your intent, one or any combination of the three can be used at the same time.

> **White light** - protective and healing on all levels.
> **Pink light** - offers healing and protection as love and compassion.
> **Yellow light** - serves as protection through knowing and understanding.
> ***Black light** - the holiness of black; cloaking and shielding for going about your world un-noticed.
>
> *** DO NOT under any circumstances use black light around your car or your form when driving or parking; don't use in places where people need to see your body like walking or riding your bike on the street.*

Now place an additional shield of glass, armor, or mirrors over the light, reaching all around you, including above your head and under your feet.

> **Glass** - slippery to allow energies in your world to fall away.
> **Armor** - a steel shield that's hard and durable.
> **Mirrors** - used facing outward, these reflect energy from the sender back to its source; very important for shielding from those who are energetically draining/psychic vampires.

Remember that your intent and belief create whatever you use for protection.

How and what did you feel as you practiced your personal *Wynebgwrthucher* with these new tools?

Journal about your experience using additional layers.

Notes:

Journey III: Angelic Posse and Auric Repair

By now you can see that we are adding important layers to your shield. This aspect of protection calls on angelic help.

If you suspect damage to your aura, begin by calling forth light to address it. Imagine your aura filled with light from the inside, cleansing any psychic "dirt" that may have entered as a result. Ask the Angels of Healing to repair any holes, tears, or weak spots. Imagine these healing helpers sewing or "plastering" areas with a pliable, living, energetically restorative compound (think of living Silly Putty). Ask to be shown how to prevent the damage in the future, knowing that this most often will include changes in your attitude and/or interactions.

Renew your protective shield that you learned about in **Journeys I** and **II**.

Now call on the Angels of Protection. An example of a request for protection may include the following:

> *I ask the Angels of Protection to protect me from all negative energies so that I may not be harmed nor do harm from within or without. Thank you. And so, it is.*

> *I ask the Angels of Protection to guard my home. I ask for an angel at each window, door, and at each corner of my home to protect me and all those within from all negative energy. I know it is done as I speak or think these words. Thank you. And so, it is.*

Write your own communication with the Angels of Protection and Healing and journal about it. Reflect on when and where you plan to use their help, knowing that they come to serve your highest good.

Journal your progress as you integrate **Journeys I**, **II**, and **III**, practicing your *Wynebgwrthucher* around others, at work, in the store, or out and about in general.

Additional notes:

Journey IV: Cleansing and Fortifying Our Aura

Cleansing our aura from negative energy serves to remove what we've collected throughout our day. The three methods this author uses for "washing" away energies include water (shower, bath), light (like **Journey I** with light to shield), and smoke from incense or burning dried sacred plants. Over the course of a day, all of them can be employed. *Ex: You meditate in the morning, burning incense to start the day and cleanse your space. Later, you're out in public and feel drawn to reinforce and cleanse your aura with light before going into the grocery store. As you settle in for the night, you shower to cleanse your aura with water.*

Because we live in a physical world, using tangible items may feel more potent. Humans also have a long history of using water and dried plants for cleansing, so it's deeply engrained in our collective consciousness and highly symbolic. Remember, your intentions and beliefs are truly the most important, regardless of what you choose.

- **Using water:** stand in your shower and intend that all energies that do not serve you be removed from your aura, released into the ethers to do no harm, and replaced with love, light, and whatever feels resonant.

- **Using light:** imagine light coming down from above, bathing your aura clean and intending that all negative energy be released into the ethers to do no harm and replaced with love, light, and whatever feels resonant.

- **Using sage/Palo Santo/incense:** use the smoke from burning a smudge stick of sage, Palo Santo, or incense, fanning it over your body in a clockwise fashion. Intend that all negative energies be released into the ethers to do no harm and replaced with love, light, and what feels resonant.

Now use what you learned from **Journeys I, II,** and **III** to renew your protective shield.

Journal about your experiences before and after cleansing, making sure to note your progress and observations as you continue to practice.

Notes:

Journey V: Cleansing Our Space

Cleansing our home and work space is an essential tool, especially if we do spiritual work, see clients, encounter conflict there, or have energetic sensitivity.

Imagine the spiral below mapped on the floor in the center of a room you want to cleanse. The arrow indicates the direction you will move to clear the negative energy. Clockwise movement is life-affirming and flows in the natural direction of energy.

Light a stick of sage, Palo Santo, or incense and begin in the center of the spiral, which correlates to the center of your room. Moving in a clockwise fashion, increase the circle as you gradually move toward the walls of the room. Ask that all negative energies from each corner, window, and door be released high into the ethers and replaced with love, light, peace, forgiveness, joy, wisdom, knowingness, laughter, etc.

Repeat this process with each room, moving from room to room in a clockwise fashion. If you don't have time to move through each room, cleanse one central room and ask that the cleansing take place in each room of the dwelling surrounding your current location and on all lower and upper levels of your home through your intent.

Now light a candle, drawing the angels to your space who align with what you need or desire in this moment. To protect your space from within and without of all negative energies, ask the Angels of Protection for help in the same fashion as **Journey III**. Remember, the most important aspect is your intent as you cleanse your space and ask for protection.

Journal about your experience, considering the following: How did your home/space feel before cleansing? How about after? How often do you intend on cleansing your space? Be mindful to cleanse after exposure to a conflict, a person struggling with negative energy and difficulties, or people visiting.

Journal about what you notice and learn as you practice.

The Soul-Discovery Journalbook

Notes:

Journey VI: Staying Clean

Center and meditate in your sacred space. When ready, ask for guidance to gain clarity about the energies you have been carrying - moods, attitudes, thoughts, emotions, reactions, and situations that would draw more of the same energies to you.

Reflect on what you receive and journal the guidance provided. Know that this may take time to reach your awareness.

Consider the following questions: What attitudes and moods are present currently? How have they been affecting your inner and outer world? What have you noticed about the energies you may have attracted (heavier and lighter) because of these attitudes you've been carrying?

How can you change your moods, attitudes, judgments, etc. to lift your energy and experience to a lighter vibration or to cultivate more positive in life? Can you create a plan or develop a contract with yourself to assist you on your path?

Faith in Ladybugs

*You are the beautiful sunshine that
naturally attracts precious little ladybugs.*
— Marta Shumylo

We are ever in a state of creating our life as a natural out-picturing of our innate power. Often, we do this unknowingly or without much thought. Many chapters intend to make these hidden aspects more obvious and **Faith in Ladybugs** adds to the list.

Manifesting - putting our creative energy into action - occurs when we sustain our idea long enough to see it birthed. We manifest constantly through our conscious as well as our subconscious intent. Remember, intent is thought fueled by feelings and emotions. Intent builds our personal world - the things we have or don't have, the situations we walk through, and the relationships in our life - as we create moment by moment, projecting our energy that unfolds before us.

Knowing the mechanics of manifesting informs us of the how and why of all that has occurred or is presenting itself in our life. To understand this, we begin by examining where we invest our energy. In other words, where are our thoughts and emotions joined in perfect chorus? Are we singing the songs of woe, worry, strife, discouragement, and negativity, or are our melodies infused with love, forgiveness, abundance, understanding, respect, compassion, joy, and wisdom? Most likely, we operate with a combination of both extremes and with many degrees between as a collective whole. Regardless, where we place our focus and energy inextricably links to manifesting by our *faith*.

Wherever you place your faith, that is where your strength will lie.[18]

In the channeled teachings of Archangel Gabriel, we are reminded of the power of faith. And while we often think that faith is merely the belief in a higher power that protects, guides, and loves, in truth our faith is determined by the energetic whole of our intent and focus. That doesn't mean that we are absent of support, guidance, and infinite love. What it does speak to is *our power* - our personal use of our Divinely inherited, creative energy as an individualize aspect of Source. We use our creative nature to direct, influence, and express the life we desire (by our faith). *Our faith is wherever we decide to place it* - in things, in people, in Source, in worry, in love, in the Universe, in ice cream (that's hunger calling).

How does the power of our faith work on a typical day? Let's take worry, for example. If we invest in worry, our faith lies in a general belief of "our ability" to manage situations by (the energy we invest) trying to control circumstances, outcomes, people's behavior, what we want from the Universe, etc. With worry, our mental grinding to solve or fix something or someone is a reactive attempt to prevent a particular "bad thing" because we believe we're on our own with it or don't trust the Universe or Source to provide. Worry at its core is really praying for the things we don't want in our lives, as we fret about situations we fear will happen. All the "what if's" our ego casts at our feet as proverbial bait keep us trapped in negativity and fear.

Remember, where we place our energy determines what we draw to us via the Law of Attraction. Energy placed in worry eventually manifests what we attempt to avoid as energy contorted into negativity through our creative abilities draws more negative to us in stressful, frustrating, turmoil-filled situations, people, and events. By using negative emotions like worry to prevent circumstances, we instead actively solicit them.

If worry is a perfect example of manifesting what we don't want, what about actively manifesting the life-affirming, loving, and positive in our life? The same faith applies, placing our energy in the *heart-felt vision* of what we desire, knowing that the Universe provides according to our intent. Here our faith is *knowing* that what we desire is ours, though it may not yet be in our physical world.

Because I too fall prey to the ego and worry, I decided to practice manifesting through consciously focusing my faith. Hatching a simple project that seemed fun and light, especially because no pressure existed to produce something attached to survival, I

---

[18] Donovan, Rev. Penny (1999). *Bypassing the Subconscious: Archangel Gabriel.* Kingston, NY: Appleseeds Publishing.

intended to manifest ladybugs. Now I know you might think, how can anyone manifest ladybugs? Ladybugs live in the world; they come and go as they please and that's that. Well, using our creative powers, we can bring what we desire into our life and yes, we can use that energy to serve the purpose of bringing ladybugs or various other critters to visit us.

Late in the winter, when ladybugs hadn't made an appearance, this proved to be an exciting experiment. Now, I love ladybugs and always have, especially the symbolism of these creatures heralding a time of abundance and fulfilment of desires; even the tiny decorative black marks on each indicate something valuable as the number of gifts coming to us. Knowing the great variation in markings, I began to wonder what the Universe would provide. *Maybe twelve, or nine or seven gifts...great numbers*, I thought, and off I went.

My journey started by entering morning meditation where I imagined a ladybug, the beautiful red crest of its back dotted with perfect black specks that contrasted its bright white "eyes". My heart connected with love and affection for these tiny crimson jewels and I envisioned ladybugs everywhere - crawling on my walls and windows, printed in books, on cards, and sculpted as jewelry or figurines. Mind and heart merged, *knowing* and *feeling* (faith in action) that I would be graced with a grand ladybug deluge...as sure as a small child's faith in Santa's special delivery under the Christmas tree...as sure as I am that each morning's sun will grace the sky. My deep, abiding gratitude and love for these little creatures permeated a consciousness beyond thought; I believed in and felt the power within me. Through faith in my Higher Self, I released expectations on any exact outcomes while holding to the original feeling-thought manifesting power and opening to the Universe's work.

Two days passed before the first signs of my project appeared, a ladybug adorned a student's decorative pin - a courier dressed in red and black paint, not breathing but a sign nonetheless. I thanked the Universe and stayed positive. Later that afternoon, a living version landed on my jacket. I felt like a kid on a treasure hunt, smiling ear to ear with ladybug fever. By the next afternoon, fifteen ladybugs gathered in the sunshine inside my patio window, my world unfolding in kind with what I had asked. A serendipitous, cosmic smile - seventeen bugs total aligned with the seventeen spots that decorated two of the scarlet gems I paused to count. Divine order...seventeen. I rested in the number and its symbolism.

Learning how to consciously manifest in our lives is an important and powerful lesson. Truth dictates that we always create and manifest, if not from our clear, conscious intentions, then from the mindset that lurks below the surface. The soul-discovery we each navigate helps us shed our shadow-self and activate the power of the positive, uplifting spark that lies within us.

You see…the key element of change in your life, in the world, is *YOU*. *You make the difference.* You hold more power than your brain can imagine. Yes, little old you can have the life you desire. You can be a beacon of light…light is your core. You, the Whole You is a vessel of love, light, and goodness. Every loving thought, every act of compassion, every forgiveness, every kindness radiates from you into your world to affect everything and everyone, *especially you*. Remember, we are One and any changes in your life affect your world.

Yes, Child of the Universe, the world is at your fingertips. Go out there and get those ladybugs!

Journey I: Reflections

Spend time in your sacred space centering and meditating.

As you are ready, reflect on the chapter material. What do you think about what you read? How do you feel about it?

Has this chapter shed any light on how you have manifested your needs and desires up to this point in your life?

Journey II: Manifesting Practice

Go to your sacred space to connect with what you desire to manifest. Allow your awareness to open to what's fun and enjoyable, beginning with something simple.

Imagine in your mind's eye what you are manifesting. As you envision it, feel the love, gratitude, and admiration for this gift. Know, as best as you are able, that the Universe provides as you give some time and space for the energy to manifest in form. Be patient and keep loving it.

While holding your intent, be sure to allow room to witness your gift anywhere...on cards, books, in person, TV, etc. Your treasure may reveal itself anytime, anyplace. Dispel all negative thoughts and remain positive that all is as it should be, allowing the time and space for your desires to be revealed.

Journal your experiences along the way - how you feel, your thoughts, what you believe - as this journey unfolds.

Serendipity and Synchronicity

Coincidence is God's way of remaining anonymous.
— *Albert Einstein*

Imagine for a moment the spark of magic that ignites when we unexpectedly find or uncover something - something old or new, previously insignificant, but now suddenly bringing happiness and seen as more valuable. This is serendipity, the energetic equivalent of a child discovering treasure in the unusual, commonplace, tiny, or even strange. Serendipity's sister, synchronicity, is a coincidence we experience as charmed fate, destiny, or good fortune. Both synchronicity and serendipity seem to possess the enchanting element of a puppeteer tugging the strings of our life, sometimes wonderful, other times star-crossed.

Simply said, from a spiritual perspective, synchronicity and serendipity remain constants, not just some mystical happenings that float in and out of our lives on a whim. Some may even say that they merely herald the action of Source or Universal Power. As we look beyond appearances, we discover the magic and value of these fated sisters by peeling back the thin outer covering of any situation to reveal the deeper lessons through symbolism. When we accept that synchronicity and serendipity are afoot, the seemingly insignificant or common events/situations can suddenly point us toward seeing everything in our life with more importance, offering gifts moment by moment.

Not to ruin your imaginings and sense of wonder, but everything (yes, *everything*) in our life is part of a grand play that we have written on another level in Spirit. What we see as coincidence is the magnificent power of our creative ability at work bringing lessons of all sizes and shapes. Despite our conditioned thinking that tells us to ignore and/or forget life's challenging circumstances or run head-long into them by blaming others, we can instead embrace all events knowing they possess value...gifts as serendipity in action. Through a subtle turn in our attitude, even the typically ignored, dismissed, and "throw-away" situations can illuminate serendipity and synchronicity at play.

Now, many would say at this point, "Last year I had the most horrific thing happen to me. There is no way I would have chosen to go through that! No serendipity or coincidence there. It was bad luck, chance, accidental pain and heartache." Yes, I understand the feeling. Let's for a moment, though, peer in from the other side.

Broadly speaking, the benefits of looking at the serendipitous and synchronous may be to put our questioning to rest, to really demonstrate how the Universe converges to give us exactly what we consciously and subconsciously desire (manifesting in action), as well as what we need to grow (spiritual evolution in action). Additionally, though coincidental events and happenings can vary greatly, sometimes the simplest symbolism appears serendipitously to demonstrate our innate power. Perhaps it even causes us to pay attention to everything occurring in our world, externally as well as internally. These fated cosmic siblings may even teach us about our own value or show us how much we are loved. At other times, they herald the arrival of a push (sometimes a shove) to use all the tools we have learned, to put into practice in the "worst of circumstances" what we know to ground the experience deep within our soul.

Always and eternally, Universal Power and our Divine helpers want to bolster us through love and urge us forward; as such, when we pay attention, we also find supportive and reassuring events. Sometimes what happens is so surreal that we can't help but stop dead in our tracks to look, listen, and heed. One such personal experience, demonstrating the many faces of serendipity and synchronicity, happened amid a tumultuous divorce during the recession of 2008. Deeply immersed in a financial wrestling match, I stood alone as a single parent with no extended family support. Because multiple part-time jobs and a lack child support left me unable to pay bills, I struggled not only financially to support two young boys and myself but battled intense fear. While one aspect of the experience was karmic, my perception exacerbated everything. And even though I was deeply engaged on a spiritual path, I still held the attitude of lack. Worry combined with current experiences reinforced my negative mindset, which in turn created more of the same. On the other side of the coin beamed two bright, imaginative, caring children, many loving and supportive friends, a rich spiritual practice, enough food on the table, and a comfortable home to mention a few. The message that this time of struggle would pass and I was/we were OK eluded me.

Now, the energetic height of this period of difficulty landed squarely in the middle of summer, a time rich with roasting s'mores, backyard games, and catching fireflies. One evening, on the way to join my children at the neighbors, I discovered a tiny, mushroom-brown frog clinging to the outside of the garage screen door. Knowing how the boys and I loved these little guys, my new friend accompanied me and became an instant hit amongst the kids before being released into the tangle of grass yards away from where our two families played fireside games. That was the last of our amphibious friend, not seeing any significance in his appearance. That is until the next morning.

Like any morning, looking forward to a nice warm shower, I climbed into the frosted-glass enclosure, allowing the water to wake me. As I reached for the shampoo, a tiny light-brown blob clung just below the shower caddy. There looking right back at me was a frog, identical to the one I found last night on the screen door. *But that one was released across the street,* I thought to myself. Yet, the creature in my second-floor, glass shower stall said otherwise. Amazing! Clearly, I didn't get the message from froggy's first visit; the second…impossible to ignore. Serendipity and synchronicity coalesced, creating a snap to attention. Strolling through resources for the deeper meaning, I uncovered potent messages condensed into the following:

> The spiritual meaning/totem animal symbolism of the frog appears in many traditions around the globe. This animal, generally associated with the water element and its attributes, symbolizes cleansing, renewal, rebirth, fertility, abundance, transformation, metamorphosis, life mysteries, and ancient wisdom. If we want more abundance and success in our life, frog tells us to change our personal vibration.
> — Ted Andrews

As we know from **In the Heart of the Jungle**, when animals make an appearance, especially in such a manner, we've been offered a powerful message. Any more obvious and I might have found him straddling a pile of scrambled eggs! This shower-hopping frog demonstrated just the lesson I knew in my head yet had escaped my heart. The Universe's reassurance helped me to examine current struggles and remember the lessons that needed to completely integrate into my feelings so I could move beyond the limitation of lack - to fully trust in Universal abundance by changing my perceptions and releasing my projected fear. The message affirmed a period of cleansing and rebirth toward transformation through the ancient Divine wisdom of Universal order - a "coincidental treasure" in the shape of *Pseudacris crucifer*, or Mr. Mushroom-Brown Peeper. Now I see synchronicity as a potent reminder that demonstrates where Spirit is leading me, urging me to grow. Whether my discovery appears "good" or "bad", it's always my choice to find the sweet serendipity and the beauty of the lesson it holds.

Journey:
Sweet Serendipity

After centering, reflect on the chapter. Journal your thoughts and feelings about the topic and all you read.

Write about a serendipitous and/or synchronous occurrence in your life. Remember that your mere intention to witness these will bring them to your attention.

Consider what this event reveals about your desires, fears, limiting beliefs, etc. - the parts that you accept, as well as reject.

See **References** for resources on symbolism to aid in your journaling.

Into the Butterfly

Just when the caterpillar thought the world was ending,
it became a butterfly.
— Proverb

Much of this book series focuses on transformation, the beautiful change of the caterpillar to the butterfly. Through learning, discovery, uncovering, witnessing, observing, allowing, letting go, and accepting, we navigate our own growth as metamorphosis. The chrysalis of our limiting beliefs about ourselves and our world transmutes into the butterfly of our True Nature, shining as a light within each of us. Working with the energy of transformation on a spiritual level is to think, act, be, and feel in conjunction with the pure energy of unconditional love (our Higher Self) through the action of the Holy Spirit.

The term Holy Spirit appears in many religions - Hebrew, Christianity, Islam, Bahá'í - though finding congruent meaning among them appears nebulous. Across these faiths, the Holy Spirit operates as the conduit through which the wisdom of Source connects with the messenger. Rich metaphor for the Holy Spirit is similarly represented throughout religious text as the burning bush to Moses, the sacred fire to Zoroaster, the dove to Jesus, the angel Gabriel to Muhammad, and the Maid of Heaven to Baha'u'llah.[19]

Growing up Catholic, the term Holy Spirit was part of my religious education. The way I heard it: There was God, the white-bearded old man in the sky; Jesus, his only Son, the

---

[19] Osborn, Lil (1994). Female Representations of the Holy Spirit in Bahá'í and Christian writings and their implications for gender roles. *Bahá'í Studies Review*. London: Association for Baha'i Studies English-Speaking, Europe.

chill dude with the long hair, robes, and cool sandals; and the Holy Spirit. All the vivid imagery related to the Holy Trinity was at least vibrant, even in Its archaically false way. God and Jesus the Christ seemed to make sense, but the Holy Spirit remained a mystery to me, and I imagine to others, too.

Shifting from what many religions teach to a different understanding, we can explore Holy Spirit as energy, the transformative power of Source/God/Universal Power. As the bridge that connects us with the energy of Creative Force, the Holy Spirit operates as an integral aspect of the Divinity within each of us. All have access to It as one facet of the totality of Source known as the Trinity - Mother-Father God, The Christ, and the Holy Spirit. From *A Course of Love*, the Holy Spirit is the helper, perception changer, and voice of truth.

> The way to overcome the dualism that threatens even the most astute of learners is through the Christ in you, through the One who knows what it is to be God's child and also to walk the earth as child of man. This is not your helper, as the Holy Spirit is, but your identity. While the Holy Spirit was properly called upon to change your perception and show you the false from the true, your recognition of the Christ in you is proper in this time of identification of your undivided Self.
>
> — *A Course of Love*, C:P.25

We can appeal to the energy of the Holy Spirit to help us let go of tormenting thoughts and emotions, to dissolve negativity and lack of love to feel peace. The Holy Spirit helps us transcend our limited, little-self "vision" to see truth and think beyond the concrete mind from a deep, internal knowingness even when we have difficulty connecting to our Self. The power of the Holy Spirit offers a helping hand when faced with experiences that appear to have the power to crush us, transforming any situation into a gift, a blessing in disguise.

> ...I have told you that you all are God and it is true, but God has but *one Son* and that is the Christ. The Christ of you is the Son of God. It is the love of God. It is the cause of all things to come into manifestation. The Father is the substance out of which all things come forth. The Christ is the *reason* they come forth because it is the love spilling out, if you will. And how do you think that comes to be? It is through the *action* of the Holy Spirit, the knowingness that brings it forward.[20]

---

[20] Donovan, Rev. Penny (2016). *I Am Gabriel: Selected Lessons from an Archangel, Volume II, 1988.* Albany, NY: Sacred Garden Fellowship.

Not so very long ago, embroiled in a painful custody battle, I spent long meditations asking for the Holy Spirit to help me release the pain created by the situation and replace it with peace. On sleepless nights, when I woke with anxiety, I'd ask again for the Holy Spirit to take my worry and fill me with love. Sometimes one hundred times a day the same call for help soothed, comforted, and nurtured me through my suffering, delivering peace…accessing the peace that is an innate part of my being (and yours, too). While I still had to navigate the lesson, I had help, as we all do.

Recall from **We Are So Loved** the vast number of angels at the ready, present to help us. Remember also that angels cannot act against our will nor can they remove the errors in our thinking, the negative beliefs about ourselves, or the behaviors that we need to shed. We must do that ourselves. The spiritual tool for navigating this kind of storm (created in this lifetime or chosen by plan) lies within us as the action of our True Nature… through the Holy Spirit.

What I learned in childhood about the Trinity as some untouchable, sanctified posse of "people" far outside of myself has evolved; I now understand these nebulous religious terms as energies, experiencing them within. Source, God, the Divine, Universal Power, or All-That-Is is the creative energy of the Universe; the energy of Divine Love is the Christ (not Jesus, but the pure love energy of the Self of us, *in us*, as a Divine Child); and the movement, comforting, and transformative aspect of Source in us is the Holy Spirit. New understanding created a change from praying "to someone" out there for what I thought I needed to expressing gratitude and experiencing an awareness of God in everything, including me. What is within is without, infusing everything and everyone with Its love, power, and joy. The once far away that "awaited me upon death" I now know from the inside as the beauty, love, and peace within me…within you…within all of us, eternally.

Everyone possesses the gift of the Holy Spirit, lovingly provided by Source for us to remember Home by crossing the bridge to Heaven within our mind and hearts now, today, and whenever we ask. All that's required is willingness - the willingness to let go of our old constructs, the willingness to surrender, and the willingness to feel the embrace of Divine Love.

Journey I: Reflections

Spend time in your sacred space, in meditation and reflection.

Consider your thoughts about the chapter. Write out what this chapter means to you and how it may align or conflict with what you previously were taught.

How do you feel about the chapter teaching?

What ideas/beliefs of yours might interfere with what this chapter offers?

Can you imagine any positive outcomes by embracing what you've read?

Journey II:
Holy Spirt Help

Returning to your sacred space, spend time centering. Journal about a situation that is challenging, emotional, or difficult to resolve.

When ready, ask the Holy Spirit to help you with this situation, helping you understand the lesson presented and transforming the entire experience into a beautiful gift. Ask that acceptance, forgiveness, peace or whatever loving state feels resonant replace the pain of the situation.

Now practice letting go of the outcome of this situation, asking the Holy Spirit to help you release the desire for control and replace it with trust.

Over the weeks to come, return here to journal how the situation has resolved, transformed, changed or how your attitude or feelings about it have changed. What gifts have you received?

Understanding Illness and Healing

The spirit is the life, the mind the builder, and the body the result.
— Edgar Cayce

Throughout our life, as well as our many, many past lives, we find ourselves on one side or another of illness and healing as either patient, caregiver, supporter, healee, or healer. We all experience days in bed with the flu or a cold. Some suffer accidents or serious health conditions. Many of us watch loved ones stalked by a disease that seems to steal their very essence.

Because we are so encased in our beliefs about suffering, bodies, and our physical world, we often find ourselves tethered to a three-dimensional mindset since thinking and feeling beyond them can present challenges. The body is so very real to us and when it seems to experience discomfort (pain actually in our emotional body that registers in the physical), our focus magnetically pulls us toward the physical sensations and holds us in the mesmerizing draw of the experience. We may even find ourselves snapped to attention under pain's cruel command.

Outside our conscious mind and conventional knowledge, however, lies another way to look at our body's symptoms and experiences, a way that points to the cause, a reason for what appears to us on the physical level. This chapter proffers a new mindset beyond our day-to-day thinking; not to remove or ignore healing modalities or people who help us in our life, but instead to provide an opportunity to change our perceptions about "disease" states, pain, accidents, and illness that result from the conditioned thinking that binds us so potently to our three-dimensional existence.

While many believe that a body is a body, metaphysics teaches that we are more than our body. You...WE are not our body. As stated before, we are SPIRIT - Spirit exploring life on a physical plane.

> We are not human beings having a spiritual experience.
> We are spiritual beings having a human experience.
> — Pierre Teilhard de Chardin

All we think and feel about our body is but rooted in belief - belief about ourselves and the world based on all current lifetime experiences combined with many previous past lives. Our beliefs generate everything we experience, including what they manifest (accidental injuries, common ailments, genetic diseases, and the mysterious illnesses that have no diagnosis or treatment) through their healing. While challenging to our very engrained ideas about fate, bad luck, and the factor of "oops", the value of exploring this metaphysical teaching can't be overstated.

> Your body in its out-picturing is a reflection of the various states of spiritual understanding. Every part of your body has a counterpart in Spirit that is not a body but rather a belief system. When an ailment attacks a certain portion of the body, you can go to a belief system and trace it back. It is that belief system which you should seek to heal, for without healing the cause, the effectual healing will only be temporary.[21]

As this teaching illuminates, what appears as an ailment is merely a smokescreen for what created the physical manifestation. Again, our beliefs as the powerful marriage of thoughts and feelings create through our mental and emotional bodies. By the time we encounter a physical manifestation as disease, accident, pain, or illness, our subtle bodies have long been "hard at work". Broadly speaking, we always encounter a belief behind physical issues whether the source is our belief system, one passed along from parents or ancestors, karma, or through the genetic patterning from our DNA. In addition, on a higher spiritual level, we plan aspects of our physical constitution prior to our birth. Before we incarnate, we use our finely tuned awareness in Spirit from across the veil to select our parents' as well as our ancestors' genetic qualities. We even plan the physical journeys of certain diseases, chronic ailments, and disabilities, all because these experiences through the body offer valuable lessons. Even karma plays out in physical symptoms, disease, and other ailments to repay deeds done in previous lives according to the exacting nature of the Law of Cause and Effect.

---

[21] Donovan, Rev. Penny (2016). *Healing: Selected Lessons from Archangel Gabriel.* Albany, NY: Sacred Garden Fellowship.

While it may be difficult to accept, this metaphysical concept is critical on our path of soul-discovery. Why? First, as we cease to look at our body as just a body, we can reach into the rich spiritual symbolism that explains this life beyond our three-dimensional existence to illuminate the truth about the living miracle of being in form. Second, the value of our body's "story" lies in its metaphors - the chapters of belief systems and dramatic plotlines of the lessons we are learning as they arise from the source of their making, beyond the flesh. Let me offer an example.

Nearly thirty years ago, I sustained several injuries in an accident (violence against self), the very same one I discussed in **We Are So Loved**. It was a rainy Thursday morning and I was just outside of Philadelphia on my way to work in the city. All along the drive, repeated "thoughts" to put on my seatbelt poked at my consciousness and each time I would think in response, *Next light*. As said before, I didn't wear a seatbelt, much a remnant of growing up in a home that never saw value in them. Passing through yet another green light, I saw a white blur. That became my last memory prior to impact. I awoke covered in glass, with a gaping wound on my face and gasping for air. Long story short, I sustained little injury considering the size of my car and the vehicle that collided with me. An eighteen-foot moving van, speeding on the other side of the divided highway, failed to stop in a rain-soaked turn and swerved in front of me. I hit it broadside, T-boned as some might say, leaving nothing but a mangled mess of a car. Despite facial lacerations, a concussion, whiplash, and a banged-up sternum and knees, I was very lucky. Certainly, my Divine helpers supported me that day - both earth angels and the finely feathered ones.

Peering through the window of my belief system, several scripts wrote the injuries of that accident. Examining some of the damage and body parts involved along with their corresponding symbolism, we find the following list as described in Archangel Gabriel's lessons on healing:[22]

> **Whiplash** (neck) - Neck is what we use to look from all directions to learn; thyroid resides here as our power center; whiplash represents the feeling that our internal ideas or personal privacy are not supported.
>
> **Severe contusion** (sternum) - Our sternum and rib cage protect our organs; these bones represent how safe we feel in our world.

---

[22] Donovan, Rev. Penny (2016). *Healing: Selected Lessons from Archangel Gabriel*. Albany, NY: Sacred Garden Fellowship.

Concussion (brain) - Brain represents our internal thoughts; brain injury is the belief that our internal thoughts have been violated.

Contusion/laceration (knees) - Knees represent flexibility as an attitude of "I'll do it but don't expect me to like it."

So, what really happened? Injury-producing car accidents demonstrate self-hatred in action. More specifically, a history of abuse and neglect expressed violently - the vehicle of my ego-based shadow self articulated as twisted, crushed metal. A tumultuous past punctuated with mental and emotional pain brutally manifested in the physical as it joined the present, a design meant to excavate old beliefs. The constant questioning and conflict with my parents who didn't support my decisions, life choices, or career path (whiplash and concussion) combined with more insidious forms of childhood abuse and neglect (severe contusion). For years I attempted to follow along with the rules and expectations my parents set, but internally I experienced a full revolt (knees). All became out-pictured in the details of self-directed injuries. Can you witness the echoes of that history woven with continued struggles through the symbolic feeling of danger, lack of support, violation, conflicted cooperation, and the accompanying anger and self-loathing they produced?

Now remember, we talked about serendipity and coincidence. We discussed that everything is a gift that can arrive first as a lesson. Some might say that a seatbelt would have drastically changed the outcome, that bumps and bruises would have replaced many of my more serious injuries. I agree. Furthermore, as you know, my angels urged me to buckle-up. Regardless, this event, no matter how badly it appeared, served as a wake-up call to stop putting my life on hold, to believe in myself, to care more lovingly for myself, and to support my own thoughts. Yes, a big price to pay; clearly, I needed an obvious, even obnoxious, lesson. Within six months, I enrolled in graduate school, ended a stagnant relationship, found a new apartment, and embarked on a whole new way of life dedicated to healing myself and others.

While my car accident serves as a more severe example to intentionally demonstrate previous points, not all our physical maladies will be so extreme or obvious, but the willingness to explore whatever we experience and take a fresh look unlocks doors that may have been previously closed or encrypted to our conscious mind. By opening our consciousness and desiring healing, anything we need - the help from "outside" us, as well as the urging and prodding from within - always presents itself in perfect timing and guides us to travel in a specific direction.

Because our beliefs create illness, accidents, and disease, healing from a metaphysical view is the removal of any belief which appears to limit, bind, and choke our very Livingness. Healing happens when we rest in the awareness of our Unity with Source, however that awakening may occur (through any healing modality or person including herbalists, doctors, shamans, therapists, spiritual healers, etc.). Resting in our intimate awareness of and with Source and feeling the Unity with that Creative Power erases the mistruths we've created and fills us with love — the all-powerful, cosmic healing elixir.

Forgiveness, compassion, and love stand at the core of all healing regardless of how our "dis-ease" or illness presents itself mentally, emotionally, or physically. The call for healing beckons to us through whispers, then nudges, and then smacks to give up our fear, love others and ourselves unconditionally, and accept our inheritance as a Child of God embodying the Christ.

You are a powerful being of light. The potency of your thoughts and feelings can shift your world and all you create in it, including your body. All healing is a change that aligns you with the Truth of your being as a Divine creative power; that potent transformation occurs as you remember your Oneness, remember your perfection, remember your holy Self.

Journey I: Reflections

Spend some time centering and meditating in your sacred space.

Reflect on the chapter material. How does this lesson differ from all you've been taught about healing and disease?

How do you feel about the chapter lesson? Did the chapter elicit a reaction or unexpected response? Why?

Explore other teachings that approach metaphysical healing from a more scientific perspective: This may include:

- *The True Power of Water*, Masaru Emoto
- *The Energy Healing Experiments: Science Reveals Our Natural Power to Heal*, Gary Schwartz, Ph.D. with William L. Simon
- *Vibrational Medicine*, Richard Gerber, MD
- www.heartmath.org/research/

Journal your reflections on what you discover.

Journey II: Metaphysical Messages

To understand what your body may be telling you, use the table below, decoding current or previous calls for healing.

1. Consider physical symptoms, illnesses, accidents, and injuries. These may range from cuts and sprains to more serious manifestations. Identify the body part, organ, or body system affected and list them on the table below.

2. Using the books *Healing: Selected Lessons from Archangel Gabriel* by Rev. Penny Donovan and *You Can Heal Your Life* by Louise Hay, write down the symbolism corresponding to each illness/injury/body part in column one. (See **References**.)

3. Reflect on what events, emotions, beliefs, etc. in your life could illuminate the cause for the illness/injury/body part listed in column one and list these in column three.

Illness Injury Body Part	Meaning/Symbolism	Beliefs, Emotions, Related Events

Injury / Illness / Body part	Meaning/Symbolism	Beliefs, Emotions, Related Events

Journey III: Journaling

Reflect on **Journey II**, journaling about your discoveries.

How do you feel about what you've unearthed?

Can you see any patterns across body parts, illnesses, symbolism, or other information from **Journey II**? Connections?

How does the information from **Journey II** help you make sense of other discoveries in **Volumes I, II**, and **III**? In your life?

How might you shift the attitude or belief of any injury or "dis-ease"? Can you write out affirmations to assist you?

How do you feel about new possibilities for healing?

Karmic Cords

As she has planted, so does she harvest; such is the field of karma.
— *Sri Guru Granth Sahib*

Our lives are not our own. From womb to tomb,
we are bound to others, past and present,
and by each crime and every kindness, we birth our future.
— *David Mitchell*

The concept of karma is much more common today in this age of enlightenment. Tag lines, jokes, and even songs speak about the benefits of "good" karma and the warning of collecting the "bad". Even my kids jab at others' ill-fated "instant karma," alluding to an awareness of the Universe at play and the importance of being conscious about personal actions.

Karma is what makes the world go around…literally. At this point in our human evolution, if not for karma, we would have no need to reincarnate to pay back debts or collect on what we feel owed. Without it, much suffering would fall away into the abyss of love and forgiveness.

Karma, a Sanskrit term, is the playing out of spiritual law - the lower energetic aspect of the Law of Cause and Effect. Remember, this Law holds that what we sow, we reap; whatever we put into the world comes back to us bigger and more potently than what we sent out in tandem with the Law of Attraction. Simply said, we are as responsible for our own unloving thoughts, feelings, and actions as we are for the beauty that blooms from our own grace-filled energy. The difference is merely a choice - a choice that only we can make.

Society often focuses on the less attractive side of karma, which it attributes to a vengeful God or hostile Maker - a misplaced blame since the dawn of time. Humankind, in fact, generated karma because of our archaic "eye for an eye", ego-based mindset. Steeped in the little self/personality, ego revels in the idea of "perfect justice". However, when we act, feel, and think in accordance with our Higher Self, our all-knowing, all-loving energy, we restore the innate balance of all things.

Looking deeper into karmic binding we first witness the players as the Actor(s) and the Acted upon(s), who can also correspond to families, large cultural groups, and nature. Keeping to people, these ties can play out through any relationship including lovers, children, parents, grandparents, siblings, best friends, work mates, neighbors, or any combination of individuals or groups.

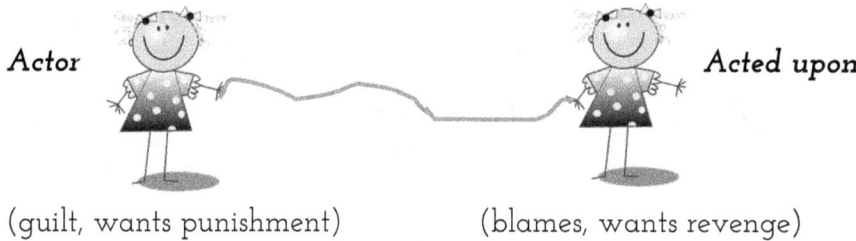

Actor   *Acted upon*

(guilt, wants punishment)   (blames, wants revenge)

As we see above, each player in a karmic relationship holds their respective end of an energetically-laden rope made of all the thought-fueled emotions that created the karma. This dynamic unfolds when the transgressor (**Actor**) recognizes on some level (in this lifetime or beyond the veil) the gravity of their deeds and guilt fills their awareness, facilitating a conscious or subconscious desire for self-punishment. The recipient (**Acted upon**) of the unloving act must also deal with their blame, anger, and resentment, which equally binds them to the transgressor, ensuring a subsequent desire for re-balancing through punishment. Not every bump in the road results in the heavy bonds of karma, which only occur where strong emotions reside; karma manifests through the lasting feeling that we owe or are owed something, a guilt-punishment dynamic duo that stems from the workings of the ego. We can witness this in the case of a child, for example, who deeply loves their parent (as children do) but feels owed if the parent doesn't care for them physically, mentally, or emotionally by the child's perceptions. Or in the case of partners, when one feels guilty that they didn't love the other enough, it may result in karma, which can carry over to another lifetime. Behind every debt of this nature lies the guilt from our misdeeds and a need to punish; where there is guilt, punishment inherently follows inasmuch as blame projects the need for the same kind of retribution.

The nature of karma that more frequently draws our attention results from feelings like hate or out of ill intent. Inflicting harm physically, mentally, or emotionally through unloving drives cultivates profoundly felt indebtedness, which again results in a need for rebalancing. Severe examples of this can be seen in random murders, genocide, and violence. The transgressor may even need to transition into the spirit realm to understand the magnitude of such deeds. More commonly, a kind of karma borne out of hate becomes projected as "love gone wrong" like abuse, infidelity, or abandonment. While love can never truly go wrong, our ego enjoys using the hard-learned lessons from what we experience in painful interpersonal relationship dynamics to convince us otherwise. Additionally, we often remain unaware of the spiritual contracts we make to grow through experiences (painful and loving) and forget that they hold great value along with their challenging counterpoints. Love, from an energetic standpoint, truly falls on the same continuum as hate, even though we see hate as love's perfect opposite. When our love for someone becomes tainted by anger, mistrust, revenge, or any other strong, negative emotion, the hate-fueled blame generates and sustains a binding tie. So, feelings of "You hurt, injured, or deceived me and now you must pay!" generously grease the wheel of karma.

Karma appears with many faces, each unique to the person and their path. Generally, we can recognize it playing out where intense situations appear to bind us together, despite times when logic, good sense, or calls for peace and harmony seem to beg for everyone involved to walk the other way. Adult children who cannot or will not leave home for various reasons, tumultuous relationships that appear extremely unfair or unbalanced, disease or illness that has no "cure" or cannot be identified or treated, murders and other acts of violence - these are often the re-balancing of karmic debt. We never truly know the path another walks or the reasons for their actions.

Though we can certainly gain clarity from understanding childhood hurts, environmental factors, family circumstances, and social challenges, sometimes earth plane appearances offer insufficient explanations of how lives unfold; what appears as a horrific act may in fact be a re-balancing of the karmic scale. That is not to imply that understanding karma serves as a replacement for taking responsibility and accepting the consequences of our actions. Instead, witnessing the possibility of karmic ties in action helps us develop compassion and offer forgiveness in increasingly challenging situations.

Deciphering karmic ties in our life can often feel cryptic and elusive. Let me offer an example. Not so long ago, I became perplexed by a persistent ringing in my head around both ears. (Remember, karma often shows itself in physical symptoms.) As a child in a home with much conflict, both eardrums ruptured during grade school causing scarring and ringing on my right side. As an adult, the intensity and frequency of this ringing became so troubling in recent years that I decided to ask for clarity from one of the Master Teachers at Sacred Garden Fellowship. He shared that in a previous lifetime, as a wealthy woman with many servants who I treated unkindly, I frequently demonstrated my displeasure by hitting them about the ears. My ringing symptoms resulted from karma I created in that lifetime, a great reminder that we have all done things that elicit regret, guilt, distaste, and downright repulsion. The immensely exacting nature of karma created a situation for me to experience what I caused in others; one that dissolves as I forgive myself for the transgressions.

Recall, the nature of karma frequently involves two players or combinations of players. Sometimes, however, it continues as personally-created self-karma, a tormented relationship with the "man in the mirror" built against ourselves and equally as binding. We create this when others forgive us but we hold onto our guilt and feel unable to forgive ourselves. Self-karma may be carried from previous incarnations thousands of years ago or be generated in this lifetime, playing out in the present as residual guilt for our wrongdoings toward others who have dropped the karmic cord. We just continue to hold the other end and close the loop with ourselves, becoming the **Actor** and the **Acted upon**...blaming, shaming, and carrying the desire to be punished as a result.

Self-karma tends to exist more commonly than we would think, showing its face in many situations. For example, if we are living a life that seems fraught with punishment, can't get ahead, find difficulty around every corner, have friends or lovers that disrespect, mistreat, or leave us, find situations that don't work out no matter our efforts, or have adult children who just don't appreciate us, self-karma is afoot.[23]

---

[23] Donovan, Rev. Penny (1999). *Karma and Love: Archangel Gabriel*. Kingston, NY: Springwell Metaphysical Studies.

With all karma, self or other, there is good news; a simple solution rests in our very hands...simple, but not always easy. All we must do is forgive others and ourselves, dissolving our guilt-punishment binding. Remember, however, forgiveness is a process whose common denominator is time. Forgiveness begins with others and follows with self-forgiveness because our little self holds self-blame more tightly than what we project out.[24] In fact, often the intensity with which we condemn others increases in relationship to how much we remain entangled in blaming ourselves.

Releasing the pain of any situation takes the courage to look at what we experienced, feel our feelings, process them, release them, and eventually release the other person, as well as ourselves. How long our forgiveness journey takes differs from person to person and situation by situation. The prison we create through blame and guilt can only be opened by our loving heart, which looks upon ourselves and others through the eyes of compassion and joins with a mind to discern the truth beyond the illusions of the ego's twisted games. Many chapters to come (**Volumes IV** and **V**) facilitate the process of forgiveness with varied tools to continue to learn, grow, and facilitate soul-discovery in this area.

As you read this chapter or perhaps in the days and weeks to come, you may recognize your part on either side of a karmic cord. Know that during any incarnation, we can choose to pay karmic debt from other lifetimes or use the opportunity to release ourselves from transgressions or perceived ills through forgiveness. True forgiveness releases all the pain we felt through the situation and dissolves our side of the karmic contract. (See **Remembering the Love, Shedding Perceived Failures**, and **Ho' oponopono** in **Volume IV**.) And if our karmic relationships escape the light of truth, we will find other ways to address these ties as karma follows us after physical death where we find a greater understanding of what we created. Crossing the veil naturally elevates everyone to a higher vibration, making visible the pain caused by our words, attitudes, beliefs, and actions. And while in truth, anything of the physical plane has no impact on our Spirit, our personality and form register the hurt and/or damage on many levels; therefore, we must accept responsibility and dissolve our karma through forgiveness or by going through a proportional and equivalent situation to rebalance the scales. Remember, we create any karma in our life and are still accountable to it because we made the beast long, long ago. The choice of forgiveness or equal action is ours to make as we grow in awareness.

By now you may be wondering if we need to know all the pieces - the who, what, where, and when - to forgive, thereby releasing karma? Simply put, no. If we need to

---

[24] Donovan, Rev. Penny (2013). *Introduction to Practical Spirituality: Selected Lessons from Archangel Gabriel.* Albany, NY: Sacred Garden Fellowship.

understand or know the details of past deeds or events, we will be guided to that discovery. More times than not, we would use the information to emotionally beat ourselves over the head. Because every day holds many opportunities to forgive, this is where the magic lies. If we stay present with how we think and feel, the negativity (anger, disappointment, blame, guilt, or resentments) we have in our interactions with the people in our life become apparent. We can explore how we feel now, allowing the experience to move through us as active engagement in soul-discovery. Any forgiveness begins to release us from our pain. We feel our feelings, deal with the anger, shed our hurts, forgive others, forgive ourselves, let it all go…one step at a time so we can embrace the valuable lessons learned.

I can hear what some of you are thinking now. "I can't do that! I'm furious with them." "He's hurt me." "She's manipulated me." "They'll do something mean again." Please don't confuse forgiveness with approving or thinking what another does is OK. And it's not about ignoring how we feel, either. Denial, lack of boundaries, and forgetting self-care are not part of forgiveness. It's not about condoning the actions of another, nor does it mean that we allow ourselves to fall "prey" to others. Owning our Divinity means standing in our power where we know how to lovingly and respectfully take care of ourselves by saying no, stop, or even by walking away. It means we vibrate at a higher frequency and the hurts that drew the situation to us are no longer part of our consciousness because we have dissolved the belief system that created them. Being loving and aligned with our Higher Self enables us to rise above the perceptions of the personality - the judgments, blame, and guilt - to take responsibility for our part in any situation and see others with discernment and love. When we forgive, we are really allowing ourselves to be free - free from blame and free from hurt - to learn, grow, and love again.

The core of our very being is eternal, indestructible, and beyond the effects of the physical world. No matter what has happened to us - what we have done to others or what others have done to us - nothing can hurt our or their Spirit. As our consciousness evolves to be in Unity, we can free ourselves by stepping off the wheel of karma to end the cycle of heartache and embrace our True Self.

Journey I: Chapter Reflections

Spend some time in your sacred space, first meditating and then reflecting on the chapter.

What are your thoughts? How to do feel about what you read?

How does it resonate with your current understanding and your past learning?

Journey II: Karmic Cords

After centering in your sacred space, spend time contemplating evidence of karma in your life through illness, accidents, difficult relationships, etc.

Journal about how you feel about the people in your life now and in the past. Is there guilt, blame, or hard feelings still between you and others? How is that experienced or played out?

Returning to **Journey II** of **The Ties That Bind Us** in **Volume I**, what relationships listed might fit with this chapter?

How might karma be playing out in any of your relationships currently?

What interactions/events in the relationships call for forgiveness to release these karmic situations?

Do you sense any self-karma? In what ways might it present itself? Do you blame or punish yourself? What forgiveness or letting go could release the karma you sense?

Journey III:
Practicing Daily Forgiveness

Spend some time in your sacred space, centering and meditating.

Ask your Divine helpers to call to your attention to small daily opportunities for forgiveness. These are the events when people irritate you, try your patience, seem to use words carelessly, etc. Stay present to all your reactions that are unloving and involve anger, irritation, blame, etc.

Journal your reactions here and the details of any relevant event.

Now rate your feelings about the event on a scale of 1 - 10, with 10 being most intense.

Can you feel your emotions and let them pass through you? What needs to change in your thinking to shift your reaction? Can you depersonalize the other person's behavior? Do you see any evidence that the event triggered self-blame? Can you let go of this "little grievance"? Why or why not? Journal all your insights.

Additional notes:

Blessings Blooming

*He is happiest who hath power to gather wisdom from a flower,
and wake his heart in every hour to pleasant gratitude.*
— *Wordsworth*

Our life is filled with blessings, some fully in our awareness, others seemingly hidden from sight. They come in all shapes and sizes, though we often generate expectations about how they should arrive or the specific ways they must look. Our lives, in fact, are filled with blessings if we but open ourselves to notice and receive.

Blessings inherently hold two interdependent and unified aspects: giving and receiving. Through giving, we extend blessings to others by acts of service, gestures of love, gifts, and deeds of kindness. Running against the grain, though, we uncover the blessings offered through challenges and conflicts; these "unwanted opportunities" call us or the people in our life to exercise forgiveness and compassion as the blessings of personal growth.

On the seemingly opposite side of the spectrum, we find receiving - taking in what's offered to us with gratitude, accepting all with love. In receiving freely, we release our notion that the scales need balancing; feeling that we owe others or aren't worthy enough to be gifted (from ourselves and others) can keep us on the karmic ride. And remember, in the same lovely packages of turmoil and difficult relationships, we find blessings wrapped in what appears to be soiled paper with a crushed bow, the treasures of receiving through what tries our patience, appears unloving, disrespects us, etc.

Some of us are much more comfortable giving than we are receiving. Even in its subtle expressions, any reticence to receive not only blocks our awareness of all the wonderful that comes to us but also diminishes what we manifest because we engage with the world out of lack - lack of worthiness, lack of deservedness, or lack of feeling loveable. In truth, the completeness of giving and receiving only occurs as giving and receiving become one. As such, giver and receiver join perfectly like the pieces of a puzzle nesting in one another to create a whole. While we may witness this union in many ways, a common example is seen through the exchange of a present - when the giver lovingly gives while receiving the blessing of giving and feeling the receiver accept, and the receiver accepts and blesses the giver with love, giving in return through gratitude.

> Others are the great unknown of living in the world. Others are those who are beyond your control, those who can influence the course of your day or your life in ways you would not choose. Others represent the accidents waiting to happen, love that is not returned, the withholding of things you deem important. This fear that you feel in relation to others is as true of those you hold most dear to you as it is of those you would call strangers. It is the very independence of others that makes your own independence seem so important to you. Dependency is not consistent with your notions of a healthy self. What, then is the alternative?
>
> The alternative is believing in giving and receiving as one.
> — A Course of Love, T2:7.2-7.3

We often feel most in need of blessings when life feels a bit challenging or even quite difficult. Assistance from our Divine helpers may be in order, requesting help to see and receive blessings. Remember, when we reach our hands and heart to the heavens for assistance, aid is *always* there. All it requires is that we pay attention to everything that presents in the moment, staying open to all possibilities and releasing preconceived ideas regarding size or significance. When shifting our attention to receive, a stranger opening the door for us is no greater or lesser than a dear friend's soup delivery when we are ill. The only difference is our perception, the way in which we define our need or desire being fulfilled at the time.

Let's be open-hearted and open-minded…see giving and receiving as one and watch the love flow.

Journey I:
Blessing Blooms

Retreat to your sacred space to center, meditate, and reflect. Ask your Divine helpers to join you, requesting that they bring your attention to all the blessings you've received in the past week.

Allow thoughts and images to come to mind of blessings, using what you envision to create a blessing bloom where each petal of the bloom displays a blessing.

Continue creating blessing blooms throughout your week and month.

Can you fill the page?

Journey II:
Blessings Reflection

Go to your sacred space to center and meditate.

Journal about your blessing experiences.

What do you find has changed from previous journeys like this that included gratitude and thankfulness?

Has your attitude toward blessings changed? Are you aware of more uplifting and loving energy in your life?

Journey III:
Giving and Receiving

After centering in your sacred space, reflect on your attitudes toward giving and receiving.

Which do you find easier, giving or receiving? Why?

What does your attitude about giving or receiving say about worthiness, expectations, feeling deserving, indebtedness, etc.?

Are there any challenges or difficulties you could consider to be blessings now, even though they didn't begin that way? Write about them and how they turned into blessings.

Let Your Love-light Shine

Darkness cannot drive out darkness; only light can do that.
Hate cannot drive out hate; only love can do that.
— Martin Luther King, Jr.

Prayers, sending light, lifting another's consciousness through positive thoughts, and holding others in love are powerful, powerful acts of compassion and healing. These we do through the love within us - the tender glue that binds the Universe together. As such, they are precious expressions of our "love-light".

What is the source of love? Of light? Of healing? Source, God, Mother Nature, All-That-Is, Universal Power…it matters not what we call It. God is the cradle from which all life is birthed. Love is the energy through which creation happens. Light is what we are created of. Each time we call upon the light and love within us, our Self, we tap into our own Divinity and our awareness of that holiness grows. The effects of our being loving toward others ripple out in ever increasing circles, touching all living things in its gentle wake.

Our collective experiences, especially with religion, commonly challenge the belief of Source within us because many creeds teach that Source lies outside of ourselves, making us seem separate from Him/Her/It. The wellspring of our Divinity and thus connection with It, however, remains eternal - safely part of us at all times, in all places, whether we live in skin or on the other side of the veil. Just as an apple contains a seed as the perfect potential of its very flesh, the everlasting energy of our being is Source - the eternal seed of our temporary flesh, as well as our Spirit.

Bound permanently with our infinite nature, our Spirit energy connects us to Source and with all living things through an invisible energetic thread, joining us to all the world and the world to us. Even as the body and our levels of consciousness linked to the physical world attempt to maintain a sense of separateness, we have been and always will be a part of Source and Source a part of us. We are a raindrop merging with the River of Life, a merger we feel by stepping into the awareness of our spiritual Union.

What does this have to do with prayer, light, and love, the expressions of our love-light? All are gifts we offer the world through our inherent Divinity - an extension of Source, an expression of our Holy Nature through Union. Spiritually speaking, *we are prayer, light, and love*, which become known and expressed most especially when we embrace our Self and the raindrop knows it is One with the River.

As fellow journeyers on the path of soul-discovery, prayer, light, and love are powerful tools of transformation and healing as our love-light. The depth and strength of what we offer lies in our Divine interconnectedness and the willingness to truly trust in the power that rests there - the "place" where our energy reaches inward and vibrationally up - as we step fully into that River. So, let's explore each gift and its application and perfect interdependence with the others.

Prayer, in its common practice, is our communication with Source through a request. When we intentionally pray, belief in speaking with a higher power fuels our conversation as we ask Source to help us or others shed something - a disease, pain, a bad situation. Other times we pray to assist ourselves or others gain something that appears absent in our or their life. And since prayer is such a powerful way to be a blessing in the world, the more people who join, the more potent it becomes. ("Where two or more are gathered…") Here's what happens:

> When you pray for someone, there goes a light to them – not from you, from God – a light to them that surrounds them and forms a kind of protection for them. And the more you pray for them or others pray for them, the stronger and brighter and wider that light becomes, till finally the situation, whatever it is in this person, it is dispersed. So, it's very important to pray for people, even if you don't know what to ask for them, and sometimes you don't. You know they need help, but you don't know what, so you pray that God will bless them and help them; and that is very powerful because that light is like an insulation and it brings healing and health. It attracts angels that can be of service. It's a very wonderful thing to pray for someone. It's a great gift.[25]

---

[25] Donovan, Rev. Penny. (2016). *Ancient Forms of Teaching and Understanding: November 2016 Retreat with Yeshua.* Albany, NY: Sacred Garden Fellowship.

While I'm not here to tell you how to pray, as that is highly personal, let me offer some help for creating a prayer practice that clarifies intent and directs the energy in a life-affirming way. Here are some suggestions:

- Hold a positive attitude and use affirming words.
- Open as much as possible to unite with the feeling of Source within, connecting with love to It, ourselves, and others.
- Ask to be lifted out of misperceptions into Truth.
- Remember that when lifting anyone into Truth, we don't need to know what causes the "problem" they are experiencing or what appears to be lacking in their life.
- Affirm that the Higher Self and Source knows what is for our/other's highest good.
- Call for the awareness of Source *in us/others* to do the work through us/them.
- Move past any perceived limitation, lack, or illness and ask to witness the person in their perfection, Spirit, or Divine Self.
- Thank God/Source and acknowledge that everything is already available. Remember to allow for time for it to manifest on the physical plane.
- Open your arms to receive, trusting that Universal Power answers and provides.

At times we may have difficulty praying without a negative attitude or fear as we allow ourselves to become fooled by the appearance of a situation. Ego can be quite tricky, convincing us of how "bad" something is or the realness of lack. But because of our interconnectedness with Source, all we need, want, desire, and experience is known by Him/Her/It and our needs are always met, even if they arise from a subconscious desire or spiritual contract to experience challenges. Furthermore, anything we ask for is already known by God and all needs are provided, just like the saying "birds don't carry backpacks".

Our consciousness (belief in limitation) is the only blockage to our receiving positive, uplifting anything in our life. And because prayer is always answered from the level at which we generate it, as we discussed in these chapters of **Metaphysical Musings**, we avoid praying from worry or lack. Instead, we can pray with the attitude of ever-present abundance, *knowing* that all we need is already present, though not in our current awareness. The infinite richness of love expressed in many ways through heart-felt acceptance and positive language for the highest and best works with Universal Law through gratitude and opens us to take in the bounty of the world.

Prayer from the heart always offers healing to others, regardless of our relationship with them. One of the best ways, in fact, to remove a difficult someone from our life, a person seen as an enemy, is to pray for them. We can ask that they be lifted out of their challenging ways into the heart of the Universe and wrapped in the love of God. As we reach *beyond* personality into our True Nature to recognize the same in them, the Divinity in us sees the Divinity in them, and this is mutually healing. If we still feel negative emotions toward them because of our own need for resolution and growth, this impedes the healing. So, we can ask that God blesses, forgives, or lifts their consciousness for us, through us. Regardless of who we send prayers to, remember to be specific, holding a vision of what we desire for their highest good. Feel the love…put your heart in it and know that each person, plant, and animal choose their own path.

Here's some examples of prayers generated with life-affirming, uplifting language and centered on gratitude:

Dear Mother-Father God,
I feel Your loving presence within me and around me.
I greatly desire to release the fear that is holding me back from my true path.
I consciously invite the Holy Spirit to work through me to release this blockage
and fill me with knowingness and wisdom.
Thank You for guiding the expression of my highest and best,
to live my purpose and do what I love for my precious time
here in this great adventure.
Indeed. And so, it is.

Divine Father, Holy Mother,
I call in the action of the Holy Spirit to lift me out of fear
and replace it with perfect trust.
I thank You for perfect health and the perfect health of my family.
I know You hear me as You always do.
Indeed. And so, it is.

Dear Bringer of Light,
Powerful Creator of the Cosmos,
I greatly desire for all those in positions of authority
to have compassion and wisdom toward all sentient beings.
Thank You for working through them to ignite their hearts
in brotherhood and sisterhood, inspiring them to act for
the good of ALL human, plant, mineral, and animal kind.
Thank You for Your guidance to all those involved in care of Mother Earth
for maintaining clean water, fresh air, strong wildlife,
prolific gardens, and healthy humans everywhere.
We envision her whole, vibrant, teeming with life,
and perfect as You created her.
We are so truly grateful for Your abundance and the Mother
You have given us to sustain our physical needs.
Indeed. And so, it is.

Adding to prayer, we have the potent practice of sending love. When sending love to ourselves and others, we can offer prayer to clarify our intent. We begin by connecting through meditation, which at its deeper levels allows a resting in the stillness to receive guidance, opens us to inspiration, and unites us with our Higher Self. This sets the stage to rest in the arms of Source, abiding there to be a conduit for Divine Power from the highest will and out of the mindset of ego. Though our heartfelt connection we offer our love as healing.

Sending love to ourselves, loved ones, those in need, or even our perceived enemies is restorative for both the giver and the receiver(s). Remember, what we give to others we cannot help but give to ourselves (giving and receiving as one). When someone is not feeling their best, sending love through prayers with a feeling of compassion and deep caring affirms the purity of their being. This offers a blessing as it is taken in. All that we intend through a heart-centered connection of loving thoughts and feelings possesses incredible healing power. And in a world in need of much brotherhood, sisterhood, and compassion, these aspects of our "love-light" make all the difference.

Wrapping people in light through and with love is also healing and protective. The same light we learned about in **Wynebgwrthucher** serves to help restore and assist others in gathering more loving, life-affirming vibrations. This practice also calls forth the energy for them to experience what they need in their life to grow. As we envision those we desire to help through light - white for healing and protection, pink for love, and yellow for knowingness - we imagine a vibrating, living brightness coming down to them from above, lovingly wrapping around them. Remember the power of the mind and heart joined together, and always, always, always do this with love.

As we "turn on" our love-light in the world, we must remember that everyone has free will. We all have the choice to live in perfect Union - in love, compassion, forgiveness, trust, and peace - or to create misaligned with our True Nature. Choosing to accept healing, love, and prayers as the blessings bestowed upon us enables the manifesting of the positive, high vibrational energy of our birthright and demonstrates our alignment with Source as giving and receiving as one. The choice is always ours.

Generally speaking, all blessings mold to the giver's as well as the receiver's intent and can include restoration of the physical form, mental and emotional healing, and positive movement in life. Consciously intending that the healing power addresses the cause of any difficulty or illness removes the weed of erroneous belief that created whatever situation has manifested and replaces it with truth and love. How the energy is "taken in" even includes being stored in the aura for future use or for aiding the person's transition to the next plane through death of the physical body. And yes, we can know the healing power of passing as we witness a loved one release a cumbersome, diseased, or failing body despite deeply grieving them.

A critical aspect to our love-light rests in the arms of perfect trust. When we trust, we know that Universe/Source hears us and always answers for our highest and best, even when we don't like the outcome. Our human nature, however, tends to desire control; when motivated by the ego mind, our drives to manipulate, rule, and dominate life directly compete with trust. Asking our Divine Creator for something and then telling Him/Her/It all the caveats tagged to creating what we want demonstrates our lack of trust in Source. For example, if we ask something like, "Dear Mother-Father God, please help me do ____, but make sure it's not ___ or ____ and it has ____ and I only want a little of ____ just after this time of ____ but not before ___," we can know that mistrust and control have moved in and taken up residence. Trust and allowing join hands in gentle union to answer our calls for love, prayer, or healing. We need only open our hearts to receive and know that as we thank our Divine Creator for all the good in our life, God hears and answers. Even if it's not the exact outcome we hope for, it's what we need at the time to be nurtured, grow, or heal.

Healing through prayer, love, and light as our love-light can be a conscious, daily practice. Again, this must be done from the heart, for without love, no helpful energy lies behind it. When people come to mind and we hear of their struggles or we witness chaos and turmoil in the news, we can send prayers, light, and love as healing. We can do the same for ourselves. Knowing Mother Earth requires our love and protection, we can send prayers and healing to her. When leaders act in challenging, self-serving ways, we can send prayers and light to them as well, that their consciousness be lifted and they act through discernment and compassion.

The world is in much need of prayers, love, and healing, a call to shine our love-light on and in the world, letting our true Self sparkle and fill the ethers with joy, compassion, and peace.

Journey I:
Creating Prayer

Spend time centering and meditating in your sacred space. Ask your Divine helpers for guidance on this journey if you are called to do so.

Write a prayer for someone whom you love who appears to be suffering or could benefit from assistance. How could you use the positive, affirming language outlined in the chapter?

Now practice praying for them.

Journal your experience. How is this way of prayer different or the same as praying in the past?

How does it feel to pray in this new way?

Journey II: Love-light

Spend time meditating in your sacred space. Ask your Divine helpers for guidance on this journey as you are called.

Before sending healing as love and light, aligning your energies with your wise, loving Higher Self through centering and meditation is very important. Removing yourself from the busyness and lower vibrations of the day frequently takes time so give yourself space to prepare.

Connect to someone (person, plant, or animal) you love or have deep and abiding affection for. Feel your love for them connecting heart to heart with the highest and best intentions for them. For help with this, revisit **Journey II** in **Beautiful World** or **Journey I** from **Mindfulness and Gratitude** in **Volume II**.

Envision in your mind's eye a light from Source that comes from above them, surrounding them completely. Ask for help from the Holy Spirit to see them as beautiful, perfect, and whole, seeing only light. They may have shape but imagine only light with no features or details. Visualize the same for you, that you are a light connecting with them. Wrap them in additional pink, yellow, and white light. Affirm the highest and best for them and let go of the outcome.

Journal your experience with this and continue as you are drawn to repeat this journey.

Practice this with Mother Earth, world leaders, government officials, those who try your patience, etc. and journal your experiences.

Additional notes:

Journey III:
Blessings for Ourselves

Spend time centering and meditating in your sacred space. Ask your Divine helpers for guidance on this journey as you are called.

Practice using the tools outlined in the chapter to call blessings into your life through prayers, light, and love - your love-light.

Journal your experiences. Consider the following: Did you find this easier or harder than sending blessings to others? Why? What do you feel or think your experience with this journey helps you understand about your soul-discovery and all you are learning?

The Substance of Stars

What you seek is seeking you.

— Rumi

Child of the Universe, you are the substance of stars - of light, of love, of pixie dust. We celebrate your connection to all and All, your expression of Truth as the purity of the Self.

Everything you experienced in **Metaphysical Musings** was to help you remember You. All your exploring, learning new, forgetting the old, and discovering the many aspects of your being brought you to this celebration of your work.

Take a moment to acknowledge all you have done. Write or draw about how you've grown and what you'll take with you as you continue your travels. Here is the space to celebrate and give yourself recognition while reflecting on the path ahead. When you're finished, move on to **Volume IV: A Deeper Gaze**.

The Soul-Discovery Journalbook

An Intimate Journey into Self

Volume IV
A Deeper Gaze

The real meaning of enlightenment is to gaze with undimmed eyes on all darkness.

— *Nikos Kazantzakis*

A Deeper Gaze

Wow! You're more than halfway there! Give yourself a big hug for working through **A Single Step**, **Constant Companions**, and **Metaphysical Musings**. You've gathered many valuable tools along the way and amassed a library of information about yourself and your world.

We continue onward into deeper soul-discovery, building on previous volumes. Looking at ourselves is much like refurbishing a piece of furniture; many, many layers of old paint reside between the colorful, etched surface and the beautiful wood beneath. As aspects of old personality become apparent, **A Deeper Gaze** provides opportunities to look closely at the paint under the paint while shaving, scraping, sanding, and stripping away the colored veneer - one, two, three steps closer to the core. Roll up your sleeves and discover layers of your soul, out of sight but not far away.

Love Your Spots

Because one believes in oneself, one doesn't try to convince others.
Because one is content with oneself, one doesn't need others' approval.
Because one accepts oneself, the whole world accepts him or her.
— Lao-Tzu

We live in a world filled with judgments - a world that judges physical attributes predicated on standards set by social media, television, fashion, and the internet. As such, men and women of all shapes, sizes, and colors can find an unwelcoming attitude in which diversity and uniqueness seem to lack value. Highly edited, tucked, stuffed, and made-up bodies adorn our magazine pages and screens. In these perfectly quaffed realms, natural human nuances become swear words.

Unfortunately, these assaults to our self-image aren't relegated to one source. The messages from our unfriendly media landscape can compound a litany of messages in childhood and teen years from our home life, school experiences, and social interactions. When these messages feel negative or pressure-producing, they infuse our psyche with a siren's song of self-criticism, matching any other beliefs of the same vibration. Unless we release the unseemly impact of them, they continue to fill our consciousness and affect us in the present, eroding our self-esteem by encouraging a lack of self-love. Living *through* this negative inner climate results in chastising ourselves with a caustic internal dialogue like "My nose is too big" or "My butt is too wide." We may even embark on a self-improvement and physical conditioning regimen but gather our motivation from the bad feelings about our appearance, worried about body fat or lack of a perfect physique. Maybe we additionally compare ourselves with what we see on our televisions, in our neighbors, at work, or with the lovely person working out next to us at the gym.

In truth, our body is the physical temple of our Divinity. As stated before, we are Creative Force in action and our body is a three-dimensional representation of it, an opportunity to live our holy inheritance on the earth plane. How we feel and speak about ourselves, about any aspect of our being, profoundly affects our self-worth and feelings of value. Steeped in self-criticism, we then unknowingly attempt to live counter to our True Nature using our creative power recklessly against ourselves.

The power of our Divinely-given energy - as our consciousness reflected in the words, beliefs, thoughts, and emotions - either energetically supports us or tears us down. When our powerful mind generates thoughts that we believe about our body, it creates exactly that or a state that metaphorically mirrors it. Loving thoughts nurture an acceptance and love of our form to express health, vibrancy, and life. Unloving energies steeped in the "not-good-enough" married with emotions of condemning our physical form creates more negative. All that we want to dispel or change then manifests either directly or symbolically as bigger or increasingly more potent.

Aligning with what we learned in **Understanding Illness and Healing** in **Volume III**, recall that on a spiritual level, our body symbolizes a belief about ourselves. As we work aligned with our True Nature, we claim perfect health, but if not, "dis-ease", illness, injury, or physical attributes manifest that reflect the belief system in play. Simply said, if we find ourselves in a battle with our physical form, the personal wrestling match in our mental and emotional bodies illuminates a lesson of self-love, acceptance, and compassion. Here's an example to illustrate.

Many years ago, I manifested a sun spot on my face under my eye. Day after day it drew my attention. No matter how much I covered it from UV exposure, it continued to grow, and I began to hate it. Every time I looked in the mirror, there it was…taunting me, representing age and imperfection, a swear word from the old family messages that held perfect, flawless beauty in high regard. The more I focused on it, the faster it grew, until one day, I noticed a disturbing change; no longer flat, it appeared elevated and more irregular. Watching friends, neighbors, and relatives deal with cancerous skin lesions, I began to worry until a friend said to me, "You'd better start loving that spot or you're guaranteeing a trip to the dermatologist."

What a gift! I became so focused on the spot, the basic spiritual premise of manifesting through belief eluded me. All my energy, focused on despising the spot, began to create the perfect spot to hate. That moment, I changed my mind and started a journey of "spot forgiveness". In two months, it completely disappeared without a dermatologist or special treatment. Now, I'm not negating medical treatment or affirming some lack of value in it. Had my path continued instead of turning the corner, a doctor would have been the next course of action in addition to changing perceptions about my appearance. Clearly the lesson of using spiritual tools - to understand the power of the mind and heart joined in Unity, especially toward myself - ranked in the forefront of this invaluable experience.

So how do we shift from pouring negative energy into our perceived flaws? First, we become aware of our unloving affirmations and recognize that we are OK. To shift where we invest in our "blemishes", ALL judgment against ourselves and our bodies as not good enough or unacceptable must be dropped. Even the subtle as well as blatant judgments or criticisms toward others must go, too, because judgments toward others simply serve as a cloaked version of those, we hold toward ourselves. (See **Leaving Our Swamp of Judgment** in **Volume V**.) Secondly, we may require help from any combination of healing therapies - mainstream, modern, or alternative. As the body appears to express something to heal and we seek help for our highest and best, the assistance we require is present before the thought is complete. Our desire to heal unites with our Self and the Universe answers. Caring for and honoring the body shows loves and respect to the Divinity within; everything expresses some aspect of sacred, loving energy, even when we distort, twist, or alter its pure nature to be something of our making. So, taking care of our form by washing, resting, sleeping, eating well, exercising, meditating, etc. honors the Self by nurturing the physical vehicle of our Divinity in its current expression.

> *If you can't remove yourself from life, what choice have you but to join with it? Love it. Love yourself. Love yourself enough to accept yourself. Love will transform normal, ordinary, life into extraordinary life. Loving exactly who you are and where you are in every moment is what will cause the transformation that will end your desire to remove yourself from life. All those frustrations you currently feel have a purpose: To move you through them and beyond them—to acceptance.*
> – A Course of Love, D:Day8.2

What if, on the other hand, we desire to shift a physical attribute? Let's say, for example, we aspire to lose weight, to be slimmer and healthier. Yes, a new eating plan, exercise, meditation, and other healthful practices provide great benefits. Perhaps though, the weight gain also represents something deeper, like adrenal stress or thyroid issues. Then on a physical level, care through a holistic nutritional practitioner, a physician, or naturopathic doctor may be in order. Emotionally speaking, as we progress in our health and wellness through honoring our body, we benefit deeply by self-encouragement and self-acceptance. Looking in the mirror and remarking on our "fatness", focusing negatively on our exaggerated curves, or cursing our "muffin top", wreaks havoc.

Instead, we picture our form at a healthy weight and hold that vision each time we look in the mirror. Again, loving and accepting attitudes are paramount, especially in the face of the improvements we desire.

Let's endeavor to embrace ourselves as different and unique - not special and better than but one-of-a-kind AND equal. Like a precious snowflake, no other person is exactly like you; how bland the world would be without the diversity you bring. You are monumentally important, a piece of the grand, cosmic Creator Who is incomplete without you! Embrace it, love it, live it!

Journey I: Body Talk Survey

Retreat to your sacred space and center. If you desire, ask your Divine helpers for support, guidance, and to be made aware of your highest and best for this journey.

Create two lists of all your words, thoughts, judgments, criticisms, and attitudes you direct toward your body: one of positive feedback and compliments and the other of the lack of love and acceptance. Next to each comment, note how you feel.
Ex: I love the color of my hair and my full lips. - happy, sexy, confident
Ex: My hips are too wide, and my eyes are too small. - irritated, insecure

Things I like about my body…	What I don't like or criticize my body for…

Journal your experience with this journey. What are your thoughts, feelings, and insights witnessing all you listed above?

Notes:

Journey II:
Practicing Love

Choose one or two of the attributes you wrote about in **Journey I** listed in your "dislike" list. Consider how you could change your mind about this quality.

How could you practice **Wise Baby Vision** from **Volume II** to see yourself without old judgments, old habitual attitudes, or programmed thinking?

Ex: These are my full hips. I accept them for what they are and imagine them smaller as I care for my body by walking 30 minutes a day.

Ex: These are my eyes, small and cute. I chose them before I was born to give me a lesson in self-love.

Include your plan for shifting your vision to self-acceptance.

Journey III:
Moving Forward

Journal about your experiences as you grow in the loving beliefs and attitudes about yourself.

What changes are you witnessing in your body, overall health, and life because of your attitude shift?

Letting Go

*Some of us think holding on makes us strong;
but sometimes it is letting go.*
— *Herman Hesse*

Our earthly life commonly revolves around collections - a personal assortment of things, rules, habits, and beliefs. Things include the various items that fill our homes - the knick-knacks and decorations on our walls and tables, the stacks of books that display our knowledge, the clothes and shoes that line our closets, and the all the food, drink, and cooking tools in our pantry, cabinets, and refrigerator. Without diminishing the significance of our current national twelve percent poverty rate, we generally have well more than we need. This may point to a sign of abundance. At other times it stands as a symptom of feeling like we never have enough, birthed from an attitude of lack.

We also frame our life around another collection - the rules we learn or adopt along our way into adulthood. Gathering instructions, laws, conventions, and regulations, we amass many through our lifespan, integrating all we collect from religion, society, work, and/or cultural groups. Many rules, in fact, are predicated on beliefs that harken back to other lifetimes, especially our immediately previous incarnation. As such, they may appear to serve us but often subconsciously remain unexamined, stored away in our little treasure trove of "what we must do" because they help us make sense of our world and/or feel safe.

Our habits - the behaviors that can give structure to our day - are also part of our eclectic collections, though we often go about our day silently engaging in them. Many healthful habits and an equal, if not disproportional, number of outdated, unhealthy, or useless ones become part of our lives. Patterns or habits of behavior (physical, mental, or emotional) are the well-worn grooves in the platinum album of our lives. Oh, how we so easily fall into what is comfortable and familiar, becoming stuck in archaic ways of operating. Perhaps most importantly, below the surface of many patterns and habits lies fear - fear of another, of the world, of ourselves, of failure, of success, of abandonment, of connection…

Finally, our beliefs, like rules, we gather from a wide range of sources. Beliefs - the thoughts about ourselves and our world fueled by powerful emotions and feelings - may be more elusive. We carry them, too, over many lifetimes, but their presence surfaces most dominantly from our most recent previous life combined with our current one. Beliefs often operate under the surface, embedded deeply within our psyche, as they drive our present moment thoughts, feelings, and actions, often without our conscious awareness. They are intimately woven with and are the motivating force behind our rules, patterns, habits, and why we keep our collections of things.

We often need to look no further than the end of our nose to discover the "stuff" that clutters our path, the very debris that we must shed to uncover and embrace our True Nature. This integral aspect of soul-discovery, revisited as letting go or releasing attachments at a deeper level than **Old Habits Die Hard**, moves us through new growth. By letting go we discard the limitations that shadow our light, helping us engage with life and the joy, peace, and love that comes with experiencing our Divinity.

Letting go inherently combines with other valuable tools that readers find included in **The Soul-Discovery Journalbook**. For example, as we practice releasing our attachments to the physical plane, its application extends to cultivating mindfulness and plays an integral part of centering and meditation by dropping all attention to our environment, concrete mind, and emotions. Applied to our emotional development, we let go of the pain of any difficult situation to move forward with acceptance and ultimately forgiveness. The deepest aspects of growth involve letting go of another sort; this work encompasses releasing personality patterns from the convincing illusionary self that finds value in appearances, control, force, and performance, to name a few. And remember, releasing anything less significant offers valuable practice for the more strenuous work ahead. Many, many opportunities and applications for letting go lie within these pages as an important part of self-development and spiritual growth that comes with soul-discovery.

Navigating the journey of releasing can highlight the challenges we all find on the path. Witnessing our need for, addiction to, or fear of losing something, even our negative emotions, shows us our sticking points in the process of dumping what no longer serves us. For example, when we keep our anger, cling to disappointment, or grip onto self-criticism, it signals a submersion into the old and a call to open our tightly clenched hands wrapped in white-knuckle fashion on the prison bars of our ego mind. In fact, as we experience letting go of anything as challenging, even items from our physical world, the depth and breadth of letting go or releasing attachments becomes apparent. Simple decluttering, dumping, or saying "good-bye" to what seems insignificant in our life also may illuminate a struggle with the subterranean levels of "house cleaning" as we move toward saying good-bye to the habits, rules, and beliefs we cling to. Only on the other side of this liberating process can we feel the sense of freedom and expansion that accompanies releasing what tethered us to the past and old ways of being.

Within this chapter lies another invitation to clean out our metaphorical closets, ditching all the collected trinkets of emotional junk, the worn-out socks of old behaviors and ways of being, and the obsolete but comfy sweatshirts of safety. In this process, we may find that releasing physical stuff is the easier, more comfortable place to start. This could be the everyday do-dad's and old clothing that surround us, keeping us seemingly peaceful but in the same old place and loaded with what we don't need any more. The shift in our world of possessions can lead to more intangible changes of our inner climate, but don't be surprised if transformation happens in reverse - when we let go of personality attachments (habits, beliefs, or thought or emotional patterns), our outer world needs a bath or cleaning out to reflect inner changes.

This chapter's adventure assists us in taking inventory, observing, and actively practicing the letting go process and prepares us for progressively deeper work. The table on the following page revisits what can stagnate our growth, clutter our home, mind, heart, and all the spaces in between. Remember, this is a process that requires patience, diligence, gentleness, and self-compassion. Any movement, no matter how small, helps us go forward, evolving by cleansing our soul.

The Soul-Discovery Journalbook

Objects	Habits	Thought Patterns	Emotional Patterns	Beliefs
Old books	Smoking	I must figure it out/analyze it	Anger	I'm/You're not OK
Clothes that don't fit	Over/under eating	I must plan/schedule everything	Sadness	I'm not safe
Newspapers and magazines	Excessive partying	Avoid it	Drama	There's never enough
Clothes/Jewelry not worn or worn out	Escaping or frequent daydreaming	That's good/bad	Fear	I'm not loved or loveable
Broken/chipped dishes	Swearing	Poor me	Anxiety	I'm not good enough
Duplicates of anything	Nail biting	Don't feel	Worry	I'm better than you
Knick-knacks	Interrupting	Hurry up!	Frustration	You owe me
Old documents or forms	Being defensive	I can't make mistakes	Hostility	I must do more
Worn-out pens/art supplies	Over-working	I need to be better	Overwhelmed	I must rescue or fix
Outdated food	Picking at your body	I'm fat	Lonely	Taking care of myself is selfish
Unwanted Hand-me-downs	Eating poorly	I can't	Guilty	I owe you
Items for showing off	Under/over exercising	I'm stupid	Vengeful	No one cares about me

Journey I: Inventory

Go to your sacred space. Center by breathing deeply to cultivate a sense of inner peace.

Call in your Divine helpers to assist you in opening your awareness to the letting go that would serve your highest and best.

Review the habits you listed in **Old Habits Die Hard** from **Volume I** and re-list them here.

Now, add to the list and include new habits, objects, beliefs, and thoughts or emotional patterns collected, using the table on the previous page for ideas.

How does your new list compare with your old one?

Journey II:
Object Cleanse

Survey your list to consider an object to let go of. Observe your reaction to the idea of ridding yourself of it. Note what it means to you and why. Does your object spark joy or some other feeling? Do you notice a fear, sense of guilt, or worry about letting go of your object? Is your object tied to a person or memories of them? Describe this connection. Journal about your experience.

Decide on donating, gifting, or selling your object and journal the feelings associated with each avenue of releasing it. If this object no longer holds a sense of joy, does it make this process easier?

Now, practice letting go.

What did you find difficult and/or easy about saying goodbye to what you decided to release? How did you feel after? A sense of loss or lightness? Why?

Be sure to journal about your experience with the whole process and the insights you have.

Journey III: Moving Experiment

Pick an item that you use frequently. This could be something as simple as the container of pens on your desk or the salt shaker in your kitchen. Place the item near where it lived before but in a *different* location.

Ex: Move your pens to the other side of your desk. Place the salt shaker on the counter instead of on the table.

After moving the object to a new location, watch the magic. Pay attention to how many times you return to the object's old location. Watch how long it takes to change your habit of looking to the same space for the item.

Journal about your experiences and reflect on how this relates to the process and challenges of letting go of mental, emotional, or other habit collections.

Journey IV: Observation

Spend some time in your sacred space, relaxing, centering, and being still.

Choose a habit that's a behavioral, thought-based, or emotional pattern to release. Write out what you are letting go of and how you believe it manifests.

Ask for guidance from your Divine helpers to be made aware and observe yourself. Watch whatever you have chosen to let go of surface over time.

Journal about what you observed. Consider the following questions: Did you notice what situations brought out your "habit"? Is there a theme or a general tone to the situation? Is there an emotion you observed behind the habit? How might those emotions keep your habit/pattern in place?

Is there a "seed" situation related to your habit, an event or series of events that correlate to when the habit started? How might this "seed" and its related thoughts and emotions keep the habit in place?

Journey V: Letting Go

Spend time in your sacred space to center and meditate. Ask for guidance from your Divine helpers to again draw your attention to the habit chosen from **Journey IV**.

Observe your habit once again. Can you stop the habit immediately? Can you remove all energy from it?

Is there a different behavior you can choose, like a healthy distraction, to promote your letting go? What affirmation can you use to replace what you are letting go of?

Journal about your experiences.

Ex: You become aware of a pattern of frustration toward yourself when something doesn't go well. Instead, you practice positive self-talk - "I can do this. I'm OK."

Ex: You decide to stop the snack attack habit. You notice it happens when boredom strikes. Instead, you replace the habit with listening to music, walking, or calling a friend.

*New habits take 30 days to get a solid start and 18 months to make them automatic, so be gentle with yourself as you replace old habits with new, healthy ones.

Journey VI: Letting Go

 Follow the guided meditation below to practice letting go. Use the QR Code on the left for the recorded version at www.pathways2innerpeace.com or consider asking a friend to read it to you as you journey within.

Retreat to your sacred space. Spend a few moments centering, setting your intent for clarity and understanding. Ask your Divine helpers to join you and guide you on your journey toward your highest good.

Close your eyes and focus on the space just between your eyes on the bridge of your nose. Relax into this space, breathing deeply and slowly. Now allow the darkness behind your eyelids to transform into an all-white space. You are surrounded by white, fluffy, energy; all you see around you is soft and safe, a nurturing space that feels as if you have just walked into a cloud.

In your mind's eye, the white transforms and a rich green forest lies before you. All around you everything is vibrant and filled with life. An active stream can be heard near where you stand and you make your way to it following the sound of the water as it travels over rocks and sticks. Walking through the ferns and grasses, you find the stream and see it gently flowing off toward your right in the direction of the setting sun. Take a moment to consider all the thoughts and emotions you desire to release, especially the ones that naturally cleanse your soul and leave you lighter and freer.

Near the streambed, old brown leaves rest on the rocks around the water's edge. You pick up a handful to represent all you are letting go of. One by one, imbue each leaf with what you are releasing, mentally offering it to the leaf, which willingly accepts it. Now place the leaf on the stream, watching it float away taking the thought or emotion with it. Feel the sense of freedom as you watch it travel from you and disappear from sight. Do this with each leaf until all have been sent on their way with your thoughts and emotions on them.

Now, at your feet, you notice beautiful little flowers growing along the bank. Ask the flower if it will serve as a reminder of the love, joy, compassion, and/or peace to replace what you released. It lovingly agrees and you pick it, knowing it has offered its gift to fill the space of what no longer served you. Feel the gift the flower has given, taking it deep within your heart and infusing every cell. As you allow the space to fade, return to the all-white space. Here you relish in the feeling of freedom of soul-discovery and the beauty of letting go. Open your eyes when ready.

Go to **Journey VII** to journal your reflections.

Journey VII: Reflections

Journal your reflections about the guided meditation in **Journey VI**.

Consider the following: How did you feel placing what you were releasing on the leaf? When releasing the leaf? Could you accept the gift of the flower?

How do you feel after the meditation? Lighter? A little sad?

Knowing that sometimes letting go can bring some sadness for what we're releasing, can you maintain your connection with the feelings of what the flower offered and rest in the love and peace?

Remembering the Love

Even after all this time, the sun never says to the earth,
'you owe me.' Look what happens with a love like that!
It lights up the whole sky.
— Hafez

The winds that sometimes take something we love
are the same that bring us something we learn to love.
— Bob Marley

We all receive love in many ways - a gentle pat on the back from a neighbor, a shared meal with family, a smile from our closest friend, a lick from our beloved pet, words of encouragement from a teacher, or a gift at just the right moment. All serve to spark feelings of being valued, wanted, important…and loved. Even when we experience challenging and chaotic times, a happy memory or a spark of love and light in what seems to be an otherwise dark and cloudy time can lift our spirits.

To do our important work shedding what does not serve us, it's vital to acknowledge and take in the love we receive from others, a reflection of the all-powerful love from Source. The love around us calls to the love within, reminding our hearts of our True Nature. It grounds us in the most healing way, giving us strength and determination to forge ahead. Love embraces, nurtures, and fortifies our being.

Recognizing loving demonstrations from others may require expanding our definition of love, stretching our perceptions about giving and receiving the joy-juice of the Universe.

For example, in the book, **The Five Love Languages,** Gary Chapman outlines the five ways we express and experience love that he calls "love languages": gift giving, quality time, words of affirmation, acts of service (devotion), and physical touch.[26] According to Chapman, our ways of receiving and giving love are often based on our own needs, so we feel cared for according to the particular ways we each define love. Simply said, we each require our unique cocktail of love - the expressions that feel most resonant to us. For example, some individuals feel more comfortable and have a greater desire for touching and being touched; others want to hear verbal expressions of affection. Knowing our love language offers a roadmap to understanding how we feel connected to another, the avenues others can travel to communicate "I love you."

Because each person's love language is unique, we also may benefit from looking through the giver's eyes to truly see how they are offering their deep affections. Equally important is the opportunity to clarify our needs of being wanted, cared for, and valued just as we are. We certainly must be honest with others and ourselves when a lack of affection, attention, physical intimacy, or shared activities impact us. Practically speaking, a fish may have the most loving human caregiver, but if that person only offers the love language that's meaningful to them, like hugging, words or affection, or quality time through hiking, and ignores the fish's need for fish food and clean water (which equals fish love), I dare say that little finned pet would literally die. Love is a two-way street. In our relationships, we must pay attention to our needs as well as those of others; finding balance, compatibility, and compromise are vital.

One landmark longitudinal study by Dr. Terri Orbuch also speaks to the qualities that deeply affect our relationships. Tracking couples for three decades, the study revealed overarching premises in relational life, vitality, and happiness that appear universal despite gender and race nuances. Through specific displays of love, our relationships become strengthened and fortified to last, making us happily and strongly bonded to one another. Echoing the work of Chapman, the following highlights fundamental components to loving relationships found in Orbuch's study. The strongest, happiest, long-term partnerships include:

- **frequent random acts of kindness** - saying "you're on my mind" in an uplifting way;
- **realistic expectations** - being reasonable about what we want from one another and the relationship;

---

[26] Chapman, Gary. (1992). *The 5 Love Languages: The Secret to Love that Lasts.* Chicago, IL: Northfield Publishing.

- ***shared adventurous activities*** - finding time together for fun, exciting, and mutually enjoyable dates that combat boredom;
- ***small acts of care and appreciation*** - communicating how much we care for each other long after the honeymoon period is over;
- ***compliments, help, support, and encouragement*** - affirming one another positively;
- ***good communication skills*** - creating lasting respect;
- ***identifying needs of ourselves and addressing the needs of our partner*** - a vital part of good communication; and
- ***dealing with conflict fairly*** - minimizing criticism, defensiveness, and blame, which dismantles one another and the relationship.[27]

While many of these findings may seem commonsensical, putting them into action can be trickier. It's not uncommon in our relationships that we can take one another for granted, become burdened by crisis, feel unhinged by unresolved turmoil, or so entangled with day-to-day living that we put ourselves and/or others on the back burner. At these times, the love in our life can feel out of reach if the pain at hand pushes the love offered by others out of our consciousness. All-consuming negative thoughts marinate our aching wounds in the caustic salt of our unloving attitudes. And like the preserving qualities of salt, this briny nature seeps into our hurts or is held there by our own lack of gratitude, appreciation, or balancing effect of remembered good. Then our pains and cuts become preserved, frozen in time and held in place by a hardened heart - hardened through self-protection, suffering, resentment, and/or withdrawal.

Believe it or not, the most important aspect of remembering and feeling the love in our life rests in how much we love ourselves. While forgiveness of ourselves requires us to forgive others first, loving others naturally happens when we love ourselves. Ironically, our lack of self-love becomes out-pictured in our projected judgments and harshness toward others or when we pour our love into someone not able to accept the love shown for them. Acting as a mirror, they reflect our absence of self-love, acted "upon us" from the outside so we can see it in the world as "a someone" who withholds, rejects, abuses, or disrespects. The scarcity of love toward ourselves fulfills our subconscious beliefs that we are unlovable or unworthy.

---

[27] Kovac, K. (2018, April). Dr. Terri Orbuch Reveals the Secrets to Happy Relationships in the Workplace and Beyond. *OTW: The Oakland Post.* Retrieved from https://oaklandpostonline.com/22392/campus/dr-terri-orbuch-reveals-the-secrets-to-happy-relationships-in-the-workplace-and-beyond/

On the flip side, remembering the love in our life, especially from those who appear to be so very challenging to our sense of peace and happiness, often requires new sight. As we recall the positive and the negative - the helpful and the opposing, the loving and unloving - we can ask for assistance to accept the whole and realize that even those who drive us crazy are human, fallible, and often struggling through life. Witnessing even the smallest act of affection by them serves to strengthen our journey to leave behind all judgments and to see with a higher vision, the sight of our Self, even if we choose to leave their orbit of influence.

Ultimately, the love of our Divine Creator sustains, nurtures, supports, guides, and provides *through us*. The very love within us...the love that we are...offers the sustenance to rid ourselves of what no longer serves us and embrace all the good in our life. Embracing the love in our relationships, as well as in our casual, serendipitous encounters, fertilizes the seeds of our holy self and nurtures us to grow life's bountiful harvest. As we rid our consciousness of the ugly weeds of discontent and embrace the love in our life, we recognize our Union with all through Self. So, let's grow beautiful love and bask in its abundance.

Journey I:
Chapter Musings

Center and meditate in your sacred space, giving time to be.

Reflect on the chapter material. What do you think and feel about the topic?

What part of the information resonated with you? Why? What didn't? Why?

What are your overall thoughts about love in your life? Is this an area in which you desire to grow or change?

Journey II:
What's Your Language?

Spend quality time centering and reflecting in your sacred space.

Read **The Five Love Languages** or take the quiz to determine your "love language" by visiting www.5lovelanguages.com.

Journal about your discoveries, writing out the details of your love language.

How did this help you make sense of your world? Your relationships?

Is there an incompatibility in any of your current relationships between what you desire and what you receive? How might you resolve what love you want from what is present?

Can you identify the love language of your partner, family, or friends?

How might you shift the love you offer to be more compatible with others' needs?

Journey III: Expanding Your Love List

Spend quality time centering and reflecting in your sacred space.

Make a list of people in your life who easily show you love. How do they demonstrate it to you?

Remember to consider how they express their love as it is meaningful to them.

Do these individuals express their love to you in alignment with your love language? How does that affect you?

Do these relationships have the qualities of strong, lasting partnerships listed in the chapter from Orbuch's study? In what area might your relationships need help? Why?

Journey IV: Expanding Your Love List More

Center and meditate in your sacred space. Ask your Divine helpers for guidance and support on this journey to help you identify where relationship disharmony is present.

Create a list of those who still feel challenging to you or with whom your relationship seems filled with discord.

Has this list changed from previous exercises like **The Ties That Bind Us** from **Volume I** or **Karmic Cords** from **Volume III**? How?

Can you find any ways these individuals express any love or affection to you, even if it's misaligned on some level?

Ex: My mom is always putting food in front of me. Even though she knows I'm on a diet, she never stops enticing me with special desserts and treats. I know this is how she shows me love and cares...through cooking and food.

Journey V: Opening to More Love

Spend time centering and reflecting in your sacred space. Ask your Divine helpers to bring loving memories associated with childhood to your awareness.

Many of us experienced a difficult childhood. Even in those challenging times, love was present.

Journal about expressions of love and caring from at least one source. This might be an animal or even support felt through nature.

How does making this positive connection feel? Does it help you develop more compassion for yourself or others?

Practice connecting to expressions of love, anchoring positive experiences to help grow in self-love and other love. Log your progress along the way.

If these loving memories feel absent, remain willing to be shown the love and return to this journey when ready.

The Mysteries of La-La Land

Dreams are the guiding words of the soul. Why should I henceforth not love my dreams and not make their riddling images into objects of my daily consideration?

— Carl Jung

Each night, as the dark hours entice our body into deep rest, a rich dreamscape awaits us. When our head finally finds its soft, landing place, the thin veil that divides our sleep time from waking hours pushes out the day and we drift. Whether our entrance into slumber is fitful or easy, everyone requires time away from heavy earth energy, so we leave our body behind to restore itself while our consciousness ventures off into the astral plane - exploring, helping others, or working on our own growth.

Dreams have long been the place where our subconscious mind replays current events and happenings from our waking hours. As a result, we often unknowingly search for meaning, order, and resolution through the mysterious la-la-land. Some of the stories that script our dreams include daily occurrences that create confusion or negative reactions like a fight with our partner, the state of the world, or decisions weighing on our mind, to name a few. Basically, any "problem" or situation that occupies our consciousness becomes fair game. Thus, dreamland offers a stage for the more elusive and hidden parts of us to express and find resolution in a way that may seem safer than head-on examination.

As we explore what surfaces in our nighttime adventures, just about any aspect or detail can offer valuable information to help our journey in soul-discovery - from seeing the hidden aspects of ourselves, to providing the opportunity to explore and accept the traits we love to hate or hate to love, to witnessing the misdeeds of others who require our understanding and forgiveness. And while looking at the minutiae and metaphors of dreams can feel like we're in the midst of a great mystery, at other times the symbolism is laughingly obvious.

So how do we interpret these cryptic tales? Before we even attempt to decipher dreamscape adventures, we must first create a record of the event. Writing down as much as we can upon first waking best captures the details and essence. Next, we explore deeper aspects of our experience - the thoughts and feelings that surface in our dream. And finally, we look at what the vivid account may be telling us, wading through the rich symbolism for understanding, guidance, and clarity.

Having an approach to dreamwork can be helpful, especially if the whole exploration is new to us. The suggestions listed below help start the process.

First, let's set our dream-catching climate:

1. Keep a journal, pen, and book light by your bed.
2. Ask for your Divine helpers to help you pay attention and even wake you enough so you can remember your dream's important details.
3. If there is a situation or question for which you'd like understanding or clarity, ask your Divine helpers or Higher Self for guidance and understanding through your dreams.
4. When you awaken, regardless of what time it happens to be, write down as many details of your dream as you remember. If you are too tired, write a few words that identify what feels important.
5. Three key questions will help jog your memory:
    a. Where was I?
    b. Who or what was there with me?
    c. What was I doing?

Next, pay attention to the following as you look at your dreams:

1. As you examine where you were in the dream, consider the qualities of the place. Was it familiar? If so, what was the same or different about it?
2. How did you feel about the places you were in the dream?

3. List the people there. Who did you expect to be there but was absent?

4. What were the relationships of those in the dream to each other? (titles, roles)

5. How were the people in your dreams behaving toward one another?

6. How did you feel about each person? How did they feel about you/one another?

7. Reflect on each person and object in the dream as an aspect of yourself. What does this show you about yourself?

8. How do you feel about how you behaved in the dream? About others' behaviors?

9. What other objects do you remember from your dream? (Also, consider your relationship, feelings, and thoughts about the object as it plays out in the dream.) What is the function of the object, knowing this helps inform the symbolism?

10. Were there any animals in the dream? (Again, consider your relationship, feelings, and thoughts about the animal as it plays out in the dream.)

What if dreaming or remembering dreams seems to be problematic?

1. Set your intention to remember. Expectations to remember a dream, thus interest in our dreams, causes us to remember them with higher frequency.

2. Remember to ask for help from your personal spiritual guidance team.

3. Make sure you are getting enough sleep to allow for REM-level activity to occur. Also, watch your alcohol and caffeine intake as it affects your ability to enter REM sleep, too.

Because dreamwork is particularly interesting to me, la-la-land adventures tend to hold a place of significance in my life. For example, looking for clarity and guidance one early winter evening, I asked my helpers to intervene, and two very vivid, symbolically-rich dreams offered answers. An unusual bear, rich brown with a vibrant, golden "necklace" entered my first dream. Deep in my sleep, the word Sumerian echoed through my mind. The next morning, researching Sumerian and bear, I discovered the furry friend in question, a Sumerian Sun Bear. The subsequent night offered another dream to strengthen the first, a deer worn on a chain as an amulet of pure gold. Looking at the symbolism, we find:

Bear - healing work with others, rest, restoration, rejuvenation, and repose;
Sun Bear - blessings in life and sweetness coming;
Deer - loving kindness and patience with self/others and trusting intuition;
Gold - abundance, deep understanding of self and Spirit, and spirituality; and
Necklace - an acknowledgement of knowledge and power.

Combining the imagery and recognizing the repeating themes, I identified a powerful lesson of honoring a deep hibernation - a rest and repose while cradling myself with kindness and patience. Previous self-criticism about repose states met with a cautionary reminder to stay steadfast in the face of judgments, especially those turned inward. Bear's indication of blessings and an acknowledgment of my healing work served as a reminder to stay positive and continue my passion for what I do. The gold on both bear and deer and repeating theme of necklace acknowledged my growth, as well as the spiritual potency of this guidance and the abundance/sweetness to be received in honoring it.

Exploring our personal, fertile metaphors of dreams, the marketplace holds many helpful materials, each with its own value. One such text is *The Book Of Symbols: Reflections On Archetypal Images* by Archive for Research in Archetypal Symbolism (ARAS); it offers a comprehensive guide to deciphering our often cryptic tales, dream life, and other metaphors of living. The following page also offers a short **Dream Dictionary** of common symbolism. Each term describes a construct, a way to approach various subjects that appear in our dreamscapes as we seek to understand. Whether any symbolism resource feels resonant and/or helps inform our study depends on us; we get to decide how much a description fits and adequately aids our soul-discovery. As such, our feelings and relationships to ourselves, others, things, and surroundings create unique experiences best understood by each reader.

Let's journey on through another deeper gaze. The exercises that follow will aid your discoveries. When you grab your pillow and blanket and drift into la-la land, remember the cosmos is standing by to support your soul-discovery. Dream on, beautiful dreamer!

Dream Dictionary

Animals - an aspect of ourselves viewed through the symbolism of an animal via their behaviors, instincts, and characteristics; an aspect of a person in our life as an animal; investigate specific totem or animal symbolism for further details via author and animal symbols expert Ted Andrews.

Bathroom - elimination of thoughts and emotions that don't serve us.

Danger - shows the how's, what's, and ways that we feel unsafe in life about people, situations, lessons, or parts of ourselves played out symbolically.

Door (Gate) - transition; moving from one consciousness, stage, or aspect of life to another.

Emotions - inform our responses/reactions to relationships; show us how we feel about the who and what in our dreams and thus life; emotions toward others often tend to be a projection of how we feel about ourselves.

Falling - feeling a loss of control; fear of a loss of control.

Father - our own father; our self-protection; our relationship with our own self as father; our relationship with our masculine, doing, protective side; our relationship with Source as Father.

Mother - our own mother; our self-mothering; our relationship with our own self as mother; our relationship with our feminine, nurturing side; our relationship with the Divine Mother or Mother Earth.

Movement (walking, running, etc.) - moving forward, growing, and evolving in life.

Nakedness - feeling exposed, unprotected, or stripped of what clothes us; loss of privacy or boundaries; free from the clothing of personality.

Others - represent an aspect of ourselves placed outside of us to observe, especially if we don't like that aspect; represents that (other) person in our life now or from the past.

Pee/Peeing - anger; fear; feeling "pissed off"; marking our territory like an animal.

Place (room, house, building, city, etc.) - our current consciousness; the characteristics of the place and our experience there informs how we may be currently operating in our world or feel about it; **house** or **room** in house represents our personal consciousness while **building** or **city/town** represents the world we live in.

Poop/Pooping - eliminating the thoughts, emotions, or situations that dirty our life; how our thoughts, emotions, or situations move through us with ease, fear (diarrhea) or held onto (constipation).

Rocks - represents history or personal past.

Self - a physical representation of ourselves; an aspect of our personality that could be hidden, accepted, rejected, or placed on others, or that asks for our attention.

Sex - desire for connection with another or ourselves; need to express love to ourselves or another.

Stuck - inability to move; feeling stuck in life; unable to move forward in a particular area in our life.

Toilet - elimination of thoughts, emotions, beliefs, etc. that don't serve us.

Water - symbolic of emotions; washing away of something we are letting go or the need to do so; level or amount demonstrates intensity or volume of emotions; our Feeling Nature or our pure unconditional Divine love aspect shown as clear, inviting, pure body of water.

Journey I:
Chapter Reflections

Retreat to your sacred space to reflect.

After centering and meditating, consider what the chapter offers and write about your thoughts and feelings on the material.

What has your relationship with dreams and dream exploration been up to now?

What areas in your life could benefit from dream exploration?

Journey II: Preparation

As the day draws to a close, prepare your sleeping space for dreams. Gather all the materials for your journey.

Set your intentions. Feel yourself connected to the dream world and the rich landscape there.

Ask for help from your Divine helpers. Thank God, the Universe, and all your helpers for their ever-present guidance and love.

Write your requests for assistance/guidance and intentions to clarify and ground them.

Journal about how you feel about these preparations.

Get ready for dreamland!

Journey III: Dream Recovery

Immediately upon waking or as soon as you are able, use the chapter's key questions and write out the who, what, and where of your dream.

Pay attention to the places dreamt about - who was there, what you and the others in your dream were doing, etc. Refer to the chapter questions for further assistance.

After writing out the details of the dream, refer to the list of symbolism in the chapter and other resources as needed, applying them to your dream.

Journey IV:
Dreamy Reflections

Reflect on all you uncovered writing out the details of your dream from **Journey III**.

Is the dream helping you discover something about yourself? What?

How do you feel about what your dream is showing you?

How does this information add to any other revelations or ah-ha's along your path in soul-discovery or daily life?

An Intimate Journey into Self

Additional notes:

Consider starting a separate dream journal to continue your explorations.

Letter of Love

*I know that if I am to write anything fine and noble in the future,
I shall do so only by listening at the doors of your heart.*

— *James Joyce*

Throughout our lives, the opportunity to express ourselves to a person who has influenced us in a positive way may slip by us. Maybe that person has passed and with them the chance to tell them or show them how much they meant to us. Perhaps we don't see them anymore because they moved or we frequently see them, but assume they just know. Maybe telling them our feelings seems awkward or embarrassing, or maybe our love for them remains hidden or unacknowledged.

Whatever the case, write a letter to a certain someone sharing how important, loved, wonderful, generous, etc. they are, as if they are present. Let them know how (past or present) they inspire, support, encourage, mentor, and love (you and others) in all their special ways. Most importantly, don't forget to express love to them for just who they are.

Journey I:
Letter of Love

Spend some time relaxing, centering, and meditating in your sacred space.

Write your Letter of Love.

When finished, read the letter to yourself, *out loud.*

Journal your experience, considering the following: What was your experience with writing the letter? How did you feel reading the letter to yourself?

Journey II: Letter Reading

Pay a visit to or call the person chosen for your Letter of Love. If they have passed or you have no contact with them, find a photo.

Move past your shyness or embarrassment and read your letter to them in person, on the phone, or to their photo *out loud*. If you have no photo for those passed, connect with them in your mind, imagining them sitting with you.

Journal your experience, considering the following: How did you feel about the idea of contacting the person to read your letter? About reading the letter to the recipient?

What did you notice in the recipient when reading? Did reading the letter to the person have a greater impact than you imagined? Who did the letter impact more, you or the receiver? How?

If the person passed or if you have no contact with them, how do you imagine they received your letter? Why? Did you know those passed can hear our communication with them, whether silent or aloud?

Joy and Happiness

The best and most beautiful things in the world cannot be seen or even touched — they must be felt with the heart.

— Helen Keller

All of humankind at one point or another desires happiness...to feel content, cheerful, and in harmony with themselves and their world. This we tend to seek outside of ourselves in careers, financial gain, partners, friends, activities, and things. As such, our feelings of happiness are transient - fleeting moments and blips on the grand map of life but not a lasting, pervasive feeling that stays, flowing from somewhere inside us.

Total joy, on the other hand, is a state that exists regardless of circumstances, things, or life events. It is the constant presence of uplifting Divine energy within interwoven with love and peace - a trifecta of pure Spirit essence. Our experience of joy as an innate aspect of Creative Force becomes dulled and constrained by our physical form, blocked by our fear (ego), and tainted by our typical, earth-life dramas.

> When you were first brought forth into Spirit, your joy knew no bounds. You were like a great symphony that played out through the ethers and touched into all of the universes. You were like a song in perfect harmony without end, a melody that could not be captured and held but rather kept going out ever further and further, touching into every avenue of space and time until at last the joy of your beingness so filled all things that life resonated with the presence of you and with the power that God gave you in this unspeakable joy.[28]

---

[28] Donovan, Rev. Penny (1998). *Knowing Absolute Joy*. Scotia, NY: Springwell Metaphysical Studies.

Reading this description of us in our joy makes me long for that deep awareness of Spirit, to feel Home within me. It harkens to times in meditation when I touch into the love of Source, heart open and head out of the way. It comes through deep connection to loved ones, nature, my house-jungle, and furry, four-footed friends. As a mother, it blooms beyond all words and remains outside the appearance of what my personality rebels against, like sassy-mouthed teenage come-backs and junkyard bedrooms. Yet despite all the wonderful moments of connecting to and being in joy, I also know that an ever-present state of it can remain hidden behind all the day-to-day tasks of living, the common distractions, little irritations, and concerns of the month. As expressed so very clearly in these teachings, not very many people on this plane experience absolute joy.

We've discussed before that as Spirit having an earth experience, we interact with our world using our spiritual energy, which comes to us in a purity we cannot comprehend. As always, our personal use of this energy influences and molds it *to create our world.* Remember, the most challenging aspects of this influence come from ego, which drives us to live according to its standards, entrenched in comparison, competition, and specialness. The ego creates rules defining how we must be in the world, calling for sundry allegiance to it and pressuring us into being agreeable, efficient, strong, hard-working, precise, and better than others to the detriment of ourselves. When ego approaches the joy in us, it strives to dampen it by squelching its expression, making us think that being so filled with joy is crazy, weird, embarrassing, etc. Ego says, "There must be better reasons for joy than just because you feel it."

Falling in line with ego's mindset, we become lured into believing that joy is a personal flaw, the kind we want to hide from society and ourselves; so, under ego's dictate, our joy can become a "thing" to keep suppressed. Equally potent is ego's urge to find false joy in a scenario of "doing better than" others. It might say, "If you just outshine this person or become richer than that person, then you'll really be happy." Instead, the grabbing, striving energy of climbing an endless mountain of "do better" according to ego's unattainable standards leaves us empty and devoid of satisfaction because someone always looks more attractive, seems more successful, or accomplishes more.

Happiness to the ego is ever reaching toward impossible heights that leave us wanting and deflated, steeped in the mindset of lack. It drives us to suppress our innate Divine Truth in order to keep itself employed. So, true joy need never be expressed according to the ego, which clings to control, driving us to "do better than" in an attempt to retain a place in our life fearful that it will be replaced by a greater "something" - Self. As such, we constrict our natural flow of spiritual energy, blocking true joy and love within us regardless of outward appearances.

So how do we deal with a life, community, workplace, and society steeped in ego's idea of happiness and suppression of our innate Self? First, we practice de-personalizing the experiences with others who try our patience and tag our ego to enter a conflict. Resolving old conflicts and hurts help us see new triggering situations with clarity and compassion. As we let go and recognize the value of our life and all events, our heart expands and vice versa. Secondly, we stay mindful of how our thoughts and emotions impact us, growing joy by paying attention to what we place before us to walk through. Cultivating joy is like planting a beautiful garden; we must enrich the soil with generous, uplifting thoughts, pull out the weeds of our discontent, and sift the soil to release the rocks of our old habits and patterns to make room for new seeds to grow full and fruitful. Third, we spend time removed from striving, worrying, and stressing to appreciate our connections to people, pets, and nature - the relishing and reveling in loving feelings toward others. As we turn our awareness toward simple connection - the smile on a child's face, the wagging tail and wet kisses from our pets happy to greet us, a hug from a dear friend or our love - we open ourselves to experience more joy and lasting happiness in our life. While these each exist outside of us, the connection through them awakens a joy that lies within as a remembrance of our Divine Nature that is always joyful, loving, and filled with peace. Witnessing what is precious in another or in life mirrors our own preciousness and undiminished state of wholeness, calling forth the joy that is and always has been in our hearts.

Journey I: Reflections

Retreat to your sacred space to spend time centering.

Reflect on the chapter reading. Journal your thoughts and feelings about the material.

What has been your relationship with joy to this point? How joyful have you been day to day overall?

How do you want to shift that? What do you feel your life will look like with more joy?

Journey II:
Free from Striving

Now list all the things that you tend to strive for…a better car, clothes, house, friends, books, job, more money, etc. Consider what drives you to do better, accomplish more, be more, etc.

How have these experiences kept you locked in the ego's game of striving to be better than others or continuing to feel less than them?

Which of these behaviors or tendencies are you ready to let go of?

If you've released the mindset of striving, what other patterns tend to pull you back to ego's game, diminishing the feeling or expression of joy in your life?

Journey III: Joyful Outlook

Let's spend some time cultivating a joyful outlook. Remember, other chapters add to this journey through exercises in letting go, releasing habits and patterns, observing, practicing non-judgment, wise baby vision, etc.

Take a current event or situation, one that clearly calls for more joy. Write out the steps of the event and your attitude or reaction regarding each piece.

Ex: I was working hard on a project and forgot to pick up dry-cleaning. Panicked and frustrated, I ran out of the office in a quite a state. When I arrived at the cleaners, it was already closed. I was now furious on the drive home, mostly at myself for not being more organized. When I got home, I snapped at my husband as he asked about the dry-cleaning. Now, he's mad at me, too. I spiraled into a hole and felt miserable the whole evening.

Now, re-examine the event with a different outlook. Re-write how it could change.

Ex: I was working hard on a project. When I realized I forgot the dry-cleaning, I decided tomorrow was a better day to pick it up anyway. I congratulated myself for being so focused on the project and nearly completing it. I decided to leave the office a little early to celebrate with my husband. When I arrived home, I let him know that I nearly finished the project and wanted to celebrate with him. When I said that I'll pick up the dry-cleaning tomorrow, I apologized for any inconvenience. He understood and was happy to celebrate. The dry-cleaning could wait for him, too. And we had a great time talking about the project and my progress.

What needs to shift or change to allow a different outlook in real time? Can you practice a different attitude when circumstances do not go exactly as planned?

Practice this in real time and journal your experience here.

Notes:

Journey IV:
Look into My Eyes

Choose a person to do this journey with - a friend, partner, work-mate, family member, etc. Find a quiet place to do this exercise so you won't be interrupted.

Inform your journey-partner that this experiment is one on joy through eye contact. For ease, set a timer for between one and three minutes or longer if desired. Sit facing your journey-partner and look into their eyes as they look into yours, maintaining the gaze until the time ends.

Journal your experience.

How did you feel gazing into the other person's eyes? How did your partner feel? Why? How do you feel now?

What might this experiment tell you about connection, love, and joy?

For more information on global eye contact events, see www.eyecontactexperiment.com.

Journey V: Receiving Joy

Retreat to your sacred space. Play some soft music and allow a few moments to relax, breathing deeply.

In your mind, go to a time when you felt the most positive and joyful or to a memory of some happy moment. If possible, return to a time in childhood when joy may be easier to access.

Allow the experience of that time to unfold in your mind and feel it as much as you are able in your heart…stay with the feeling.

Now write about your experience. What created that moment?

Allow yourself to ground that experience, opening your awareness to other opportunities to be more joyful in your life.

Journal about your journeys in joy.

Shedding Perceived Failures

Has this world been so kind to you that you should leave with regret?
There are better things ahead than any we leave behind.

— *C.S. Lewis*

Regret comes in many shapes and sizes. It often visits us as a lamentation regarding the people, events, and situations in our life - the opportunities we think we missed, the choices we made on our path, the actions we took, or the ways we seemed to cause another or ourselves pain or embarrassment. Whether regret points to what we believe we did or didn't do, it often results in a feeling of failure.

While looking at what we feel we've done wrong or the mistakes we've made, know that regret can be a temptation, another trick of the ego, pulling us down the path of self-beatings and pain. Under the influence of regret and failure, we might travel into the land of "if only" and torture ourselves about what we could have done, what we did, what we might have said instead…all the ways we wish we would have chosen differently.

We can, however, use regret constructively by reflecting on our past to examine our perceived "failures" with the mindset of compassion and growth. Regret that helps us make better choices, be more loving, set boundaries, and repair relationships offers fresh beginnings and a means for self-development. Employed wisely, we can choose to see any hurt we may have caused to ourselves or others with an open heart and mind instead of self-criticism and loathing. As we understand and take responsibility for all our choices, new opportunities to shed old "junk" fuels our forward movement and raises our consciousness.

When our heartstrings feel pulled to explore the past as lamentation, the very emotions and thoughts we uncover can offer fertile soil to plant new seeds. The simple (but not always easy) process of embracing how we feel and think, facing our regret authentically, opens the doors to self-acceptance. Merely acknowledging our inner climate and declaring how we feel also starts the process of self-forgiveness with the energy of, "Yes, I did it and here I am owning it. I will grow from this and be wiser and kinder." In addition, the potent act of sharing - verbalizing our regrets with another who can offer a *safe, non-judgmental* witness to our perceived transgressions - dissolves the potency of our emotions and helps us accept ourselves. The key to sharing rests with a neutral, loving audience as we intend to move forward in acceptance and off the trail of self-criticism.

Long ago I was asked to write down every mistake or failure I felt in my life. As pen met paper, a lengthy list filled line after line; Pandora's box mysteriously opened and the old pain of missed chances, poor decisions, misspoken words, and ugly deeds was laid bare. It became clear that a rat's nest of misgivings still subconsciously haunted me. Stealthfully hiding, they loomed in a dark corner of my "closet of unworthiness" like an ugly but secretly loved Christmas sweater. These failures happily held hands with my ego, poised for action and ready for any chance to remind me of what I saw as self-created "bad" things in my life. After looking at the list and feeling the mounting guilt, the teacher asked me to destroy it and forgive myself. Tearing the page into little bits, I asked for help to finally release these pieces of my past…to let them be removed from my memory as a history long gone and allow what I learned to remain as a light on my path to guide me forward.

While I'd like to report that I've been free from seeing failures or mistakes, I cannot; however, my perspective shifted. Now, I carefully look at what all experiences teach me. Each time "failure" tries to knock on my door to take up residence, I let it know there's no room for that kind of tenant. If I'm preoccupied and it sneaks in and sacks out in the basement for a short while, I make the space for responsibility, self-forgiveness, and acceptance to move in, recognizing that any choices I made were the best I could do at the time. I accept that another growth opportunity delivered in perfect timing offered exactly what I needed, even if I have yet to understand it. In those moments, I shed a little more of ego's hold and move toward a consistent awareness beyond all the thoughts and emotions that belong to the world of illusion.

> A man of genius makes no mistakes;
> his errors are volitional and are the portals of discovery.
> – James Joyce, *Ulysses*

As Joyce so eloquently states, mistakes are merely a choice on our path, the decision we make in the moment based on current circumstances and knowledge. They can propel us forward into a higher consciousness, discovering new beliefs, a different mindset, or more innate ways of being. *Every experience we have in life, even a "mistake", is an opportunity for growth.* To witness the positive lessons in any situation, we must be willing to admit the flaws in our internal, negative climate and reactions, be accountable for the ways those flaws can affect ourselves and others, and then let go of the guilt or shame of the wrongdoing. Mistakes, flaws, failures may be the best way we learn; at other times they are the exact way life needed to happen. Our perceived failures and the accompanying situations may be painful, but what we gain in the process moves us forward on the path of soul-discovery, leading us to the Self we are meant to express.

Journey I: Cleansing Ritual

For this journey, find the following:

- a quite space
- some time (about 30 minutes or more)
- access to a bathroom or to a small bowl of water
- a clean towel
- an empty, fire-safe plate, Pyrex dish, or fire pit
- a lighter or matches.

Read through steps 1 - 7 below to become familiar with this ritual and the materials that feel most natural to you. Affirmations used throughout the process are chosen for the power of their wording and declarations. (For more on affirmations, see **Creating Affirmations** in **Volume II**.) Choose the tools and setting that feel most comfortable to you, making sure all materials are ready before you begin.

1. Ask for your Divine helpers assist you on this journey, especially Archangel Uriel, the Angel of Repentance.

2. On a separate piece of paper, write down at least one event, behavior, or choice in your life that you see as a failure or mistake.

3. Journal how you think and feel about what you wrote in #2 above.

4. Write out who you believe was hurt, intentionally or unintentionally, and how. Describe how you feel about that.

5. What did you learn from your experience (listed in #2)?

6. Now, say out loud:

    I release these perceived failure(s)_____.
    (read what you listed in #2.)

7. Tear your list into little pieces.

8. Place the pieces into a fire-safe plate, Pyrex, or fire pit and light them on fire.

9. While the list burns, allow the emotional sting of perceived failures leave you. Say out loud:

   I apologize to those I may have hurt in the process including _____ (name the people). I accept responsibility for my part in _____ (event/failure). I know that I took certain actions because I thought that was the best for me and/or others at the time. I did the best I could with what I knew then.

   I forgive others who took part in the lesson including _____ (list people connected to the event/failure from #2).

   I forgive myself. For whatever forgiveness that feels too difficult to release, I ask Father-Mother God/Source to forgive for me.

10. Make sure your papers burn to a level that feels comfortable to you. When burned, as such, say the following out loud:

    I have learned from my actions, thoughts, and feelings. I remember the valuable lessons. I release all pain from these experiences to embrace and grow in love, compassion, and wisdom.

11. Throw the remaining pieces and the ashes into the toilet and flush them away or make sure they burn out.

12. Wash your hands in the bowl of water. Say out loud:

    I wash my hands of shame and guilt. I am forgiven and free. Thank you for the blessings of this lesson and all I have gained through it.

Dry your hands. Take a nice deep breath. Allow yourself to feel the freedom from all you released.

Move on to **Journey II**.

Journey II: Reflections

Write about your experience with **Journey I**, journaling all your observations and insights.

Considering the following: What did you experience writing the list?

How did it feel to tear the list into pieces? To burn it? To flush it?

How did it feel to wash your hands of guilt and shame?

Did your negative emotions diminish?

How might you use this cleansing ritual to release other beliefs, thoughts, emotions, or attitudes?

Journey III:
Dear "Old" Me

Retreat to your sacred space, spending the time to relax, center, and meditate.

Ask your Divine helpers for guidance on this journey to understand and appreciate what you gained for your highest and best.

Write a letter to the "old" you, the you that journeyed this far.

Make sure to offer gratitude for your bravery and for letting go of the past as you experienced in **Journey I** of this chapter.

Can you offer gratitude to the "old" you for learning through the experiences you listed in **Journey I**?

Journey IV: Celebrating New You

Let's take some time to celebrate and recognize the you who has grown.

What are the positive outcomes of your perceived failures or mistakes listed in **Journey I**? What skills can you write about because of all you learned?

What could you do to celebrate yourself and the lessons that brought you to where you are today?

Journal about your celebration.

Remember, releasing negative emotions and self-forgiveness often happens over time. Use the ritual and journeys in this chapter as often as you desire with as many negative experiences as you are drawn to heal, allowing them to be cleansed and transformed.

The Final Frontier

I write for those women who do not speak, for those who do not have a voice because they were so terrified, because we are taught to respect fear more than ourselves. We've been taught that silence would save us, but it won't.
— Audre Lorde

We are reminded that in the fleeting time we have on this Earth, what matters is not wealth or status or power or fame, but rather how well we have loved and what small part we have played in making the lives of other people better.
— Barack Obama

Your task is not to seek for love, but merely to seek and find all the barriers within yourself that you have built against it.
— Rumi

On the earth plane, we have countless borders and boundaries of various shapes, sizes, and qualities. Many are physical, even more are spoken or written into laws or religious dogma, and others remain stamped in our consciousness as silent barriers. From the walls that divide countries to the guidelines of cultural expectations, boundaries divide, regulate, and define us as different than others in order to maintain a sense of separation, intentional or otherwise.

On a personal level, our body delineates the frontier between ourselves and others by looking through our physical eyes to witness separateness and independence. Even though we don't start out in this world as separate, an integral aspect of our experience here lies in our movement from an intimate physical connection to feeling separate from others to coming full circle to our spiritual Union. For example, through the beauty of nature we experience the innate human boundaries of our expectant mother nesting creation in her protective womb as delicately guarded, holy fruit. Bound to her, we are nurtured apart from the external world. Birthed out of this sea of safety into a wild landscape, we learn of individuality and separateness while striving for identity and belonging. And despite the fleshy encasement of form, we subconsciously hold a deep desire to move beyond perceived separation. This becomes most evident as our physical and emotional boundaries blur in intimate relationships, the most obvious being lovemaking as the tender union of body with body. Through our deep connection to Source in meditation, prayer, and healing, we return to our truth; wholeness and spiritual Oneness dissolve all boundaries and we become subsumed into the mind and heart of Divine Love, a union most believe to be relegated to our physical death.

At the opposite pole, through our physical nature and earthly experiences that forget the spiritual Self, the ego's drive for separation pushes us to the dark side of human boundaries. This includes assaults through misogyny, prejudice, homophobia, and xenophobia, as well as physical attacks, murders, molestations, and rapes. These are the omens of misused power acted out on our fellow beings as force. Painful lessons for all involved, the dishonoring and degradation of others illuminates a lack of love, blocking the honoring of self, Self, and others.

Understanding and respecting human boundaries serve an important part of our inward journey. Simply defined, these limits in dynamic interactions identify what feels acceptable to us or not regarding our whole self. Boundaries determine, through our choice, how we participate in giving and receiving in five general areas - physical, emotional, mental, social, and spiritual. The brief descriptions and accompanying questions below help us identify and clarify the more tangible lines of contact, as well as intangible boundaries, in our relationships.

> *Physical* - The space around our body that encompasses our physical form as it relates to our comfort with physical touch and proximity, it includes giving and receiving a hug, a kiss, a hand on our shoulder, etc., in addition to more intimate sexual contact like kissing, petting, and love-making.

Ask: Do I respect others' personal space and how they want to be touched? Am I clear about what kind of touch is OK for me? Do I communicate my personal boundaries with others when necessary? Are my physical boundaries respected?

Mental - This includes both knowing our own thoughts and opinions and sharing them with others. How respectfully we communicate our thoughts in our intimate relationships and how our personal opinions become expressed at work, with friends, and in the community are as important as how respectfully people communicate their opinions to us. Mental boundaries extend into accepting responsibility for our thoughts and allowing others to be responsible for theirs.

Ask: Do I respect others' and my own thoughts and opinions? Do I accept responsibility for how I think? Am I clear about my thoughts and opinions? How do I communicate my thoughts and opinions? Do others respect my thoughts and opinions? Do others show respect in how they share their thoughts and opinions with me? Do others attempt to make me responsible for their thoughts, and do I allow others to own what they think?

Emotional - Emotional boundaries involve how we handle our own and others' feelings in relationships and interactions. This includes how we share our feelings and emotions with others and how respectfully others share with us. Emotional boundaries extend into accepting responsibility for our own feelings and understanding how our words and actions might affect another.

Ask: Do I know my own feelings and honor them? Do I communicate my feelings? How do I feel about others expressing feelings and emotions to me? Do I respect the feelings and emotions of others? Do I feel responsible for others' emotions, or do others attempt to make me responsible for how they feel?

Social - These boundaries center around the way we interact with our world. How we/others respond to our social selves includes handling peer pressure and interacting with strangers, acquaintances, friends, and intimate partners. Both our introverted and extroverted natures inform how we set social boundaries, which include our needs for participating in and removing ourselves from social interactions.

Ask: Do I respect others' social interactions? Am I clear about my needs and desires for social interaction? Do others respect my needs and choices regarding social interactions? What is the role of peer-pressure in my life?

Spiritual - This includes the respect we offer regarding our/others' beliefs we hold about religion and/or spirituality, as well as the respect and tolerance we/others demonstrate toward others/us regarding their beliefs.

Ask: Do I respect others' spiritual and religious beliefs? What are my spiritual and religious beliefs? Do I feel free to communicate them and do others respect them?

All boundaries, our personal frontiers, become clearer as we get to know ourselves. Attention to our internal climate and patterns in life illuminate both the simplicity and the complexity of our being. Remember, non-judgmental observation informs us moment by moment so we become intimately aware of our whole self - our essential Truth and the shadowy, unwanted aspects that limit our growth.

Only in knowing ourselves can we identify the boundaries that serve our highest and best. Through our evolution, the many ways our boundaries transform with us come to the fore; as we change, our boundaries change and vice versa, sometimes more fluidly as a soft transition, other times as a sudden, definitive line or some non-tangible place between.

While understanding our personal frontier comes easily for some, others struggle with setting limits, saying "No", speaking up, and/or asking for needs or desires to be met. When opportunities arise to exercise these necessary forms of self-care and respect of others, our history and personal patterns (childhood messages, past lives, and conditioning) again come into play, affecting how we set boundaries. Faced with authority figures who exerted more control than encouraging cooperation, for example, influences us to mirror their patterns with ourselves and others; we may also revert to a childlike state of feeling and/or operating as if we have no power or ignore our own or others' boundaries in the process. Other adults who disregarded our independence, overprotected us, demanded that their needs were more important, or elevated us to operate as an equal again impel us toward repetition of the past in our current relationships, unhealthily applying the same boundaries or lack thereof.

All these subtle dynamics that weave their way through both our intimate and casual interactions can create either harmony or conflict. Soul-discovery aids us in examining these boundary-related patterns to break the archaic cycles that don't serve us. First, we must come to know ourselves to be able to clearly set our boundaries, understanding what we want, need, or expect from life's situations, ourselves, and the people around us. Knowing, while a formative and vital piece, doesn't always translate into action. Times will arise that call us to forge past our own shyness, guilt, and fear of speaking up to stand in our power. At other times, we may need to hold our temper (and tongue). A deep and abiding sense of self-worth married with the responsibility to grow helps us honor the need for a boundary over the fear of angering or upsetting another. And when we don't feel the courage to act, taking the plunge to do or say what we know in our gut cultivates the very bravery we seek. In other words, when we move beyond the internal barriers that hold us back, we often feel the courage *after* we change our behavior, not before. Yes, we can grow by "doing it differently" despite our fear.

Life, for some, presents very challenging boundary violations, striking at our core by cutting into self-esteem and trust. From unwanted advances and toxic emotional dumping to all forms of abuse and assault, the range we can encounter is wide. At its most extreme end, the impact often feels like soul-crushing turmoil. And while a reoccurring theme within these pages illuminates the synchronicity and disguised opportunity of any situation, repetitive and/or violent assaults on our personal frontier requires delicate care. We cannot immediately rise from these deep, earthly wounds to see the lesson or value, especially at the very beginning of our healing. Many steps constitute the process of healing, a journey that's highly individual and personal. This includes the frequently suggested and traveled tool of non-judgmental observation, the practice of "passing-through" or witnessing the hurt we need to release and allowing our thoughts and emotions to move through us, and accepting where we are at any given moment. Let's not forget, the importance of setting new boundaries and reclaiming the power that we feel we lost or misused are vital parts to our restoration.

Learning about boundaries remains one of my most potent lessons, especially because it encompasses so many painful and impactful family dynamics. Only now can I recognize those who offered their loving service before incarnating to teach me these lessons - my mother, grandfather, and three "fathers", to name a few. Through time and healing, I graciously and humbly accepted what they gave. That wasn't always the case, and despite my hesitance to further discuss a deeply personal history of abuse, I decided before publishing to include the following passage, knowing that the value of helping others overshadows the perceived risk of sharing.

I came from a family of little resources prior to my parents' generation, as many lived through wars, the Great Depression, and economic recessions. My driven and hard-working mother put herself through school, finding more success and abundance than her parents and grandparents. She is and always was bright, highly intuitive, and creative. On the other hand, from an earth plane view, she appeared to be a product of her environment. Generations of violent, alcohol-fueled family dynamics took their toll, along with the sudden accidental death of her sister during their teens. In addition, she carried the family lineage of assault, compounded by a history of abuse. Because family patterns and mindsets reach out generations, the echoes of hers can be heard from the distant past.

On my father's side (in appearance, not biological), the same patterns of alcohol-fueled violence ensued; though I'm unaware of his history, I assume it was filled with much of the same. The relationship with this father, a man I never really knew, ended well before I turned four. Old memories of one such assault on my mother made a very tenacious, strong woman look helpless, like a rag-doll being shaken in an angry child's hands. In another, a brandished knife pierced one sun-soaked kitchen with its stark metallic glare; my mother stood on the pointed end antagonizing him in her idiosyncratic way while I froze silently in the doorway. My father's presence in the house even terrified our little white dog so much that he sometimes peed in the lap where he sat. The painful legacy he left reverberated well into my forties, though only in recent years ago did his potent influence become apparent.

In grade school, a step-father, whom I call Dad, brought a more peaceful presence to our family. He was gentle, loving, and intelligent, though afraid to be the protective force that I needed. My relationship with him became complicated and quite unlike the one with my mom. Not until my adult years did we come to some kind of silent understanding about the turmoil in our family, the one he so generously adopted. Sometimes I wonder if he suffered the most, not really knowing what to do, verbally suppressed and afraid of any consequences.

My mother was a force to be reckoned with. I love her dearly, while one part of me remains safely detached. She could be vibrant, comical, and nurturing, though these traits largely became outweighed by her need for control, Machiavellian charm, and often violent temper. The dynamic between us during my childhood and adolescent years centered on control and manipulation, heavily colored with emotional, mental, and sexual abuse. While the emotional and mental turmoil remained well in my awareness, the other stayed a covert force until my children arrived on this plane.

It's amazing how well our mind protects us from the most devastating parts of the past while the rest of us can feel shredded by various and sundry symptoms that seem connected to nothing and everything all at the same time. As a child I suffered from strange gynecological symptoms and separation anxiety. During my teens, I experienced generalized anxiety, nightmares, and even more trips to the gynecologist. While in graduate school, the therapeutic vignettes of sexual abuse sent me into full-on anxiety attacks.

I never knew of anyone I could confide in; the gag order issued by the clear message that all family business belonged within the four walls of our home seemed to keep others out. By the time I entered my first session for counseling while still in graduate school, the huge misfire only served to reinforce old messages. My therapist, a young psychiatric resident, responded to all my evidence of abuse as a case of "watching too much television." Needless to say, I didn't return. Months later, I found another therapist and help through traditional methods. Not until I found spirituality through the comprehensive teachings of Sacred Garden Fellowship (SGF), the lectures of Eva Pierrakos, and full immersion in SGF retreats and intensives, however, did I experience the deep healing necessary to finally overcome the traumas and more holistically utilize my experiences to help others.

Gradually, I came to understand how "victim" and "perpetrator" designations belong only in our earth-based thinking as a manifestation of our perceptions steeped in ego and personality. I came to learn the power of why *we choose all our experiences*. At times I wondered what I was thinking when I hatched my plan from Spirit, though the other part of me knows that I wrote my contract to "live from the inside" all I needed to help others - the plight of the wounded healer. As always, I came to see that from Spirit, before incarnation, the immense value of a lesson is clear, but in our personality, life can look like a circus of mad clowns and vicious tigers. While challenging and painful, all my experiences provided immeasurable insight - to understand suffering, to walk through shame and pain, to know the risk of sharing, and to emerge on the other side smarter, stronger, and wiser - the insight one can only experience after navigating the hurdles of healing and embracing the gifts of a lesson.

Boundary violations such as these call for dedicated healing on all levels - physical, mental, emotional, and spiritual. Support, guidance, a safe place to talk, tools to process our hurt, and self-care all lead us through restoration and growth to fill the hole and soul knot left behind by such deep wounds. One cannot move directly from "being a victim" to knowing that spiritually there are no victims. This jump in consciousness would require denying our experience and the pain of it - the definition of spiritual bypass. The ladder of our evolution upward requires that we stay present with where we are and be real, not to get stuck there, but to give ourselves the time to navigate what's in front of us and climb one rung at a time. The weight of our experiences can only serve to make the climb heavy and slow if we remain mired in our pain, but the rungs cannot be skipped, requiring authenticity, presence of mind, trust, and cultivating positive thinking, among other valuable psycho-spiritual tools.

If you are reading this and recognize similar challenges, know that help is available. Counselors, therapists, crisis workers, and support networks offer valuable assistance for this intense phase of your journey. The numbers listed offer help at the national level. To access assistance in your region, contact your family doctor, local crisis line, or county government. For continued reading, refer to the Appendix.

National Domestic Violence Hotline   (800) 799.7233   www.ndvh.org

Rape, Abuse & Incest National Network   (800) 656.4673   www.rainn.org

National Teen Dating Abuse Helpline   (866) 331.9474   www.loveisrespect.org

A valuable tool for any situation, knowing and setting boundaries is a vital piece of soul-discovery. Through honor and respect of everyone and everything in our world, we are ultimately called us to see the Divinity of all things. As such, we naturally care for others and ourselves, which organically unfolds as heart and mind joining in Unity. In the final frontier, we merge with the perfection within us – the Self that knows our Oneness with the Father-Mother – and bask in the infinite ambrosia of Love that is eternal.

Journey I: Reflections

Spend some time in your sacred space meditating.

Reflect on the chapter material, journaling your thoughts and feelings about what you read.

How does this chapter resonate with you? Why or why not?

Journey II: Boundary Survey

Spend time centering in your sacred space. Ask for guidance from your helpers, causing you to be aware of the boundaries that require your attention.

Remember to give yourself time, when necessary, for this assistance to be recognized.

Return to the questions listed in this chapter regarding boundaries. Answer each question from the five areas and journal any reflections.

Journey III: Well Laid Plans

In this journey we continue, utilizing your observations from **Journey II**.

Read through your answers to the chapter questions that you journaled in **Journey II**.

What changes would you like to make regarding your boundaries?

What action steps are you willing to take to ground your desire for change?

Ex: I will observe my interactions with my children to clearly state what I am asking them to do.

Ex: I will honor my need for self-care.

Ex: I will attend two social activities per month with friends instead of isolating myself.

Ex: I will say "No" to events when I feel the need for alone time.

Journey IV:
Plans Unfold

Spend time centering and meditating in your sacred space. Reflect on the previous weeks and/or months. How have you grown in setting healthier boundaries?

In what ways would you like to continue to grow? Can you list any calls for action to change old boundary patterns? What beliefs or thoughts/feelings about yourself or your world are keeping those old patterns in place?

Ex: I feel guilty when I say "No". I'm afraid I'll hurt other's feelings so I say "Yes" and then get mad at myself. I feel responsible for others' reactions.

Can you identify a new affirmation that could help you change your mind about how you tend to think, behave, or feel about the boundary identified above?

Ex: All feelings are OK. I am only responsible for how I feel and not for others, providing my intentions are to do no harm.

Ho'oponopono

He kehau ho`oma`ema`e ke aloha
Love is like a cleansing dew.
— Hawaiian Proverb

We all experience some level of conflict in our lives through interactions with others, a byproduct of living in a world with people who may not see things as we do and where situations don't unfold as expected. Turmoil and discord call us to release negative reactions from our hearts and minds through forgiveness - a prominent milestone on our path.

Many years ago, a friend introduced me to a different version of forgiveness through the Hawaiian healing process of *Ho'oponopono* (HO - oh - Po-no - Po-no). This ancient practice has two distinct methods of application, both possessing great value. To begin our exploration, we first look at the more modern version of *Ho'oponopono*, heavily influenced by Christian missionaries and still practiced in its homeland of Hawaii. Rich with ritual, the tradition aids all who utilize it in navigating relationally. This path of forgiveness engages everyone involved in transgressions so all individuals can take responsibility for the problem at hand.

> The process begins with prayer. A statement of the problem is made, and the transgression discussed. Family members are expected to work problems through and cooperate, not "hold fast to the fault". One or more periods of silence may be taken for reflection on the entanglement of emotions and injuries. Everyone's feelings are acknowledged. Then confession, repentance, and forgiveness take place. Everyone releases (kala) each other, letting go. They cut off the past ('oki) and together

they close the event with a ceremonial feast, called pani, which often included eating limu kala or kala seaweed, symbolic of the release.[29]

In our day-to-day interactions, utilizing this modern *Ho'oponopono* offers a potent means for healing as love and forgiveness spread a soothing balm on wounds we experience through our personality. The resolution-style approach asks all who participate in the process to be accountable. As we accept responsibility for our part in what appears to cause hurt, we also must listen to others' experiences. After labeling what we have done, said, or projected, we connect in love to put ourselves in another's shoes. The opportunity to share our hurts, as well as release the guilt we may have accumulated through our interactions, are vital steps in the ritual. Although this Christianized version diverges from the original *Ho'oponopono* intent (outlined in the text to follow), it remains a loving and powerful way to resolve conflict. And even when we cannot interact directly with another, we can still engage in this prayerful process in our mind through a heart connection by entering a meditation to ask for forgiveness for our part in any entanglements, softening our feelings to heal perceived transgressions. (See **Oh Merciful Heart** in **Volume V**.)

Looking back to the ancient practice of *Ho'oponopono*, we discover its very cosmic roots that return us to our Divinity by moving past the tricks of ego and straight into the mind and heart of Source. Speaking directly to God for all we see in the world as imperfect facilitates a relationship with Him/Her/It in us, working through us to erase the error in our perceptions as we desire to transform our beliefs.

A key reference to the practice of *Ho'oponopono* in alignment with its original intent can be found in the book *Zero Limits*, as authors Joe Vitale and Dr. Hew Len simplify the deeply shamanic and ancient holy practice. The theme of personal responsibility remains central to its practice, resonating to its modern counterpart, while widening application of our accountability to everything in our life not aligned with the perfection of Source.

> He (Dr. Hew Len) seemed to be acknowledging that everything is a mirror of yourself, but he also was saying that it is your responsibility to fix everything you experience, from the inside of yourself by connecting to the Divine.[30]

---

[29] Pukui, Mary Kawena; Haertig, E.W.; Lee, Catherine A, (1972). *Nana I Ke Kumu* (*Look to the Source*). Honolulu, HI: Hui Hanai.
[30] Vitale, Joe and Len, Ihaleakala Hew (2007). *Zero Limits: The Secret Hawaiian System for Wealth, Health, Peace, and More.* Hoboken, NJ: John Wiley & Sons, Inc.

Dr. Len contrasts the differences of *Ho'oponopono* where the more modern practice is modified from the ancient because it diverges from its roots.

> Today Ho'oponopono is just like family therapy. This has been really influenced by the Christians. But I am talking about the real Ho'oponopono from before they came. [Back] then the Hawaiians didn't need to talk anymore. They could go straight to the Light. This is very ancient. It goes back to the start, because that's where Hawaiians came from.
> — Dr. Hew Len, Shamanic Wisdom Keepers

Dr. Len's explanation of *Ho'oponopono* emphasizes our intimate relationship with Source and the knowing we have within us to access that connection. The vision of our Divine Nature is clear and pure and Dr. Len recognizes that we must shift our perceptions to God's vision to heal ourselves and others. We can witness the power of *Ho'oponopono* evidenced in his landmark work "with" patients in Hawaii State Hospital, a psychiatric facility for the criminally insane. As Dr. Len explained, that healing occurred through specific devotions as he prayed to release himself of his "vision of the inpatients' illnesses". He didn't treat them, counsel them, or interact directly with any patients or staff. Instead, he took responsibility for how he "saw" them, connecting with Source to heal the cause of his perceptions through four statements:

> *I'm sorry.*
> *Please forgive me.*
> *Thank you.*
> *I love you.*

The result...the patients gradually healed; the staff experienced personal growth - an otherworldly transformation. Today the hospital is closed, all of Dr. Len's "patients" released. The abiding premise of his work and *Ho'oponopono* as a deeply spiritual Union rests upon, as always, taking responsibility for what we create in our life - all of it. He released his perception of the patients as flawed, ill, and criminal by transforming his illusionary beliefs, the beliefs of a collective consciousness that created the "illness" in the first place. Resting in a state of Unity and Oneness, he saw his perceptions as the problem and dedicated four years to his beloved brothers and sisters, healing them through healing himself.

Through God's grace we clear the personal, illusionary debris that inherently manifests problems in our life. As we appeal to Source, we must recognize that our perception of a problem is created by a belief that is misaligned from spiritual law. Healing through *Ho'oponopono* takes place by asking that all negativity be dissolved through releasing something in ourselves using the four statements in prayer to Source.

While in truth God never needs our apologies, we believe in guilt and wrongdoing. Taking responsibility and asking forgiveness, we release ourselves from the binding belief that we have dishonored, forgotten, or abandoned He/Him/It in our thoughts, words, and feelings. In the words of this author, *Ho'oponopono* shifts our vision to see with the eyes of unconditional love, healing ourselves, which ultimately heals the world as others in it embrace what we offer.

Let's thank the rich cultural heritage of the ancient Hawaiians that brought us *Ho'oponopono*, a powerful healing practice. Connecting to the same Creator, we let the Light within us shine the way.

Journey I: Reflections

Spend some time in your sacred space, meditating and reflecting on the chapter material. Journal your thoughts and feelings about what you read.

Can you think of situations where *Ho'oponopono* could be helpful or healing? Why?

Journey II:
Hawaiian Way

Use *Ho'oponopono* to heal a conflict within one of your relationships. Invite one person to meet with you to use the modern practice outlined in the chapter. Before starting, spend some time in your sacred space, meditating to ready yourself for the interactions, asking for help to come from a place of love, compassion, and discernment.

Below is a suggested way to navigate the prayer when put into service with another person(s) providing they are willing to participate.

1. Begin with each person taking turns to offer...

    I'm sorry that I _____.
    (State what you did to start and/or continue the conflict.)

    Please forgive me for _____.
    (Ex: Hurting your feelings, causing pain, insulting you, etc.)

2. Engage in discussion to express how the conflict affected you and then encourage the other person to do the same. Be sure to honor whomever is speaking by not interrupting, using a talking stick for the person who has the floor if necessary. Using "I" statements to communicate feelings helps the person speaking to own their reactions and inner climate, as well as facilitates active listening from the audience.

    I felt _____ when _____ happened or when you said/did _____.

3. When each person has been heard, voicing their part in the conflict and how the conflict affected them/you, move on.

4. Each person now states how they can repair the relationship. Take turns naming what each of you can do differently.

5. Each person offers forgiveness to the other. Drop the issue, blame, and guilt.

    Thank you (for listening to me and forgiving me).

    I love you. (End with a hug or handshake.)

Journal about your experience.

Notes:

Journey III: Ancient Hawaii

Spend time in your sacred space meditating.

Pray the *Ho'oponopono* in alignment with the ancient tradition of speaking to Source, dissolving problems in your life.

The four statements of the *Ho'oponopono* can be said in their simple form or made into a prayer of your own creation. *Example:*

Dear Divine Light Within,

I am sorry *that I created a vision of something that misaligned with You and my Natural State as Your Child.*

Please forgive me *for forgetting Your love within me that's present every moment of my life, no matter where I am.*

Thank you *for being patient with me as I grow in Awareness, and for Your abundance and trust in me.*

I love You.

Journal the changes that occur as you pray the ancient Hawaiian way.

Chagrin

There is a sacredness in tears. They are not the mark of weakness, but of power.
They speak more eloquently than ten thousand tongues.
They are the messengers of overwhelming grief,
of deep contrition, and of unspeakable love.

— *Washington Irving*

During the 17th century, chagrin leather, an untanned rawhide made of wild animal skin, created a lasting barrier to whatever it adorned. Chagrin decorated the hilt of knives and swords, provided a strong casing for luggage, snuff containers, and books, ensuring that rough handling made little impact. Originally derived from 17th century French, the term *chagrin* means grief or melancholy. Like its tough, physical counterpart, our own grief may develop into a strong outer layer, a leathery skin that resists softening and ultimately blocks us from receiving or giving love.

Grief is a part of life; it makes us realize the importance of someone or something on this grand journey. A faded romantic tryst, a passed loved one, a crumbling relationship, an ailing child, relocation, a fire that consumes our possessions or home, a career that ends…these are just some of the situations that elicit feelings of sadness and mourning. All speak to the notion that someone and/or something has gone - a loved one, a possession, an opportunity, and/or time. As a result, we may plunge into a deep well of sorrow where love feels eclipsed and turns to pain. Even though our grief and loss hurts, as we emerge from the shadows and turn to the light, toward the higher octaves of spiritual understanding, we can remember that love cannot be lost.

Life, in its cyclic nature, is a series of beginnings and endings. Everything and everyone flux through change. And in the ever-changing nature of life, of letting go, of loss, and the passage of time, one thing always remains - love. Love, in its state of constant unfolding, is eternal; yet, we still experience grief at many points in our lives that each person must navigate in their own way.

While our movement through chagrin or grief is highly personal, authors and experts on death and dying, Elisabeth Kubler-Ross and David Kessler, define five non-linear stages that shed light on the process:[31]

- **Denial** - This is the stage where we experience the world as overwhelming, confusing, and meaningless. Denial and shock aid our process of navigating loss to allow it to filter through our consciousness in a safe way.

- **Anger** - The anger stage may be filled with many, many layers, especially emotional pain, giving a sense of power or palpable experience to the overwhelming feelings of loss.

- **Bargaining** - Filled with "what if's" and "if only's", this stage recognizes the deals we make to avoid a pending loss or to escape from our current pain.

- **Depression** - A typical response to a major loss, this stage shows the depth of our grieving journey, especially the emptiness.

- **Acceptance** - In this stage, the reality of the loss is accepted. This doesn't mean that we believe the loss was OK or we don't miss what we are grieving. Instead, we accept our feelings, create life anew, and move on.

So, what can we do to navigate through our grief? First, we remember that grieving is a process. Moving through the above stages follows no set logic or clear, linear pace. We may repeatedly cycle through various phases, only to find that we land again in one or another until we move into acceptance. Secondly, recognizing what we are experiencing, labeling the feelings and emotions, feeling them, and finding outlets to release them (crying, yelling, laughing, journaling, and movement) help heal our pain. Giving ourselves the time and a safe place to process is also important on our healing path. When we allow expression without blocking or frequent retreating to our bubble

---

[31] Kubler-Ross, Elisabeth and Kessler, David (2005). *On Grief and Grieving: Finding the Meaning of Grief Through the Five Stages of Loss.* New York, NY: Scribner.

of safety, we give ourselves the space to walk through what we are experiencing and put it to rest. Discomfort with our own emotions, fear of feeling out of control, being overwhelmed by our emotions, and judging ourselves just sets up roadblocks. We must keep in mind and know that all feelings are OK. Our gentle embrace of whatever we experience offers a loving hug to ourselves, giving room to just be where we are at any given moment. Acceptance helps everyone move through grief, one day at a time.

As we reflect on how chagrin or grief enters our lives, we get a sense of our general trends in healing from loss. Perhaps allowing the process of grieving feels freeing and we move through it with a sense of relief. On the other hand, maybe we become hard-hearted and angry because the pain feels so great that we look for ways to guard ourselves from further loss. If, instead, we stuff our emotions, they stagnate; allowing them to move us toward transformation requires our consent and participation to unchain them. So, whether we have pushed past the death of a friend or loved one or shoved down feelings that we did not want to feel, remember that unprocessed emotions can turn into encapsulated energy held in the body as any number of physical symptoms from pain to infection and "dis-ease". (See **Understanding Healing and Illness** in **Volume III**.)

The following are signs that fixed energy and unfinished grieving could be afoot:

- intense reactions to minor issues;
- feelings of numbness or flatness (not to be confused with neutrality);
- a sense that emotions are just below the surface, but we cannot access them;
- moving too quickly toward acceptance of a situation or loss;
- frequently or habitually pushing emotions out of the way; and/or
- dis-ease or pain.

As we progress on our path of healing, sometimes we may find ourselves caught in grief's grip where we release and accept our feelings but seem stuck in a pattern of grieving after we feel it's time to move forward. Setting an intentional block of time to give expression to whatever we are experiencing through journaling and physical outlets shifts our energy. Honoring the time set aside as personal contracts of self-care means that we halt the mental spinning or emotional storms when they manifest in the spaces outside of our periods of reflection or movement. Choosing again, we instead select healthy distractions – hobbies, socializing, reading, music, etc. As we continue to gently remove our focus on negative energy (even if it returns repeatedly) and honor our contract of self-care, healing happens. Remember, mental and emotional states become part of our aura; the ones we're drawn to frequently result from the energy we feed and maintain through our reactions to every situation, grief or otherwise. So, withdrawing our energy from a pattern of mental and emotional grinding is necessary to heal and grow. We all can be tricked by the ego into thinking that spending copious amounts of time in the "problem" renders solutions, but that's just not the case. Setting aside the time for emotional discharge, as well as conscious periods of re-directing our focus, allows us to take charge of our inner climate instead of it being in charge of us.

At times, prolonged periods of emotional turmoil may leave us worn out, swirling in our own sticky, thick miasma; exhausted by our inner climate, we may feel lost, not knowing how to leave grief behind. If this occurs, we can find help in the form of a counselor, therapist, or group treatment. At any point, really, in our grieving process, an objective guide can aid our navigation, especially if a period of depression refuses to lift.

It takes courage to reach out, especially if we believe that we should pilot our troubles alone or must aggressively protect our privacy. Most importantly, if we become engaged in thoughts of hurting ourselves – passively considering leaving life or actively contemplating suicide – a serious inquiry for healing (crisis intervention, counseling, therapy, hospitalization) is necessary to secure our safety and movement through this difficult time. The benefit of seeking help when burdened with feelings of hopelessness and/or thoughts and feelings of hurting ourselves or others far outweighs the risk to our independence as well as the fear of sharing our pain by breaking our silence.* The numbers for national hotlines and website information below offer contact points for receiving professional help:

National Suicide Prevention Lifeline	(800) 273.8255	1-800-273-TALK
I'm Alive Nat'l Suicide Hotline	(800) 784.2433	1-800-SUICIDE
Veterans Peer Support Line	(877) 838.2838	1-877-Vet2Vet
Spanish Speaking Suicide Hotline	(800) 784.2432	1-800-SUICIDA
Teen to Teen Peer Counseling Hotline	(877) 968.8454	1-877-YOUTHLINE
The Trevor Project (LGBTQ Crisis/Suicide Prevention)	(866) 488.7386	1-866-4-U-TREVOR
Post-partum Depression Hotline	(800) 773.6667	1-800-PPD-MOMS
Grad Student Hotline	(800) 472.3457	1-800-GRADHLP

International Association for Suicide Prevention
www.iasp.info/resources/Crisis_Centres

National Center for School Crisis and Bereavement
www.schoolcrisiscenter.org

* If someone has talked to you about suicide and you believe they are currently a threat to themselves or someone else but won't take your help, call 911.

We need time for gentle self-care and nurturing, especially during our healing from grief. This part of our journey in soul-discovery again clears away the emotional pain of chagrin to help us remember that love is eternal. This healing process moves us forward on our path, feeling more connected to our Self and our world, as well as increasingly open to freely give and receive the love that is inherently ours. Imagine the all-loving, Divine Light wrapping Its gentle arms around you…a healing hug for your travels.

Journey I: Reflections

Retreat to your sacred space to relax and center.

When ready, reflect on the chapter material. Journal your thoughts and feelings about what you read.

Journal about situations and events in your *entire* life, the beginnings and endings that can bring a sense of loss. Remember, sometimes great beginnings also have accompanying sad endings.

Consider the following:

>major transitions
>physical changes
>disease
>aging
>births
>deaths
>marriage
>divorce
>empty nesting
>graduation
>retirement/job change
>ending of a friendship
>financial change
>accidents
>relocation
>downsizing
>trauma/abuse
>custody changes
>children becoming independent

Journey II: Identifying Chagrin

Going to your sacred space, do a brief meditation asking for Divine guidance and help to uncover situations that call for healing.

Do any situations you listed in **Journey I** or others not addressed there still bring emotions associated with the grieving process to the surface? Journal what you uncover.

If no emotions surface, use the chapter materials to explore blocked guilt and journal any signs or symptoms that indicate such. When did these signs/symptoms arise and can you identify whom or what they linked to?

* If this journey reveals an absence of emotions or neutrality to the above questions and no blocked emotions exist, move on to the next chapter. If not, see **Journey III**.

Journal III: Letting Go

Set aside at least thirty minutes of time in your sacred space. Before you begin, find photos, music, movies, videos, or other props that resonate with you, a reminder of the person or situation you would like to work with. Also gather self-care items to soothe you along the way - hot tea, a blanket, tissues, essential oils, flowers, etc.

Use your props to bring out emotions - listen to the music, look at the photos, videos, etc. Give some space for blocked feelings to come to the surface.

Now, write about your experience - all the thoughts and emotions that come to you and through you as you experience anything attached to the person or situation. Without censoring, just allow yourself to write, draw, scribble, color, etc. and feel whatever it is you need to express.

Writing about situations or people who trigger many emotions can be overwhelming. After writing, consider taking a nice warm shower with the intention of releasing any unwanted or heavy emotions that remain with you. When standing in the water, cleanse your aura. If desired, cleanse your soul memory of all the negative energies relating to the situation you explored. Employ your memory to retain only the gift of the lesson while releasing any related pain. Remember, you can ask for the transformative action of the Holy Spirit to help you let go of any remaining grief and replace it with peace, comfort, love, etc. Be sure to also energetically cleanse your sacred space using incense or sage. (See **Wynebgwrthucher** and **Into the Butterfly** in **Volume III** and **Shedding Perceived Failures**.)

Repeat **Journeys II** and **III** and the follow-up cleansing as needed.

Dearest Friend

To love oneself is the beginning of a life-long romance.
— Oscar Wilde

What you are is God's gift to you.
What you do with yourself is your gift to God.
— Leo Buscaglia

By now, dear soul-discoverer, you have been exposed to many writing exercises, discovering the potency and value in them. In **Letter of Love**, we explored another powerful tool - sharing your feelings in direct communication with an inspiring individual in your life. In considering letter writing, we tend to only think of communicating with others. Offering the same to ourselves from the perspective of a wiser self or dear friend, however, serves as another way to express self-love and acceptance. Looking from the "outside" with fresh eyes, compassion, appreciation, support, and encouragement can replace the common self-talk of criticism or the constant, nagging, internally-directed pressure for improvement.

Letter writing to ourselves can help us forge a new path, developing valuable insight in surprising ways. Recognizing our virtues and all the things we feel good about call us to witness our grace. Dedicated to a new opportunity to speak to ourselves from an "outside" vantage point, the journey to follow facilitates connection with ourselves as a dear friend. As such, we find another way to express self-love and acceptance, speaking from the heart about all we learned, our virtues, and the wonderful gifts we share with the world. If this opportunity to recognize "goodness" and embrace self-love is met with shyness or avoidance, this chapter is for you! Let's boldly look and see your grace, shining like a diamond in an indigo sky.

Journey I: Dear Me

Take a pen, envelope, postage stamp, and a blank piece of paper to your sacred space. Center and meditate, inviting the transformative power of the Holy Spirit to help you be open and loving.

Address the envelope to yourself and place a stamp on it for mailing. Now write a letter to yourself acting as a dear friend. Include all positive deeds, beautiful qualities, growth, etc. in their varying sizes and shapes. Allow yourself to feel connection and love to the dear friend in you.

When finished, put your letter in the self-addressed, stamped envelope and mail it to yourself.

Journal all your reflections.

When your letter arrives, move on to **Journey II**.

Journey II: Reflections

Go to your sacred space with a hand mirror or a private location in your home with a mirror. Center and meditate.

Connect with the "self" that wrote the letter. When ready, read it out loud while facing the mirror. Periodically look at yourself to anchor what you are sharing and to whom you are sharing it with.

Allow the positive feelings of self-love and growth absorb into your soul, imagining the energy embracing you as a big, warm hug.

Journal about your experience and don't forget to thank your Self for shinning a light in you, the light you share with the world.

Waters Deep and Wide

*No man ever steps in the same river twice,
for it's not the same river and he's not the same man.*
— Heraclitus

The current is swift and deep in these waters of soul-discovery. As you ready yourself for more exploration, take a moment to acknowledge the trail behind you. You've been working diligently, exploring who you are, all of you. Remember, those shadowy parts are temporary, a thin grey silhouette that fades in the new dawn of your brilliant Self.

Reflecting on your adventure through this volume, which chapters or topics felt the most significant? Which were the most challenging? Which held the most value? What discoveries, experiences, or changes can you acknowledge as jobs well done? An unveiled aspect of your Self calls for celebration; which facet of your Self will you embrace and revel in?

Take a moment to applaud all your work, chutzpah, and courage. Write or draw about how you've grown…how you've navigated the deeper waters in **A Deeper Gaze**. When finished, move on to the last volume, **Hip Boots and Waders**! Woohoo!

The Soul-Discovery Journalbook

An Intimate Journey into Self

Volume V

Hip Boots and Waders

*There is an eagle in me that wants to soar,
and there is a hippopotamus in me that wants to wallow in the mud.*

— Carl Sandburg

Hip Boots and Waders

Amazing! Here you are in the final stretch with four books under your belt. Excellent work!

Drawing once again on potent metaphysical principles, **Hip Boots and Waders** offers additional psycho-spiritual tools and techniques as it joins the soul-discovery of **A Deeper Gaze**. This powerful and transformative work helps us explore some of the most hidden parts of our being.

Fishing in the mire of our past, in old attitudes and challenges, we find the bottom feeders of our personality - blame, regret, heartache, guilt, and shame. Here our lost little child wanders in the forest, looking to connect with and be nurtured by our adult self.

Sometimes stomping through this personal swamp requires special gear. It's not just any adventure; prepare to get a little muddy. All the while we march onward and upward to sunny, dry ground. And remember, as we grow in soul-discovery, we can bask in the freedom that places the antiquated and long forgotten where it belongs - in the past. So, get out the hip boots and waders. They will help you navigate the morass, providing invaluable benefits as you continue soul-discovery to let your Light shine.

Meeting Peter Pan

"Pan, who and what art thou?" he cried huskily.
"I'm youth, I'm joy," Peter answered at a venture,
"I'm a little bird that has broken out of the egg."
— J.M. Barrie

A beautiful, little child lives within each of us. When we laugh, they laugh with us. When we cry, they too cry. Our inner child knows our supreme, true Self; it knows how close heaven really is…right in our own backyards…right in our hearts.

Sometimes when I work with others and describe the child that lives within each of us, I'm met with an understanding nod. At other times, it's a smile and cautious head-bob to a "This lady is crazy" thought. However, when clients finally meet their inner child, an eternal Peter Pan, some find surprise and delight, as if they just re-discovered a long-forgotten friend. Even so, the first blush interaction with our inner child, as a mind's eye figure from childhood, can breed confusion and strangeness at the "realness" of the experience. Commonly, some people even worry that their imagination took hold or worse.

The energy of our inner child seems quite unusual in a world that loves linear, logical thinking. Regardless, all humans carry this state, which embodies unhealed, as well as healthy, well-functioning qualities that influence us moment by moment at our current age. We can witness the impact of our healthy inner child as we play through sports, artistic endeavors, or clowning around. This is the loving, curious, happy child who loves life, people, learning, and growing.

On the other hand, highly emotional, over-indulged, over-criticized, and/or unnurtured parts of our inner Peter Pan exist, too; they often appear in our self-beatings, tendencies to demand, or adult temper-tantrums as the parts of ourselves that require help to grow. The energy of this child remains in place, held in our psyche by our lack of maturity, understanding, or the tools to heal - a piece of our childhood self that energetically became and stayed "stuck", frozen in time through difficulty, trauma, loss, chaos, or some combination of experiences that stagnated our growth. While most like to think that a major, insidious life event manufactures these fractured time-capsule parts of our early life, any circumstance or recurring (subtle or overt) interactions can create a split-off piece of us, breaking the continuity of development that appears to lack wholeness. In other words, we all have an inner child state impacted by people who failed to nurture or teach us in the ways we needed or by those who violated our boundaries and hurt us. Other experiences scar us through damage accumulated over time, like a persistently dripping water pipe that slowly weakens the floor and wall around it. Either way, we can reclaim our little kiddo, offering Peter Pan new ways to feel nurtured, grow, and heal.

So how do we find this little child who seems to lurk in the shadows? Typically, an initial look comes from two avenues of exploration. First, through a journey to scan our personal archeology, traveling through memories, photos, and stories. Discovering these snapshots from childhood informs us about our early climate and family landscape. They weave the canvas on which we steadily paint the story of how we became the adult and even the parent of today.

Secondly, we travel through a model to unravel our inner child as an aspect of a whole, identifying one of three operating personality or ego states: Child, Parent, and Adult. Developed by Dr. Eric Berne, the father of Transactional Analysis, this paradigm of distinct but interactive aspects of our personality operate according to our navigational abilities. In other words, how we behave, think, and/or feel in any situation (navigating our internal and external world) identifies our current Child, Parent, or Adult ego states in both their mal-adaptive or well-functioning patterns.

In this chapter, we focus on the qualities of our inner child in its two expressions, the Natural Child and Adapted Child. Looking at the table, the Natural Child demonstrates the one given freedom, nurturing, appropriate structure, and guidance - our innate self organically expressed through exploration, play, creativity, healthy boundaries, nurturing love, and appropriate discipline. In contrast, the Adapted Child responds in ways that indicate their world lacks the safety and/or love they need, reflecting all our unhealed aspects exhibited in fearful ways. This child experiences life with anxiety, doubt, and thwarted expression via criticism, taunting, hovering parents, unhealthy structure, and neglect, among others.

Natural Child is expressive, creative, and loves life	*Adapted Child* fears being judged, punished, and/or humiliated
Exploratory	Anxious
Playful	Awkward
Free	Defensive
Uninhibited	Apathetic
Funny	Hurried
Imaginative	Moody
Energetic	Whiny
Loving	Demanding

Expanding this model to the metaphysical realm, we find an additional layer to consider. So, even though we as children (chronologically speaking) are naturally expressive, creative, and exploratory in our love of life and would like to think we are a clean slate at birth, on a spiritual level we bring many, many beliefs from previous incarnations that influence us, even in youth. As we mature into adults, we continue to function with some combination of our Natural and Adapted Child impacted by two sources - the past of our early current life and the past we bring with us as a collection of past-life baggage. These sources, with all their various influencing details, coalesce to create the results in the personality we express today. Regardless, circumstance by circumstance, our reactions and responses to the world come from either the energy of freedom, creativity, and love or from judgment, punishment, and humiliation. Seeing the world through the lens of our collective past affects us moment by moment, bleeding into the now on multiple levels in every new situation.

Make no mistake…discovering our Peter Pan is not some witch hunt for the "less than perfect" parents and guardians in our lives. No parents can meet their children's needs one hundred percent of the time. No parent. All make mistakes and act according to their own history as the effects of their own inner child filters through their decisions in parenting. Walking through the halls of forgiveness, we come to realize that they only did the best they were able to do with what they had in their own toolbox.

Remember, we all are exactly where we need to be at any given time, growing in understanding toward our highest good. So, let's meet Peter Pan or Patricia Pan and give him/her a great big hug for getting you this far!

Journey I: Reflections

Spend some time in your space resting, centering, and meditating as you are drawn.

Contemplate the chapter information. What are your thoughts and feelings about what you read?

Journey II:
Natural/Adapted Child

Journal the characteristics of the Natural and the Adapted Child in the space here. Circle all the qualities that fit you as a child.

Take each quality one at a time and write about your unique expressions of that quality.

Ex: Exploratory - I loved to play for hours outside, finding bugs and looking at flowers and plants.

Ex: Anxious - I felt very anxious at school, especially first grade. I didn't like being away from home and found the schoolwork confusing.

Journey III:
Pan Unveiled

You will need a photo from childhood, choosing one that was taken between the ages of 3 and 7 years, if possible. Make a copy of it or use the original, bringing it to your sacred space.

Now paste the photo or copy here or in a journal for soul-discovery.

Journal when and where the photo was taken. Who is present in the photo with you? What do you remember about it? Is there a family story about you or the event it's capturing?

How to you feel looking at this photo? Describe what you see?

Does the photo identify the Natural or Adapted child in you?

How does this photo help you better understand your inner child?

Journey IV:
Inner Child Music

There are many ways to connect with our inner child. This journey uses the music of Shaina Noll, who wrote healing songs for him/her.

Travel on the web to www.shainanoll.com where you can find her music. Download *How Could Anyone Ever Tell You* and take it to your sacred space. Listen to the song while connecting with your inner child. Imagine holding your little girl or boy and loving them with this song.

Journal your experience here.

Transforming Drama

Never argue with a fool.
Onlookers may not be able to tell the difference.
— Mark Twain

We love drama, plain and simple. We (or at least a part of us) enjoy the experience as ego magnetically draws us into the news, soap operas, and emotionally tumultuous movies. Drama with family, friends, acquaintances, and strangers all lure us like a mesmerized moth into the flame to the excitement of pain, safety of judgment, and/or the upheaval of conflict. We need not look far to witness how often human interaction becomes laden with drama - the ego-fueled dichotomy of thrill and trauma we experience with our own struggle, turmoil, and chaos, as well as that of others.

Though seemingly messy and complicated, exploring drama through the work of Dr. Karpman offers clarity. A psychiatrist and student of Dr. Eric Berne, Dr. Karpman developed a model of dynamic human interactions called the Drama Triangle (DT) based on the idea that conflict needs players and players need roles. The consequential objective of each player's role is to meet needs, even if temporarily, to feel justified in their rationale, behavior, and/or emotional experiences. Understanding Karpman's DT helps us untangle from sticky, conflict-laden relationship dynamics. Moreover, our own attachment or attraction to drama may be illuminated, further assisting us in removing ourselves from the kind of situations that cause us turmoil. Any interaction, whether real or imagined, can be explored using the DT. Here's how it works.

Three main roles exist that a person can play during conflict or drama: the Persecutor, the Victim, or the Rescuer. (See diagram) The Persecutor is happy to allocate blame and point to the other players' wrongdoing. Typical Persecutor behaviors include judging, blaming, demanding, attacking, gossiping, controlling, and criticizing. To have their needs met, The Persecutor requires someone onto whom they can place their irritation and anger, known as the Victim.

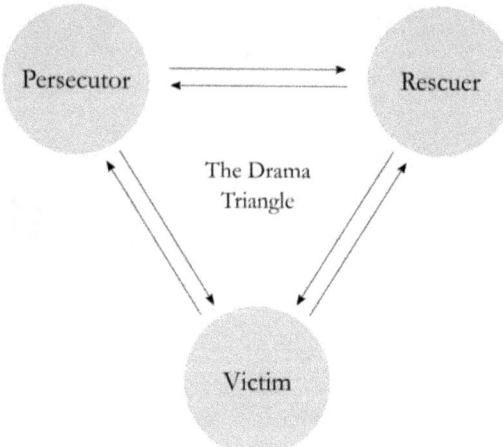

The Victim takes the brunt of the Persecutor's anger and aggression and feels swindled, powerless, attacked, ashamed, and helpless. Despite being a position of anxiety for most, playing out this role brings a subconscious comfort (mostly out of habit, conditioning, and belief) that stays hidden from the Victim's conscious mind. Rooted in seeking parental-type support, guidance, and/or sympathy of others, the learned personality traits of the Victim serve to keep them helpless. If this role feels natural to you or you find yourself in this role repeatedly, then you will innately draw Persecutors and Rescuers to you.

The Rescuer, often deeply affected by guilt, needs someone to help distract them from their own anxiety or other hidden emotions. Acting as the hero, the wise one, the guru, the advice giver, the expert, or the teacher, the Rescuer appears to be the Victim's "savior" from the Persecutor. The Rescuer helps cement everyone (including themselves) in negative behaviors: the tormented (Victim), the bully (Persecutor), and the white knight (Rescuer).

Look at the diagram of the DT above, considering the qualities of each role. Notice the dual arrows; this signifies that a participant in the DT *can rapidly switch* between Victim/Persecutor or Victim/Rescuer or Persecutor/Rescuer within any conflict or drama.[32]

For example:

> "Why do you always treat me so badly?" (V) she sobbed. "Don't you ever say that again to me or I'm gonna cut your tongue out!" she screamed. (P)

---

[32] The Official Site of the Karpman Drama Triangle (2005). The Karpman Drama Triangle family of sites. Retrieved March 18, 2015 from https://www.karpmandramatriangle.com

"You're always so lazy, never taking care of your car," he criticized. *(P)* "I don't know why you just don't appreciate anything I do for you," he whined. *(V)*

Do you see the change in the first example as the Victim (V) switches to the Persecutor (P) and vice versa in the second? Here's another example, switching from the Rescuer to the Persecutor, a conversation between two fictitious sisters:

"You know, you really need to stand up for yourself and not let him treat you like he does," Mary said. *(R)*

"He's just in a bit of a depression because his father died. He's not usually like that." Sally explained.

"You're such a pushover. No wonder your marriage is a mess," Mary criticized. *(P)*

(Note: The response given by Sally could be a Rescuer response if she's making excuses and protecting a partner who behaves abusively. We don't really know here, so it's left blank.)

Looking more deeply into the DT, many readers may already be aware of current positions or common roles. Even so, what can we do about our involvement? First, we must become conscious of when and how we become DT participants. The following questions offer guidance:

- What are the situations that trigger our emotions of feeling victimized?
- When do we feel inept?
- When do we feel stuck in chronic complaining or want others to fix our problems?
- Do we want to save others from their troubles, problems, or from doing their own work in projects or circumstances?
- Do we easily slip into a parent role for those who can take care of themselves or need to learn to be independent?
- Are we hostile, judgmental, and/or critical of what others do? What behaviors in others bring that to the surface in us?

Awareness of ourselves is the first key, becoming informed of our participation in the DT by stepping back to witness our interactions during conflict, in daily situations, and when supporting others. By taking responsibility for the parts we play, we begin to shift our perceptions and stand in our truth. Through authenticity and accountability, we grow in courage, clarity, and honest self-evaluation. Becoming willing to communicate, compromise, show compassion, as well as let go of our negative grip on others, we learn to be in relationships in a healthy way. This may be reflected in self-care, setting appropriate boundaries, owning our needs and wants, embracing flexibility, refusing to gossip, disengaging from negative situations, and communicating with kindness. As we come from a place of truth and discernment, we move beyond punishing others for "wrongdoing" to holding them accountable when their actions or choices directly affect us. Remaining completely neutral in the face of conflict, walking away, and offering forgiveness instead of criticism removes us from the DT as well. Most importantly, we support others and ourselves to live from a state of honesty and power. Accepting and honoring the belief that everyone is OK and possesses competencies, as well as their own Divine guidance, even in the most challenging of circumstances, helps removes us from the entangled dynamic of whatever role we tend to play.

In the journeys to follow, we first identify and work with the DT, reviewing the qualities of each role. Then moving deeper, we apply it directly to our life experiences. Only then can we begin to see how to remove ourselves from drama's lure.

Remember to be patient and gentle with yourself. Know that all we uncover through exploration of the DT was learned and adopted through years of practice. We have but repeatedly chosen fear over love to feel better about ourselves and our world. In approaching this part of soul-discovery, trust that any present roles or patterns are transient. They took time to develop and require time to transform. With the gift of the DT, we can see with fresh eyes, take responsibility, and dissolve the old to shed what no longer serves us.

Journey I: Triangle Understanding

Next to each role (Victim, Persecutor, Rescuer) below, write out all the respective qualities described in the chapter.

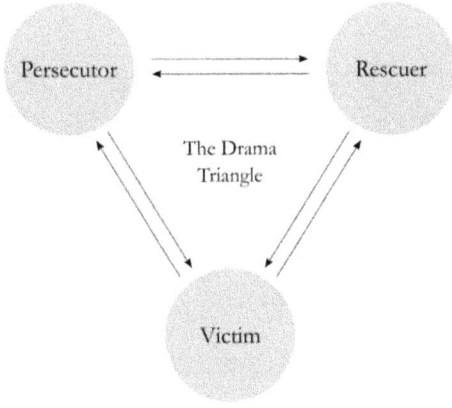

The Soul-Discovery Journalbook

Journey II: Role Assignment

Using the triangles below, identify people in your life as they play out roles in the DT. Consider two different events or situations and write a title above each triangle. List each player's name next to their role(s), remembering that any player may flip-flop from one to another. Where do you fit on the triangle? Use a colored pencil/pen to mark your role in each drama. Do you tend to gravitate to one role? Do you fluctuate between two or more?

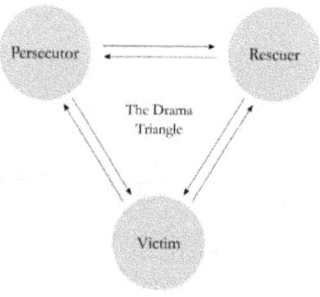

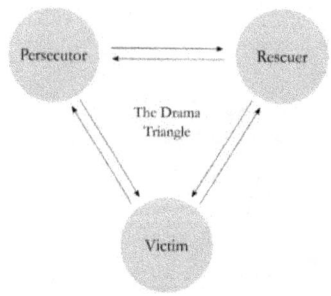

Journey III:
The Now Drama

Take one of the dramas from **Journey II** and write about each person's role(s), including your own. What behaviors or attitudes are you and others exhibiting that fit with the DT?

How do you feel in your role? How are you contributing to others keeping their role(s)? Are you comfortable in your role and why?

Journal any other reflections.

What action steps would be helpful for you to take to remove yourself from your role?

How do you imagine being out of the drama or conflict would feel?

Repeat this journey with the other drama from **Journey II**.

Do you notice any patterns between the two dramas?

The Soul-Discovery Journalbook

Digging into our own mud is uncomfortable and humbling. Give yourself recognition for being courageous, authentic, and committed to shedding those shadows! Good job!

The Letter That Won't Be Sent

...the words I can't say are the holes I punch in the walls of my psyche...
— John Geddes

A long time ago, I deeply felt the need to express something painful to a certain someone in my life. Communicating with them, however, seemed nearly impossible. Broken ties created by many painful events built the damaged landscape of our relationship. Even the possibility of reconstituting some shred of a connection faded along with their denial and refusal to assume any responsibility for their actions. Like many who experience abuse, my path to healing was a solo flight - solo in my lack of accompaniment (from the person with whom I desired the greatest reconciliation) - yet thankfully supported by other nurturing co-pilots and attendants along the way.

Many of us face situations where direct communication is either anxiety-producing, unwise, or unproductive. Challenging co-workers, neighbors, acquaintances, or family members can stir feelings that may be best handled solely with ourselves, even if only in preparation for later interactions. Furthermore, when our emotions reach a height that circumvents effective communication, processing them before we approach others helps us manage our reactions and turn them into responses.

As we seek deeper healing, we may naturally desire to openly discuss our hurts or challenges with specific individuals in our life, especially those who feel connected to our pain or who appear to have caused it. As we consider the consequences or outcome of such sharing, many factors come into play, including previous relationship dynamics, underlying belief systems, and personal conditioning, as well as our comfort with direct communication. For example, thinking a future interaction will only be met by intensely negative or unwelcoming energy, we may hold our feelings hostage and operate under a veil of fear created by our perceptions. If we experienced abusive relationships, we may feel frightened into silence because of possible retaliation. We may also fear loss of love, concerned that our words may hurt the other. On the other hand, an intense rage that seems contained only by silence can affect our decisions to share because we are fearful that uttering a single syllable might unleash an aggressive or violent outburst. Perhaps the person with whom we seek reconciliation has passed over, or perhaps historical conversations were extremely unproductive or downright volatile. Quite commonly, fear of judgment or skepticism can cause us to shut our shame and pain away from everyone.

Allowing ourselves the space to express in a non-judgmental and safe manner is fundamental to being able to heal past hurts. Remember, emotions are energy, and left without a means of release, can lead to resentment. Continued compartmentalization or stuffing how we feel traps emotional energy, which literally leaks from our psyche masked in other forms like anxiety, rage, or depression. At other times it stays stuck in the body, manifesting physically as headaches, body pain, or other illnesses. Eventually, our compartmentalizing, hiding, denying, or ignoring of these emotions becomes a locked cell and we feel more and more trapped behind heavy iron bars.

Whether we uncover our feelings to free ourselves from self-imprisonment or we just need a space to express, another journaling tool can serve as a constructive way to navigate our inner mire. This form of healing gives us permission to express what needs a voice, again allowing the process to transform difficult situations into valuable life lessons.

Regardless of our story, when we seek to heal, communicating our thoughts, emotions, and feelings becomes a vital step in the process. When our audience seems unable to engage or is absent - physically, mentally, or emotionally - communication with them requires a bit of creativity. So, opening the door to expression through "a letter that won't be sent" gives our inner climate safe release until we decide to move beyond ourselves as the singular audience.

Here's another opportunity for authenticity and chutzpah to express whatever needs to be said, shedding another layer of our shadow and stepping forward in growth.

Journey I: Un-mailed Mail

Set aside some time in your sacred space centering. Ask for guidance and support from your Divine helpers.

Make a list of people and corresponding situations where you feel the need to speak up, voice your thoughts and feelings, or get something off your chest. Choose one person on the list and write "a letter that won't be sent". While the space here can be used for your letter, using a separate piece of paper may feel more comfortable.

Imagine this journey as a free, get-out-of-jail pass. Share how you feel - openly, honestly, and without self-judgment. *Do your best to not censor your words.* This means including *any* words that feel inappropriate, mean, selfish, etc. *Giving yourself the time, space, and permission to express all, no matter how silly, irrational, or angry it sounds to you, is vital to this part of your soul-discovery.*

Remember, this is meant only for your eyes. **Journey II** provides the opportunity to destroy your letter should you desire to do so. Remember to stay present with your inner climate. Use music, photos, videos, movies, old cards, etc. to help you connect with all your emotions for the person to whom you are writing and your relationship with them, whether it was in the past or is happening now.

Great job! This is tough work, so give yourself a big hug. Move on to **Journey II** to complete the process.

Journey II: Cleanse

Now is the opportunity to release the energy from your unsent letter.

Pay attention to what feels helpful to you by using the steps from **Shedding Perceived Failures** in **Volume IV** to finish the process of letting go.

Reflect and journal on your whole experience.

When finished, cleanse your living space using the steps in the chapter **Wynebgwrthucher** in **Volume III** to remove any remaining heavy energies. Take a bath or shower to complete the cleansing process.

Be sure to do something nice for yourself to acknowledge your courage and honesty. Great job!

Journey III:
Time Heals

Give yourself two weeks or more to allow your experience with **Journeys I** and **II** to integrate.

As you are ready, spend time in your sacred space to journal any reflections on how you feel now.

Did your heavy emotions toward the person or any situation with them diminish? Do you feel lighter, less burdened by your inner climate?

Knowing this process may be repeated to continue to express and to let go of old hurts, consider writing another letter to the same person to explore deeper layers, or to another person on your list. Do you feel one surfacing?

🐞

What reflections do you have on your part in the interaction with the person in your letter? What behaviors and/or attitudes could this relationship be calling you to change?

Visiting Never Land

The secret of genius is to carry the spirit of the child into old age, which means never losing your enthusiasm.
— *Aldous Huxley*

Armed with crayons and magic white sheets, I watched my children scribble to their heart's content as creative, growing beings. We made yogurt into paint, mixed homemade playdough (which the youngest happily ate, too), created rice trays, built with blocks, Legos, trains, and Tinker Toys. My boys could explore for hours, freely, messily, and happily. Though I imagine I might incur their wrath for sharing this, I still smile at memories of our oldest proudly marching out of the bathroom, hat on head and spoon in hand. This two-year-old "cook" made "soup" in the toilet, luckily free from any unsavory additions. Phew! The youngest, imbued with his own flair for adventure, discovered a personal mini, porcelain, hot tub (minus the hot, of course); I found him grinning ear-to-ear and fully immersed, arms resting on the toilet seat taking a good soak. All the while I giggled, still thanking the powers that be for the absence of poop or pee in the mix!

Regardless of the many ways we express, creative energies are an integral part of our being, inspired by the Universe as our Divine Nature, as we've discussed before. Filled with the breath of Life as inspiration, Spirit is the very source of our creative flow. As children, we organically embody creativity, expressed through play, art, music, and crafts. Left to our own devices, we will use just about any medium allowed - hence the fascination with a box over the toy that came in it because of its limitless possibilities, painting with jelly, or staging grand scenes of imaginary creatures with fantastical, magical abilities. Not until the adult world sets regulations and issues assessments does our expression become dampened.

We all navigate our childhood the best we can with our developmental triumphs and struggles, growing on many levels. Remember, however, that parts of us stay stuck in the past, too. Recall from **Meeting Peter Pan**, when we (as adults) create, play, use humor, and remain curious, imaginative, and loving, our Natural Child speaks through us as innate joy and creativity. On the other hand, if we're anxious, whiny, or defensive, our Adaptive Child demonstrates the threat, burden, or lack of love we feel. As old energy remains stagnant, our own personal Peter Pan who "won't grow up" reminds us that he/she is alive and well, running the drama of our adult life and blocking our creative flow. (See **Meeting Peter Pan** and **Snow White and The Evil Queen**.)

When I started to do my own inner child work, a four-year-old self bounded out of the shadows. This tenacious but delicate blonde wisp loved animals, art, and nature. She was the little waif who built homes for the ants out of leaves and sticks, carried wooly bear caterpillars through forest hikes on sweater-clad arms, and drew and painted for hours; she loved cats, dogs, and bunnies but mostly fantasized about raising a whole village of mice (not allowed, of course). One day in a meditation, she arrived angry and mistrustful, immediately letting me know how I long ignored her. Over time, I learned to listen to her needs, to protect her by honoring myself in the now, and to become the nurturing parent that she desperately needed during her childhood. We became reconnected through drawing, writing, and meditation, and frequently through non-dominant hand work.

Non-dominant handwriting is a powerful tool that reveals our subconscious energies by tapping into our inner child state. Whether we are right-handed, left-handed, or ambidextrous, one hand always serves as the developed and "grown-up" writing tool (or adult/parent state). Our non-dominant hand, with its generally primitive writing abilities, accesses our inner child and all the qualities that lie therein. Alternating our dominant hand with our non-dominant hand (used in the journeys to follow) allows a dialogue between current adult states and our hidden inner child. What surfaces may seem like a long-forgotten dream that gives rise to a wealth of information. In the dynamic exchange, youthful treasures, early joys, and favorite pastimes surface along with old resentments, hurts, attitudes, and hidden beliefs. All step out of the shadows through a neurological integration as past and present meet on our journaling page.

What becomes evident through our non-dominant handwriting journey is the power of our inner child. He/she can orchestrate our attitudes and reactions like a hidden puppet master, illuminating the experiences of our adult life that we can't seem to navigate well. When we find ourselves lacking maturity, creativity, motivation, responsibility, playfulness, or well-grounded thinking proportionate to each situation and in balance with life, the influence of our inner child becomes apparent as he/she feels threatened by a danger from times forgotten but not resolved.

By now you have experienced the healing power of handwriting through the many journeys within these pages, discovering the ways it gives a home to everything swimming internally. Observing our experiences and digesting them on paper, we also make associations, connections, and gain understanding that often escape us when we stay in our head alone. Sometimes it is this very paper "home" and witness to our inner climate that gives rise to the transformation we seek. The map of our inner being laid bare in the light results in knowledge, insight, and acceptance.

Here is a deeper journey into Never Never Land.

Below is a brief meditation to connect with your personal Peter or Patricia Pan. Depending on your childhood, you may find more than one inner child delineated by age. One, for example, may be five and another may be eight; often they may come forward one at a time with lessons most relevant in the moment. They may also present themselves like siblings, helping each other as they connect and work with you in your adult/parent state. Know that whomever comes forth to feel your love and attention is assisting you in your healing. Trust that you are moving forward in perfect order toward embracing wholeness.

Note: For ease of reference, the inner child spoken about in any journeys of this chapter are addressed by *they* or *them* to encompass all gender references.

Journey I: Flying to Never Land

 Review the instructions in the following paragraph before proceeding to ground the imagery for your journeys. Use the QR code for a recording of this meditation or find a trusted friend to read it to you as you journey.

Begin with a writing tool/pen/marker in each hand. When you start the journey on paper, you will use your dominant hand to write from your adult self (the you now) and your non-dominant hand to write from the inner child. For example, if you are right-handed, write from your age now with your right hand and use your left to write from your inner child. If you are ambidextrous, consider the hand you write with most often and use it for your adult state. Have your tools ready as you begin the meditation below:

> *Sitting in your quiet space, close your eyes and take a slow, deep breath to center yourself. Invite all your Divine helpers for support and guidance on this journey for your highest and best.*
>
> *In your mind go to a place you feel protected, relaxed, and at peace. Perhaps this is a room in your home, a favorite outside space, a vacation spot, or a place in your imagination. As you rest in this space, look all around to witness your surroundings. Just allow the image to form in your mind as if you are recalling a memory. Take another deep breath and relax into the safety of this space, knowing you are nurtured, loved, and well cared for here.*
>
> *Invite your inner child to visit with you. Ask them to come out to spend time with you so you might get to know them better. If your inner child is shy or*

nervous, let them know it's OK if they place themselves in a place where they feel safe. This may be under a blanket, behind a tree, or around the corner from you.

As you meet with your inner child, take a long look at them. Notice their clothing and their hair. Look at their face. What do you see or feel in their eyes? If they stay hidden, note what you feel from them.

Begin a conversation with your inner child. Consider how you would get to know a child you haven't seen or talked with for a long while. What could you ask them? From yourself now, with your dominant hand, write a question to your inner child. Some questions to consider include:

- How old are you?
- What do you like to do?
- What is your favorite food?
- Who do you like to play with?
- What makes you happy?
- If you could do anything, what would that be?

Now allow your inner child to answer with your non-dominant hand. Just relax and feel the answer come to you. No need to strive for or grab at an answer, especially answers you'd like to hear. Listen from your heart for your inner child's answer and write it with your non-dominant hand.

Ask as many questions as you are drawn to ask of your inner child, continuing in the same fashion. When you or your inner child wants to stop, thank them for the visit and their help. Assure them that you'd like to spend more time with them and learn all about them. Ask if they are willing to meet with you again.

As your inner child leaves, allow the scene to fade. Take a nice, deep breath and open your eyes when ready.

As you give your inner child the permission to answer without censoring, the process may feel awkward and unnatural. Stick with it as best as you can to include misspellings, messiness, and childlike writing.

Note: After some dialogue and practice with your inner child, you may discover that you can connect with them in your mind and speak with them in the same fashion, holding a conversation. Allow yourself to be guided as to what is most resonant in this manner.

Move on to **Journey II**.

Additional notes:

Journey II: Reflecting

Write about your experience with your inner child.

What did you learn about yourself?

How did you experience your inner child? How did you feel about the way they expressed themselves?

Did you notice any judgments of that expression? Did you feel nurturing or critical of them?

How did your inner child feel about you? About other adults?

What insights might you make from this journey?

Journey III: Exploring Feelings

 Herein lies another opportunity to connect with your inner child using non-dominant handwriting to explore feelings and emotions. Writing materials (paper and markers, pencil, or pen) required for this journey depend on what you and your inner child prefers. In other words, use what feels right. The QR code offers a recording of this meditation at www.pathways2innerpeace.com or find a trusted friend to read it to you.

Sitting in your quiet space, close your eyes and take a slow, deep breath to center yourself. Invite all your Divine helpers for support and guidance on this journey for your highest and best.

In your mind, go to a place you feel protected, relaxed, and at peace. Perhaps this is a room in your home, a favorite outside space, a vacation spot, or a place in your imagination. As you rest in this space, look all around to witness your surroundings. Just allow the image to form in your mind as if you are recalling a memory. Take another deep breath and relax into the safety of this space, knowing you are nurtured, loved, and well cared for here.

Ask your inner child to join you. Connect and inquire if you can spend some time together.

Using your dominant hand for your adult self (you now) and your non-dominant hand for your inner child, ask what name they prefer? What age are they?

Ask with your dominant hand how they feel today. If your child seems unsure, prompt them with the four general emotions - mad, sad, glad, scared. Let them write out the answer. Pay attention to whether you can feel what your inner child feels. What are you aware of?

Ask your inner child to draw a picture about their feelings. See your "now-self" as the new parent that loves, nurtures, guides, and accepts this little child fully, healing any unfulfilled and wounded parts of them.

Hold the space, allowing your inner child to feel hurts that they never expressed as a child because they felt unsafe, feared punishment, or loss of love. What hurts of your inner child felt brushed aside? Let your inner child draw/write all about these feelings and emotions, even if that's scribbling and cursing.

When your inner child is finished drawing/writing, ask if there is something that would help them feel better - a hug, a stuffed animal, a visit from a beloved pet, a soft blanket, a favorite toy, etc. In your mind's eye, offer it to them.

Now, thank your inner child for visiting with you, asking if they will come to talk with you again.

Allow the scene to fade. Take a nice deep breath and open your eyes when ready.

Journal about your experience with your inner child. Were you surprised to discover how they felt? How did it feel to help them express? To nurture and love them? How did they feel receiving your love and acceptance?

Additional notes:

Journey IV: Playdate

Take your inner child out into the world for some fun. Connect with them again, asking about what they would like to do. Consider the activities that children of their age enjoy, like drawing, painting, board games, outside escapades, sports, dolls, crafts, ice cream outings, candy store adventures, etc. Encourage your inner child to choose what feels good and enjoyable, supporting their choice. Do the activity in real time, staying connected with your inner child throughout.

When your adventure concludes, journal about your experience. Consider the following questions: Did your inner child have a difficult time choosing a toy or activity or were they free and carefree? How did your inner child feel about playing?

How could you allow your inner child to play now, as an adult, expressing through you? What activities would they choose to help you connect with them? To nurture them?

An Intimate Journey into Self

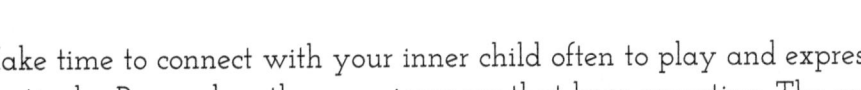

Make time to connect with your inner child often to play and express verbally and creatively. Remember, these are journeys that bear repeating. The more your nurture, pay attention to, and give voice to your inner child, the more you heal their old hurts and help them grow. As your inner child grows, so do you!

Snow White and the Evil Queen

The curious paradox is that when I accept myself just as I am, then I can change.

— Carl Rogers

A young expectant queen sits by the window of a drafty stone castle, sewing with an ebony embroidery frame as she looks out upon the iridescent winter landscape. She gazes into the distance while white flakes fall like fluffy wafers. The sharp needle she holds precariously in her hand pricks her finger. Three red pearls of blood fall beyond the window frame onto snowy crests, impelling her to wish that the child moving within her be born with snow white skin, rosy red cheeks like blood, and ebony hair and eyes matching her embroidery frame. Before long, a daughter is born with the endowments the queen wished for, but the young mother loses her life in childbirth, leaving the king a widow. A year later, the king marries again. His new queen, very beautiful but vain and proud, depends on a magic mirror to assure her of her superior appearance - superior until...

"Mirror, mirror, on the wall, who in this land is fairest of all?"

It answered:

"You, my queen, are fair; it is true. But Snow White is a thousand times fairer than you."

The queen took fright and turned yellow and green with envy. From that hour on whenever she looked at Snow White her heart turned over inside her body, so great was her hatred for the girl. The envy and pride grew ever greater, like a weed in her heart, until she had no peace day and night.

This famous tale by W. Grimm captures the essence of our inner critic in the tale of *Little Snow White*. Let's not, however, allow the obvious, racially-biased commentary on beauty cloud the significance of this passage. Leaving our focus there, the point of this chapter will be lost. The intent, instead, lies in recognizing how the vain, evil queen - consumed with jealousy and filled with disdain for her beautiful step-daughter - became intent on destroying her. Why? Because metaphorically, our own inner negative voice blames, chastises, shames, and guilts our beautiful inner child, seeking to destroy it, too. The same voice may even convince us that its disapproval serves our own good, eradicating what appears undesirable in us. All the while, our inner child's zest for life threatens the rigid ways of this unloving narrative known as our inner critic or evil queen (or king). Moreover, somewhere in the deep recesses of a subterranean mindscape, our critic (in alignment with our ego) suspects that our glorious Natural Child possesses something it doesn't - a direct line to the Universe. This is quite true, which makes our inner child even more threatening.

Criticism - the expression of disapproval of someone or something predicated on perceived faults or mistakes - tends to be part of human nature. It may surface as the little nagging voice in our mind or the terse words flung inward in frustration. Regardless of how it rears its ugly head, we learn criticism as part of our multi-faceted upbringing. Children, perpetually in a state of exploration and learning, need guidance and teaching. They scatter toys, play with food, create dirty diapers, draw on walls, spill milk, etc. Even though on some level we know the adventure of having children, as parents we often forget what it was like to be a child. Among the adult-labeled "messes" lie infectious curiosity, rich exploration with art, the awe of newly discovered nature, the deliciousness of snuggled pets and parents, as well as testing boundaries. Though well intended, parents fraught with exhaustion, frustration, or impatience demonstrate their challenges with childrearing in words, body language, and/or attitudes that negatively affect little hearts. Some parents and adults even direct their own self-judgment outwardly, overtly criticizing their offspring, which harms developing minds and leaves hurts that need healing.

Like many, my inner critic can spring to life in a flash. Some days she's dressed like a comedy club comedian, sarcastically commenting on some remarks she's deemed as inadequately censored. Other times she's poised as a hostile slave driver, mentally grinding away at "failed" tasks or "unsuccessful" endeavors. She was most alive during the throes of challenging relationships and immediately at their ends, berating me for tolerating other people's hostile and abusive behavior.

Our inner critic sometimes lurks in the dark shadows. Other nights it's smoking a cigarette under a nearby streetlamp, waiting to knock on our door when we feel most vulnerable. It carefully observes us until it judges our "failed attempts" worthy of intervening...the "mistakes" of not living up to the standards it set. Frequently, our inner critic conjures up qualities or behaviors deemed offensive, harshly chastising us for minor infractions, insignificant incidents, or less-than-perfect anything. Fortunately, at times this critic can help us move out of situations that don't serve us by drawing attention to our shadow self, but if not used as a learning tool, it can propel us into self-loathing, anxiety, and other unhealthy mindsets.

So how does our inner critic develop? In this lifetime, it becomes adopted like a wild pet from interactions with our parents, family, and other significant adults in our childhood. Our parents (when they are our primary caregivers) play the biggest role in the formation of our inner critic. Well-meaning yet influenced by their own struggles, all parents' present moment circumstances blend with their personal past. Their own unhealed and wounded inner children contaminate their parenting, perpetuating a legacy that may be generations long - one internalized inner critic built on another, over and over again back through the family tree. We, in turn, adopt their critical nature (Critical Parent) as our inner critic; their critical parenting operates inside our mind as we absorb them, unknowingly creating our very own version of the evil queen or king.

To deepen our exploration, we return for a moment to **Meeting Peter Pan**. Remember, our inner child expresses as both Natural and Adapted forms based on our own childhood experience. The Natural and Adapted Child together represent one of the three ego states (the Child, the Adult, and the Parent) that identify how we operate psychologically in our world. As a grown individual, our personality can be understood as the collective energy of these three states, but as a child (chronologically speaking), we begin our journey of forming the Child, Adult, and Parent by interacting with the Child, Adult, and Parent of each parent. Through our *perceptions* of these interactions, we form the belief system of our grown-up self - the very belief system that informs how we interact with our world, as well as ourselves. Exploring our Child, Adult, and Parent offers another layer of decoding our belief system that manifests through personality - trifecta of psychological ego states in action.

The table below outlines characteristics and behaviors/qualities of each ego state. While quite simplified, it extends a basic understanding of the aspects held within our personality as the Child (Natural and Adaptive), the Adult, and the Parent (Nurturing and Critical).

We may operate from any ego state, even fluctuating between more than one, too, situation by situation. Typically, our physical, mental, and emotional states combine with how our moment-by-moment experiences align with our past, coalescing into a consciousness that converges with a current ego state. For example, let's say our boss asks us to write a report. If this is something that we feel competent navigating, we may easily operate from our Adult and our Natural Child - a beautiful combination of rational, well-grounded, problem-solving creativity demonstrated via logical, organized qualities, and the appropriate doses of imaginative, energetic input. If, however, we feel insecure because a history of projects garnished perceived negative feedback from him/her operating as a Critical Parent, we may quickly revert to the Adapted Child - fearing judgment and humiliation, becoming anxious, moody, and defensive, and/or getting lost in our emotions enough to sabotage fulfilling the request or being able to complete it without significant stress.

	Nurturing Parent	Critical Parent	Adult	Natural Child	Adapted Child
Behaviors	Loving, encouraging, and comforting of others	Negative; harsh judgments of others	Rationally approaches life; well-grounded; able to solve problems and make choices	Expressive, creative, loves life	Fears being judged, punished, and/or humiliated
Characteristics	Affectionate Forgiving Gentle Kind Loving Tolerant Considerate	Bossy Nagging Opinionated Prejudiced Demanding Severe/Stern Forceful	Logical Capable Organized Fair Reasonable Neutral	Exploratory Playful Free Uninhibited Funny Imaginative Energetic	Anxious Awkward Defensive Apathetic Hurried Moody Whiny/Demanding

While it's easier to notice obvious and overt negativity throughout our growing years, unspoken and covert message become a potent, stealthy force in our life as well. All forms of criticism - censure, condemnation, denunciation, disapproval, fault-finding, disparagement, and attack - often contribute to feeling inadequate or even battered. Equally damaging, though less recognized, include the covert operations of the sneaky critic who consistently "shushes", redoes chores, uses "death stares", criticizes others openly, nags, and projects another's faults onto others. Additionally, while a critical environment may begin in formative years, every subsequent similar event and relationship feeds the monster created through early negative communications.

Knowing that a Critical Parent can lurk within all of us, how do we break its grasp and cycle of self-criticism? We must first become aware of our inner critic, the voice of our internalized Critical Parent. Non-judgmental witnessing, once again, offers a friendly hand; as we watch the details of our interactions, the silent or overt chiding of ourselves can come to awareness. We can even observe how we criticize others, judging them similarly to our fault-finding parent(s). The details of this internal dynamic then continue to surface as we watch personality traits and behaviors unfold. How we criticize, when and what circumstances draw our negative reactions, and the characteristics or behaviors that awaken our inner beast paint the picture for us to clearly see. Ultimately, our discoveries serve as opportunities to trace current happenings to their roots. As the messages from our early years become apparent through patient and dedicated observation, we can work with the beliefs about ourselves and walk through our accompanying emotions. Our criticisms then gradually transform through acceptance, tolerance, and compassion, as what we had rejected in ourselves or others finally finds a home, embraced in the moment. Through reflection and non-judgment, we explore what we so aggressively desire to discard, for *only what we accept*, even if temporarily, holds the potential for change. Awareness, acceptance, letting go, and forgiveness take back the power stolen by our inner critic to propel us upward on our path.

We now open the doors wide to our restrictive, perfectionistic prisons. As the "never satisfied" egoic chatter fades into the background, the voice of our True Nature is heard in the silence. Freedom comes as we accept ourselves as we are, clearing away the debris to awaken to our Self.

Let's let that evil queen pack her bags and move. It's time to shine your Light, Snow White.

Journey I: Reflections

Spend some time meditating in your sacred space.

Reflect on the chapter materials. Journal your thoughts and feelings about all you read.

How does this chapter relate to or add to other journeys or chapter materials?

Journal your reflections on the chapter table.

Can you identify characteristics of critical parenting in your mother/father from childhood interactions? What was that like for you?

What common criticisms enter your mind toward others? Yourself? Can you trace their origin to childhood through interactions or feelings of being criticized?

Journey II: Answering the Evil Queen

Gather writing materials for this journey (markers, colored pens or pencils).

Take a moment to sit quietly in your sacred space and center. Choose two writing tools that are different colors. Appoint one color to represent your inner critic (evil queen or king). The second color represents your inner child. Place the color for your inner critic in your dominant hand and place the color for your inner child in your non-dominant hand.

Spend a few moments considering a common self-directed criticism. As this comes to your mind, witness the criticism by writing it down with your dominant hand.

Now, feel your reaction to the criticism and respond to it with your non-dominant hand, allowing your inner child to speak up. If your inner child feels the need for more nurturing assistance, call in your Nurturing Parent to actively engage and protect. Consider how a loving, nurturing parent or friend would respond and use that connection to access the loving self-acceptance of your inner child. Continue with as many criticisms as you are drawn to address, using dominant/non-dominant handwriting. Let's silence the evil queen, calling on the power of your inner child and a loving force within.

Example:

    Evil Queen: *You're not very smart.*

    Child: THAT'S MEAN.

    Evil Queen: *Well, it's true.*

    Child: I DON'T LIKE YOU RIGHT NOW.

    Evil Queen: *Now who's mean?*

    Child: YOU MAKE ME SAD.

    Nurturing Parent: *Don't listen to her. I love you. You're brave and smart and creative.*

    Child: YES. I CAN DO IT.

NOTES:

Journey III: Reflections

Journal about **Journey II** and your experience with it while considering the following:

How did you feel when the criticism of your inner critic first arose? Do you notice these feelings or emotions registering in your body? Where?

Who made those criticisms in your past? Are there others in addition to you who make them now?

How did you feel when your inner child answered the criticisms in **Journey II**? How about now after the exercise? Could you access the strength, courage, and power of your inner child or the support of the Nurturing Parent in you to love your child now?

What tools from **Volume II** or **III** could you also employ to help you shed the grasp of your inner critic and support your inner child?

Remember to repeat this exercise as you are drawn. Our inner critic can possess a strong foothold that takes time to release, so be patient in supporting your inner child's growth.

Message in a Bottle

*Feelings of worth can flourish only in an atmosphere
where individual differences are appreciated, mistakes are tolerated,
communication is open, and rules are flexible —
the kind of atmosphere that is found in a nurturing family.*
— Virginia Satir

Floating in a subconscious fog of rules, images, and memories, the vaporous wisps that make up messages from childhood profoundly influence every level of our being. These messages are stealthfully hidden in thoughts, emotions, behaviors, and beliefs toward ourselves and others and become the internal MP3's (records or tapes for us old farts) we carry.

Most of us function quite unaware of the messages from our past and how they so heavily impact our perceptions in life. To complicate matters, many families communicate rules, mores, and ways of being in conflicting ways. For example, some parents and caregivers may clearly state their expectations but might behave contrary to the spoken messages. Others rarely issue clear rules, but their corresponding behavior remains subtly acted out. Some may even communicate one way to live life but openly support another. Whatever the case, we can learn much from examining the scripts of our past as we discover their broad and immense effect.

In previous chapters, we began to unravel these complicated communications from our early life, looking at the voice of our inner critic, the energy of our inner child, and the characteristics of ego states (Child, Adult, and Parent). Now, we are ready to dive into specific trends of our early interactions, the internalized messages of our youth.

Broadly speaking, communication with parents and caregivers can be categorized by two messages: the "do" messages or permissions, and the "don't" messages or introjects. Like all forms of communication, these operate overtly, subtly, or covertly, creating the living canvas of our lives; permissions and introjects help paint every attitude regarding ourselves, others, and our world.

This model for the messages in our life returns us, once again, to the work of Dr. Eric Berne (Transactional Analysis), who developed a way of looking at them through what he called drivers - the motivation for human behavior as primary compelling forces, especially dominating us when we are under stress. Through specific messages, drivers compel their "owner" toward actions or ways of being. More specifically, the table (shown on the following page) outlines the five most common drivers: **Hurry Up**, **Please Me**, **Try Hard**, **Be Strong**, and **Be Perfect**. It further characterizes each by the typical *Permissions* and *Introjects* (*Do's* and *Don'ts*), as well as summarizes their corresponding familiar *Strengths* and *Difficulties* that challenge us.

Let's take the **Please Me** driver, for example. We see from the table that this driver's *Do* messages or *Permissions* are be considerate, be kind, and be helpful. *Strengths* of those who operate with the **Please Me** driver include following rules, doing the right thing, and getting along with others. The *Don't* messages or *Introjects* for those with the **Please Me** driver include don't be important, assertive, different, or say "No". *Difficulties* of individuals operating under **Please Me** include the compulsion to be rescuers, as well as the struggle with indecisiveness, setting boundaries (or saying "No"), and putting others' needs over their own.

Many individuals operate under the influence of more than one driver, which may surface in various potencies and combinations. Most profoundly impactful and encompassing is the **Be Perfect** driver, which stands as the sum total of all others and primarily operates as the collective force of **Hurry Up**, **Be Strong**, **Try Hard**, and **Please Me**. Those with a **Be Perfect** driver must do everything without mistakes by whatever standards they absorbed and incorporated from environmental influences, especially those from parents and primary caregivers - to be fast, efficient, strong, hard-working, considerate, reliable, independent, compliant, happy...an exhausting combination.

Many years ago, when first examining these drivers with respect to my own little self, I immediately recognized the operation of Be Perfect. The influence of this message reached into and influenced how I felt about appearances, behavior, career, parenting, housekeeping, grades, art, music …every corner of my life became shadowed by working hard to meet some "never good enough" dictate. The only way I could give myself any room to not be perfect came through a lack of interest. If my curiosity in a subject/activity waned or was absent, the subsequent pressure to perform crumbled. That's not to say that I still totally avoided the "should have" traps like "I should like this better" or "I should do better at this anyway"; I just didn't have the motivation to push myself. On the other hand, if a deep and abiding curiosity to pursue something surfaced, perfection always met me with whip in hand. My own soul-discovery helped me slowly release this damaging driver, so I could drop my membership to Perfectionists Anonymous. However, on the days some remnant crawls out of the shadows, I now have the tools to dissolve its influence with confidence and courage.

Examination of messages and drivers behind the scenes of our day-to-day experiences illuminates many of the subconscious forces that cause us to create our life events. The extensive nature of Transactional Analysis reaches well beyond the scope of this series; however, we continue to gather other valuable tools for soul-discovery by exploring the operation of drivers in our life to make the messages that compel us more conscious. Because all that remains subconscious and hidden keeps us stuck in old patterns at the mercy of these inner MP3's, we instead expose, witness, and survey their impact on our life. The courage to look and really explore opens the doors to freedom — the freedom to be ourselves with grace, authenticity, and love.

We bravely stand on the shores of a new consciousness to discover all the messages in our bottle - the bottle of our shadow self. Take a deep breath, as one washes up before you. Uncork the glass harbinger and read the yellowed, damp paper in the light of day. The opportunity to observe and dissolve its messages is at hand. Unlearning what it taught us, we gradually move beyond its influence and grow.

Understanding Drivers*

	Do's or Permissions	Don'ts or Introjects	Strengths	Difficulties
Hurry Up	Be faster Be efficient Be responsive	Don't take too long Don't relax Don't waste time	Enthusiastic Energetic	Misses important details Can't sit still Gets burned out
Please Me	Be considerate Be kind Be helpful Be whatever I ask	Don't be assertive Don't be important Don't be different Don't say "no"	Rule-oriented Cooperative	Rescues others Indecisive Can't say "no" Puts others first
Try Hard	Be persistent Be committed	Don't be satisfied Don't relax Don't give up Don't goof off	Self-motivated Likes to start projects	Overvalues effort Gets lost in details Makes tasks difficult
Be Strong	Be reliable Be courageous Be happy	Don't feel Don't show feelings Don't give in Don't ask for help	Self-sufficient Helpful/reliable Good in a crisis	Avoids feelings Stifles self-expression Avoids being vulnerable
Be Perfect	Be accurate Be independent Be successful	Don't make mistakes Don't play Don't be natural Don't take risks	Detail-oriented Achievers Ethically driven	Picky and precise Doesn't feel finished Doesn't feel satisfied

* Table information compiled using information from authors D. Cuicur and A. F. Pirvit,[33] along with the work of Dr. Eric Berne.[34]

---

[33] Ciucur, D. and Pirvut, A. F. (2012). The "Big Five" Personality Factors and the working styles. In Mihai Anitei, Mihaela Chraif, Cristian Vasile (Eds.), *Procedia - Social and Behavioral Sciences* (pp. 662-666). Amsterdam, Netherlands: Elsevier B.V

[34] Berne, Eric (1964). *Games People Play - The Basic Hand Book of Transactional Analysis.* New York: Ballantine Books.

Journey I: Message Survey

Set aside quiet time in your sacred space, centering and meditating. Ask for guidance from your helpers to reveal the messages that would best help you toward understanding and growth.

Refer to the **Understanding Drivers** table, familiarizing yourself with all the do's, don'ts, strengths, and difficulties. Using the information, highlight or underline which messages you received from in childhood and adolescence.

Now list them here and write out the unique way they were delivered to you. Keep in mind, these messages came directly or indirectly, acted out or spoken.

Next to each message, identify who gave it, who reinforced it, and how. Make special note of mixed or confusing messages.

Journey II:
Then and Now

Return to your quiet space, giving yourself time to center. Ask for guidance from your helpers to reveal how messages from childhood and the driver behaviors operate currently in your life. Stay present to and allow memories, impressions, thoughts, and emotions to unfold over the next week. Remember that your intentions and requests set the energy of discovery into action.

Journal about driver behaviors and the messages still in operation. What situations, events, or relationships tend to trigger your identified drivers to surface?

How do you feel about what you discovered?

Journey III: Dissolving Message

Set aside quiet time in your sacred space, centering meditating. Ask for guidance from your helpers to aid and support your transformation of limiting messages.

Return to your list in **Journey I**. Next to each message, rate the strength of it on a 1 - 10 scale, with 10 being the strongest.

Choose one message from your list to transform, considering one that's less intense. What tools from previous chapters and volumes would help to unlearn and/or dissolve the message? Remember, even catching the message in action provides immediate assistance toward growth.

List the tools you want to employ and put them into action as you are drawn. Journal your progress.

After a period (months), note the intensity of the message. Did it lessen? In what way have you witnessed your drivers and their messages becoming less influential?

Journey IV:
Breaking the Cycle

Set aside quiet time in your sacred space, centering and meditating. Ask for guidance from your helpers to aid and support your transformation of limiting messages by breaking the cycle it travels.

Choose one message from your list in **Journey III**. Identify the patterns of thinking, feeling, and behaving that happen when your inner message and its driver becomes activated.

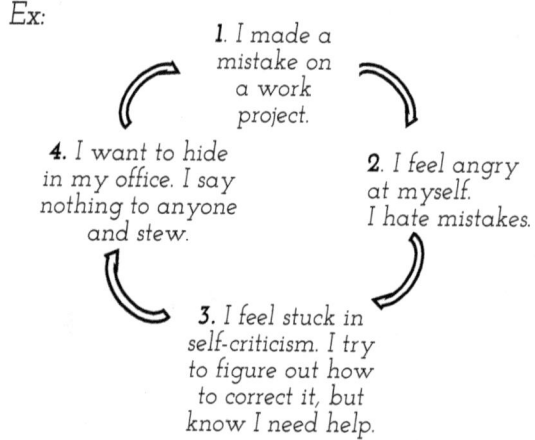

We can see from the cycle above, nothing gets resolved, returning to where the problem started to remain stuck with the Be Perfect driver in operation. Now that you identified your cycle, choose to break it by doing something differently - changing your self-talk, taking a new course of action, etc. It doesn't matter where in the cycle you choose to break it; that's up to you. Journal your experiences and progress.

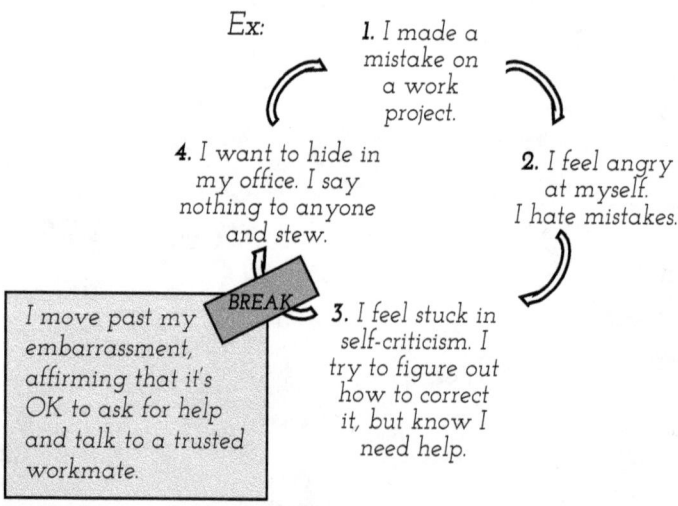

Notes:

The Merry-go-round

No longer riding on the merry-go-round, I just had to let it go.
— John Lennon

The person we believe ourselves to be appears as a complicated combination of behaviors, emotions, thoughts, and matter. The intricate yet illusionary manifestation of form is but a shadow to our True Nature, but one we deeply believe in when our physical form and personality become the "I" we think of as our Self.

One way to embrace our True Nature calls us to dissolve those challenging aspects of our personality, particularly the ones which no longer serve us. (By now, you recognize this as soul-discovery in action.) Remember, these personality traps create entanglements in our soul and draw similar energies to us. As a result, they create patterns of circumstances, events, or relationships that go "around and around" within a lifetime or across many. This merry-go-round, in psychological terms, is called the *repetition compulsion*.

The repetition compulsion describes our attempt to heal past hurts by "re-creating" them through our subconscious desire to master relationships - a grand theatrical production of repeating situations and events. As part of this process, we find ourselves time and again interacting with people whose personality traits possess an uncanny resemblance to each other in order to replay the same themes of old traumas or pain. In other words, we magnetically draw those who reenact transgressions and drama from our past because they have beliefs and thus behaviors of the characters in our early life - those who carried out the trauma or damaging interactions in the first place.

With each subsequent relationship (or repeating challenge, as it is typically seen), we attempt to "do it differently" through our conscious thinking and decision making. However, we continue to live out the past in our present, bringing the past's influences into our current relationships through subconscious forces, and create a merry-go-round that we can't seem to step off of. Repeating identical patterns through the underlying beliefs that sustain them generates the same problematic relationships. And the merry-go-round continues to spin because each player we feel drawn to becomes a "new" replacement for the original ones. In other words, we use the same learned behaviors created by old beliefs to solve or overcome the same problem or challenge, simply with different players.

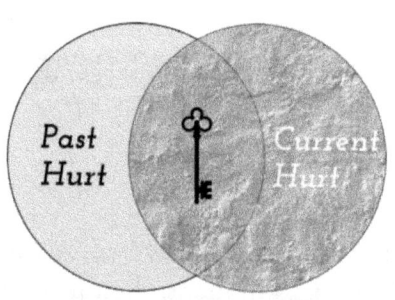

The diagram to the right demonstrates one way to look more simply at this complex dynamic. (That is not to say that simple means easy to unravel.) To all of us, current events may seem different and isolated from those in the past, but as we look closely, they divulge their connection. And while the details of each event or scenario vary, the underlying mystery theme serves as a key to resolution. Here current (Current Hurt) and past (Past Hurt) share common ground, an intersecting component that illuminates the belief system (key ⚷ belief) from the past still operating in the present. Take any current, emotionally-laden situation or relationship, strip away all the extraneous pieces, and look at the dominant patterns. What remains is a belief about ourselves from childhood (and often past lifetimes, too) but very active in the now, repeating to demonstrate unlearned lessons or to reveal progressively deeper layers of what we desire to change.

I, too, spent time at the relationship fair, riding the proverbial merry-go-round. The start of this dizzying ride began, at least in this lifetime, with my mother's first husband, known to others as my biological father. (See **The Final Frontier** in **Volume IV**.) This hurting soul suffered with an addiction to alcohol and behaved very abusively. A handful of memories from my childhood involved domestic violence - fear and danger. I was barely three years old when he and my mother divorced, but the lasting impact on my life simmered potently under the surface. My awareness of his negative effect remained hidden like a black hole in my memory bank. When I finally recalled (along with much help from my Divine helpers and Higher Self) and felt the knot he helped ingrain in my soul memory, I could see how an internalized pattern of subconscious choosing magnetically drew men that repeated the same personality patterns that mirrored my past images of him. Not only did stepping off this merry-go-round take some time because of the depth and breadth of these early experiences, but the dizzying aftermath of repeating relationship dynamics created the need for much healing, a journey of psycho-spiritual, soul-discovery work.

Within this chapter lies another opportunity, exploring the maddening orbit of old patterns to facilitate our step forward - the movement to get off the merry-go-round. We certainly can't stop the world from spinning, but we can learn how to create a ride that doesn't make our life speed by in one big, confusing, distressing blur. And while each person's journey may be filled with bumps along the way, the adventure is always worth it. After all, something valuable lies at the core - learning as we grow in awareness and letting go of the past to "see" from a higher perspective, creating a bright future filled with love, forgiveness, and many, many gifts.

**Journey I:
Watching the
World-go-round**

Spend some time centering and meditating in your sanctuary.

Reflect on the chapter material. Journal your thoughts and feelings about what you read.

Do you have any new understanding of how the world works or of situations in your life?

Journey II: Merry-go-round

Give yourself some quiet time to relax and center. Ask for your Divine helpers to provide the guidance and memory necessary to uncover what is for your highest and best - *only what is necessary for you to invite forgiveness and accept the gifts of your lessons.*

Allow the memory of events in your life that fit into a recurring pattern come to mind. These are the situations that make us ask, "Why do I keep doing that or why does that keep happening?"

Write about recurring events, situations, or patterns of relationships. Several previous chapters may assist your reflections and insight.

Be sure to journal the reactions to people and all the emotions/thoughts about yourself and others associated with your memories. Also, consider what emotions and thoughts are hiding under the initial reaction. *Ex: I'm so mad! On a deeper level, I feel hurt and sad about how she treats me.*

Journey III:
Retracing Steps

Re-center yourself in your quiet space, asking again for guidance and assistance from your Divine helpers.

Allow your thoughts and memories to surface about childhood. Use any props that may assist your journey - photos, music, old family movies, books, videos, etc.

What events, situations, or interactions from childhood demonstrated these same emotions, beliefs, and/or thoughts you wrote about in **Journey II**?

Consider your early years, especially ages 3-7, but don't ignore any time throughout your young life up to age 18.

Write about whatever you uncover and the connections and responses to what this journey reveals.

Journey IV: Uncovering the Key

In this journey, we look at the past and the present visually. The diagram on the following page assists your journey.

In the **Present** circle, write short descriptions of situations and events from **Journey II: Merry-go-round,** noting important points or trends in what you examined. Now in the **Past** circle, do the same, noting what you uncovered in **Journey III: Retracing Steps**.

Move to the ⚷ area where the circles intersect, connecting the past to the present. Journal the similarities of the past and present, the key to understanding your merry-go-round. Journal about how these two seemingly different scenes have distinct similarities, though the people or details may differ. The following questions may aid your discovery:

- What are the characteristics of the people involved in both the past and the present?
- What feelings, thoughts, or behaviors do I experience in relationship to those involved in the past and present?
- Are there similar patterns across the events I listed, like an overall theme?
- Do I see trends of abandonment, betrayal, neglect, or mistreatment?
- Do I feel misunderstood, invisible, unheard, unsafe, entitled, or demanding?

Journal your feelings about the discoveries of past and future joined through exploration of the key ⚷. What have you learned about your personal merry-go-round's key to stepping off old cycles and moving into healing, even if it's a deeper layer of the same lesson?

What beliefs about yourself emerged from your insights about all you uncovered in this chapter and the journeys? What negative beliefs, thoughts, or emotions replayed throughout the situations journaled about in **Journeys II** and **III** that require your active release?

What tools have you learned that can help you move forward to break the pattern and embrace yourself in love?

Journal about the tools you choose to employ and how they are facilitating growth. Be sure to note your progress along the way.

The Soul-Discovery Journalbook

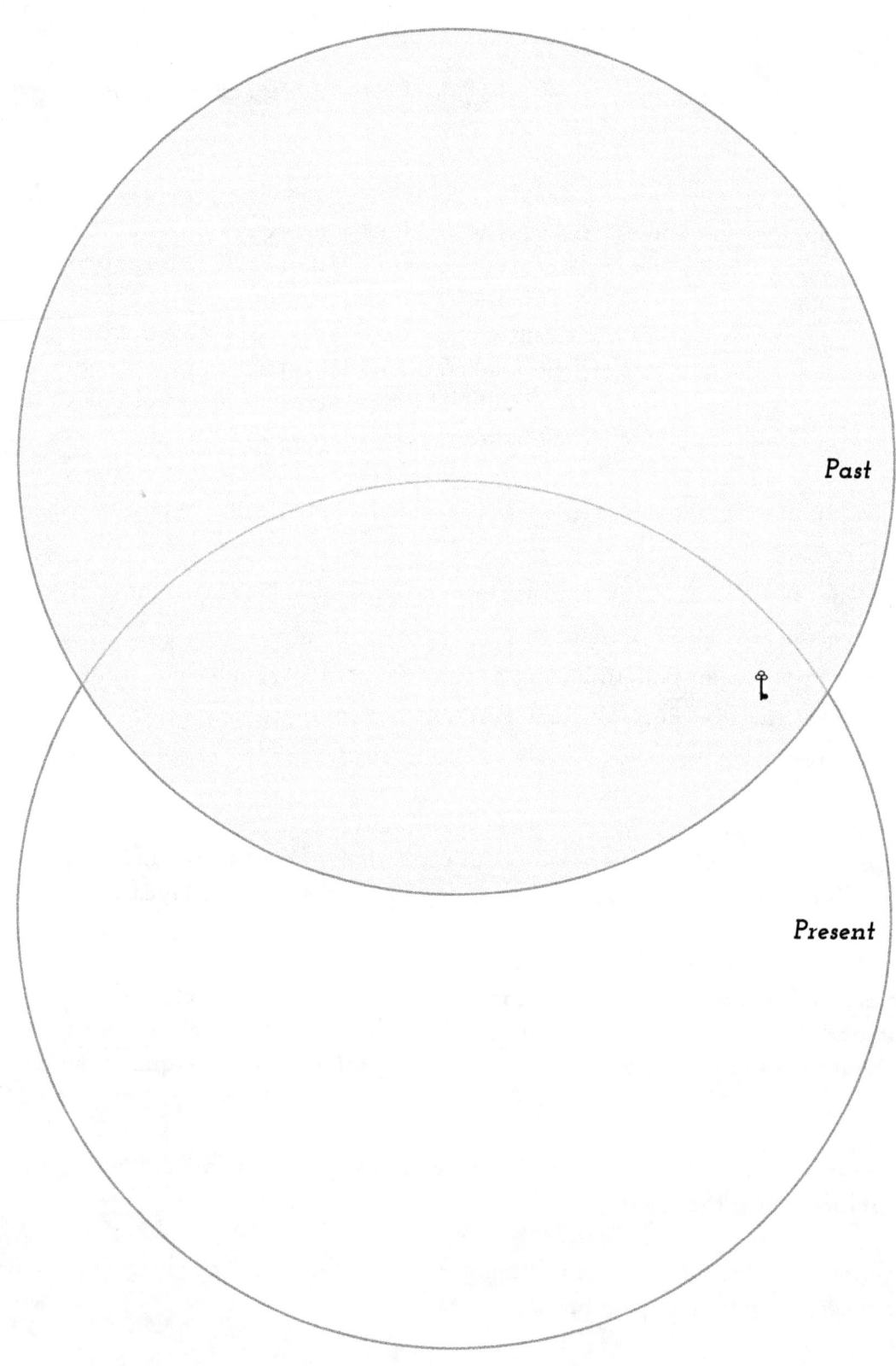

Past

Present

Notes:

Leaving Our Swamp of Judgment

*The self-righteous scream judgments against others
to hide the noise of skeletons dancing in their own closets.*
— *John Mark Green*

Under the very energy of our moment-by-moment decisions and interactions with our world lies the labeling of all things. We've explored labeling before and its prominence in this three-dimensional plane by looking at ways our daily living revolves around identification. On another level, this process is intimately woven with an adopted measuring stick used to evaluate everything and everyone around us in judgment.

Through judgment, the elevation of opinions to a factual status, we often decide what is right or wrong and good or bad about our world, innately comparing, contrasting, competing, and choosing how we see anyone and anything. Based on beliefs predicated on a conscious or subconscious sense of danger and/or fear, judgment frequently becomes a way of navigating life that makes us seem safe from others and our own rejected shadow side. Unfortunately, it instead separates us from one another, from the aspects we want to hide (remember, what we resist persists), and ultimately from our awareness of Source.

Because judgment is a tricky favorite of our ego, uncovering how we practice it toward others and ourselves can feel a bit slippery. Sometimes our ego convinces us that the casual labels of "good" and "bad" are innocuous because they really make us feel more secure in our own skin and environment. On other occasions it might aggressively reject qualities, traits, or various groups because they fall against our homegrown rules and social lines. Our slick ego, the little viper who so coyly whispers in our ear, can even justify the insults against those who seem to call us to condemnation by breaking social mores, committing egregious crimes, etc. This is the voice that might lull us into a sense of complacency with the ways we treat or think of our brothers and sisters, especially those who we feel should do better (again activating the voice of our inner critic).

However judgment surfaces in our life, paying attention can reveal obvious prejudices, misogyny, gender bias, or jibs and jabs as the more easily detected slights that separate us; less obvious, though, are self-condemnation, comparisons, or lack of self-compassion - the muddy footprints left behind by self-judgment. When the comparisons with others that make us feel entitled, inflated, or better than escape our attention, hopefully the ones that elicit a sense of lesser than or unworthiness rise into our consciousness and we can begin to see the damage of ego's games.

Exploring the covert games of judgment, we find the real source of our unloving attitudes, a cloak created by ego to hide negativity turned inward. Following the psycho-spiritual premise that judgment against others mirrors our own discarded, shadowy self, we find a hidden cause. In other words, what we see in others that generates feelings of contempt, disgust, irritation, and/or any other negative reaction shows us what we don't accept in ourselves as mirroring or the mirror of judgment. This looking-glass, regardless of the discomfort it breeds, becomes a valuable soul-discovery tool that helps us look more deeply into how we evaluate others so we can leave the swamp behind.

When our disowned, negative side surfaces in the mildly less-than-desirable, we might embrace the concept of mirroring more easily, but when others behave in extreme and highly distressing ways, mirroring feels like a stretch. Let's look, for example, at the judgments we hold against those who hit or beat others, a challenging scenario to consider. Imagine, for a moment, reading one of the many accounts of abuse or violence we so often see in the news. No doubt, each reader is affected based on their personal past. For argument's sake, however, let's assume we experience a contemptuous and strongly visceral reaction filled with various emotions including hate and a desire to punish. Applying the mirror of judgment, we, of course, look within. Some might say, "How could this be about me? I don't hit or beat anybody; I never did." Yes, that may be true. If, however, we explore this metaphorically, a deeper look may uncover our mental and emotional flogging about a mistake or the beating we give ourselves with criticism when tasks are incomplete. So, judging those who behave violently toward others can be a perfect mirror to our own inner critic who never gives us a break, driving us onward until we are sufficiently bruised and feel beaten. We must simply remember that to unearth our own mirrors of judgment, the behavior in others need not be an exact representation of our own; the symbolism, which can sometimes can be tricky to uncover, suffices.

Let's not, though, mistake any such exploration as an acceptance of violence, harm, or injury done to another. What we gain in understanding doesn't disregard consequences on the physical plane or the karmic threads created or played out, nor does it mean that we must condone or like the actions of another. Instead, we can lift our perceptions out of and past the literal, physical presentation of violence and into a higher vibration. Recognizing any negativity, threat, or harm as an expression of fear, we can "see" it as a lack of love. Hurting another, regardless of its intensity, appearance, or form, occurs because the person behind the act lacks the self-love to treat others with respect, dignity, and care…a mirror to an attitude about themselves.

Knowing that all judgment is generated internally, why then can we so easily get pulled to harshly evaluate others or ourselves? Because the eyes of judgment look upon the world through the ego and cannot witness truth, they instead see physical reality. Damage, harm, injury, slights, suffering, pain…these are the visions of physical difficulties on our earth plane that trip the alarm bells of fear, the sirens of ego looking for a way to safety. That's not to say that situations and incidents are a figment of our imagination. Events happen and we must navigate the mire of what difficulty they create, offering opportunities for growth, healing, and a chance to employ all our tools.

Through our ego, we can only view the world through labels in alignment with the lower aspect of The Law of Polarity - the mindset of seeing the world as good or bad, right or wrong - drawing in the equal and opposite energy as part of a whole. Whatever we then label on one end or another of the spectrum still possesses the perfect opposite. In other words, we can't just identify a situation or person as "good", isolating it/them from all other aspects including what appears as an energetic counterpoint.

Truth realized, however, through the higher octaves of our loving consciousness goes beyond earth plane appearances and is irreconcilable with our ego's measuring stick. With our higher perception, vision through our Higher Self in accordance with Source, we can leave judgment behind to "see" past our ego-based personality labels. All judgment then becomes merely a choice - a choice that only we can change moment by moment. Ideally, we eventually learn to respond instead of react, removing ourselves from the knee-jerk jump to judgment. But in those times when reactions surface, we can use them to learn and grow - observing ourselves, recognizing what in us requires healing, releasing our negative attitudes, and forgiving. Remember, dropping judgments to practice non-judgment develops over time and naturally unfolds when we are grounded, centered, and loving. It, however, can become more challenging when we're emotional, tired, hurried, stressed, and in crisis; then we must be gentle and forgiving of ourselves while choosing again the voice of love and understanding over fear. Nevertheless, growing in non-judgment can be a big challenge to our personality's mindset; sometimes moving past it is simpler said than done.

Now, I can just about hear what you're thinking, "Well, there *are* bad situations and bad people." Remember, ego loves to use our physical world's reality to bring us in line with its thinking; however, this chapter is not advocating a naïve look at the world, putting our head in the sand to pretend that difficult situations don't exist or that feeling pain or loss isn't real. Discounting what's in front of us - physically, mentally, emotionally - is not the answer. So, whether we must navigate a distressing accident or the actions of others that bring us to dark places we'd rather not see, remembering that we came here for adventure and to learn, experience, and grow helps soothe us along the path. We can intentionally address our hurts and eventually reign in our ego without negative labels or self-criticism to come to understand that what lies before us is a valuable lesson. Step by step, we move from judgment to non-judgment, embracing love over fear along with two additional mutually complementary practices: common sense and discernment.

Common sense, an important companion to judgment, becomes essential in increasingly difficult situations, like interacting with challenging personalities or those who wear the ego trends of force or fear. Spiritual common sense asks us to remember that everyone arrives on the earth plane encased in personality and so we employ *all* our faculties as we go about our days. Walking in a part of town fraught with crime, for example, we use our innate wisdom and common sense to lead us in any number of ways, even if that means avoiding particular blocks. We *especially* hold the vision of everyone as a Child of God despite appearances, "seeing" with eyes beyond our ego. Love and innate wisdom - the eternal aspects of Self - complement and support one another as we allow guidance from within (combined with common sense) to steer our way.

Even as we interact with the most challenging of characters, through non-judgment we free ourselves from emotions and ego-mind. Raising our consciousness to move into loving perceptions brings us to our second companion of non-judgment - discernment. Beyond the siren call of ego and between our perceptions of non-judgment and the all-loving, all-knowing energy of Higher Self lies a passage of neutrality and wisdom - the energy of discernment. Through it, *we come to know* that negativity manifests from the ego-based personality and not from our true Self, so much so that we become devoid of labels and the lure of our ego. This is a practice that requires dedication and intention to stay outside the reach of judgment and unloving thoughts.

Discernment at times feels like a tricky tool, but once we experience it solidly, a data point for subsequent interactions emerges. This may be best explained by an example. One Sunday my husband and I were running our monthly spiritual group. A member, struggling with a word particularly triggering to them, reacted toward me in what would appear to onlookers as angry and attacking. Though I witnessed this someone speaking to me and appearing upset, I applied no labels to the interaction, nor did I experience a personal reaction with my ego chiming in. I felt calm, peaceful, and centered, answering as best I could to aid the person's understanding. It wasn't until that evening that I realized the potency of my discernment and alignment with Self. Reflecting, I found that any labeling of the person's reaction felt discordant. Devoid of emotions and filled a *feeling* of compassion, I saw beyond all judgments and labels, without any commentary or emotions fed by personality. This is true discernment in action.

Using discernment assures us that spiritual decisions for our highest and best not only involve us in situations but also remove us. Even when someone has ill intent or operates with negativity, our centeredness and higher vision guides us. For example, let's say we know someone who tends to operate manipulatively; they lie to get their way and tell damaging stories to get attention and seemingly cause harm. Perhaps we've even stepped away from this person in all our interactions because of what we've witnessed. Living from discernment, we see with clarity, compassion, and love how their personality operates, knowing that life always comes with consequences. They cannot escape spiritual law without taking responsibility, whether that's in this lifetime or one in the future. To employ our common sense, we may continue to keep a distance emotionally and/or physically; always we embrace our sacred safety. If, on the other hand, we feel angry, sad, or scared about encountering them and/or their behavior and are pulled into condemning (operating from our ego), then we use the opportunity to grow. Reflecting on how our inner child is affected, taking time to nurture, support, and soothe him/her, we live authentically with ourselves about how our inner child/we felt wounded. Or we sit with how our pride became bruised, which helps us take responsibility for our reactions to extricate ourselves from focusing on others negatively. Remembering that all events and circumstances come through us to teach and help us evolve on our path facilitates a deeper level of responsibility. Always, we bless them to their highest good, sending love and light or asking Source to do so for us.

Navigating our swamp of judgment often requires hip boots and waders. The mirror of judgment can be the most bug infested part, wading through those parts of us we love to hate and hate to love. And as we step out of our judgment into higher perception, use common sense, and employ discernment, we learn to leave behind and even avoid our own ego traps to come from a consciousness that approaches our Divinity. Aligning with the Truth of our being, greater vision guides us moment by moment to recognize any deed for what is - love or a call for love to embrace another past their fear. As always, how we live is our choice - through acceptance and the embodiment of love or by choosing again and again, learning and growing with each step.

Journey I: Reflections

Take some time to reflect on the chapter's information. Journal your thoughts and feelings about what you read.

Which parts were most difficult? Which challenged your ideas about judgment?

The Soul-Discovery Journalbook

Journey II: Our Mirror

Use the space below to examine your mirror of judgment. In the left column, create a list of all the qualities, behaviors, emotions, opinions, etc. that you don't like in others. Consider what you find bad, wrong, inappropriate, etc. On the right, examine what this mirrors in you, literally or metaphorically. When finished, journal your insights.

What I don't like about others	What this reflects in me

Notes:

Journey III: Releasing Judgments

Spend time in your sacred space meditating after asking your Divine helpers for assistance.

Create a contract with yourself to release your judgments. Write out the contract in detail, including how you will use tools learned in this chapter, as well as previous tools like observation, willingness, acceptance, inner child work, calling on the Holy Spirit, seeing with Higher Vision, and forgiveness.

Journal your progress as you grow in self-awareness and non-judgment.

Journey IV:
Leaving the Swamp

Spend time in your sacred space meditating.

What are your experiences with common sense and innate wisdom?

Can you identify any times when non-judgment allowed the energy of discernment to unfold?

Ask your Divine helpers for assistance to be made aware of situations that call for love and non-judgment. Put the tools of this chapter into practice (non-judgment, common sense, innate wisdom, and/or discernment) and use them to peacefully navigate a difficult situation. Journal your experience.

The Power of Belief

*Believe that life is worth living
and your belief will help create the fact.*
— *William James*

Belief is a word loaded with many associations. By common definition, belief is an acceptance that something is true or exists with or without evidence. Belief may be an opinion or a trust and confidence in someone or something. Often it reflects religious tenants, creed, or faith.

Spiritually speaking, belief is thought powered by emotion or feeling, a combination that matches the formation of intent, derived from the same potent duo. Our beliefs are created through our view of life, an out-picturing of all our collective experiences (predominantly from this lifetime but with many, many other lifetimes' influence) as well as the thoughts and feelings we have about them. Our intent then flows from our belief system, which is a collection of our beliefs, a kaleidoscope of deep and long-held thought-emotion energies about ourselves and our world. For this chapter, we work with belief on a spiritual level.

As stated in previous chapters, events, situations, and experiences occur to teach us lessons so we can remember who we are in Truth. Because our belief system molds and creates every situation we encounter, it holds valuable information to help us decode much about our world. Like a multi-colored, multi-layered, cartographic masterpiece, our belief system can identify what makes us tick.

Throughout this series, we looked at our beliefs as they manifested through our patterns, habits, messages, drama, and inner child work, to name a few. Here lies another facet of the diamond of soul-discovery and an opportunity to join with previous chapter explorations and journeys, gazing even more deeply through this psycho-spiritual lens. While the first glance at such an esoteric and often elusive collection of thought-emotion/feeling pairings appears complicated, we begin with our standard and frequently used tool - observation. Observing ourselves, witnessing moment by moment, we become aware of situations and our varied accompanying reactions to what seems outside of us. Then, we connect our outer world to our inner world, seeing that life doesn't happen *to* us but *through* us.

> As above, so below,
> as within, so without,
> as the universe, so the soul...
> — Hermes Trismegistus

The spiritual laws within this quote bring into focus how every situation holds something valuable to teach us about ourselves. And while this may sound crazy or ridiculous or illogical, my hope is that each reader will come to see this in action and reap the benefits of understanding it. The potency of transformation (and thus soul-discovery) rests in the treasure of coming to know our own power, remembering that Home lies within.

When we shift our ideas about life as an outside experience (us in the world) to an inside experience (the world in us), we cultivate the limitless potentiality of change and growth. Looking to our belief system helps us discover the magic it holds. Exploring metaphorically, we envision our life as a movie and our belief system as the film projector that filters and displays the world as we view it; how we see the movie completely depends upon the projector (our beliefs). Only then can we know that ALL things in our life are lived through us and that nothing truly exists outside our inner world except in appearance. The old adage that "bad things happen to good people" comes into sharper focus as a trick of the ego, an attempt to keep us from realizing our Divine power. What better way to block us from discovering our True Nature than for ego to trick us into denying that we have any say over the seemingly arbitrary events in our lives when at our core we are power, truth, peace, joy, and love.

Granted, we all think that pointing a finger at what exists outside us as a source of our discontent offers relief or happiness. At the risk of being redundant, spiritually speaking, *everything* stems from the beliefs we hold about ourselves and our world, gathered from this lifetime and past lives. When we can embrace this with understanding, the mysteries of our lives - of strange events, overpowering emotions without apparent cause, or what occurs as traumatic happenings - feel less mysterious, arbitrary, or unnecessary. And though I've said this before, I'll say it again…we can shift to looking at circumstances as the lessons we need to move forward and grow or contracts we created spiritually to help us evolve, or we can stay in the mindset that things just happen to us and we are powerless to change our life. If we're not in a place to accept the former because too many painful experiences still keep us weighed down in pain, then we must work with what's standing before us. In addition, avoiding our struggles and building a spiritual belief system on a faulty foundation creates spiritual bypass. Meeting ourselves in the now with authenticity helps us circumvent this by dismantling old beliefs before adopting new ones. In the same vein, our willingness to be with ourselves in the now and work through our challenges also facilitates our steady climb upward (which is inward) instead of jumping the rungs of our spiritual ladder. Eventually, soul-discovery helps us embrace our power and the gift of ALL situations, no matter their size, weight, appearance, or seeming significance.

Regardless of where our path leads us, the choice is always ours. Our Spirit offers experiences for our growth and we have free will to navigate them however we see fit. We can align with our Self and be in accordance with It or make choices in step with our ego. Nevertheless, our Spirit will use everything as an opportunity to help us move onward and upward. So, as we continue to evolve, challenging circumstances may still unfold in accordance with what we draw to us, because a deeper layer of healing requires our attention, or through an opportunity that asks us to put new tools into practice. The new vision of total responsibility in and for all our life and the subsequent shedding of beliefs that limit us propels us toward resolution, revealing the gift in all experiences. Then we gain proficiency by applying our spiritual tools and most especially by stepping beyond the influence of our ego. As a result, the glittering coin of our growth and transformation dances in the sunlight, a lighter soul with one less limiting belief.

By now you may be gathering the matches for a bonfire, feeling like this chapter hit a nerve. If **The Power of Belief** seems offensive, infuriating, saddening, or totally outrageous, I hold the hope that you'll return for another look in the future. Additionally, if current pain, trauma, abuse, or other life events weigh heavily on you, traveling through this chapter may need to wait until more healing occurs, perhaps even through therapy or counseling. I dare say that if anyone shared the material within this chapter with me at the beginning of my healing journey from abuse, I would have handed them their head on a plate.

If you're still reading, I imagine you're curious how this chapter will end. Maybe I've caught your attention and now you're thinking about your life. Perhaps you're still considering burning this book. It's safe to say that none of us really want to believe that everything is an out-picturing of our internal world. "Life is complicated enough!" we say. "You want me to believe that the nasty, hostile things Aunt Sally said last Christmas were because I created that?" Well, in so many words…yes. The concept, while simple in principle, can lack ease in application or navigation. Let me clarify.

Let's dive deeper into Aunt Sally and imagine a nasty Christmas tirade on someone or something in our life - boyfriend, husband, job, children, new hair, outfit, etc. Looking at how we "see" Aunt Sally, for example, may be part of the lesson. In other words, do we take what she or other people say personally, or after our initial reactions, can we look at them with compassion and realize they may be coming from a place of fear, sadness, or frustration - a consciousness that demonstrates *their* pain? The Aunt Sally's represent an opportunity to use our spiritual tools, which include non-judgment, discernment, and forgiveness. If, however, we find ourselves engaged in an ego reaction, then the situation has offered a different, valuable lesson, one that directs us to a belief system about ourselves of feeling unworthy, lesser than, attacked, unloved, judged, etc. as the cause. That is not to say we categorically must like how another behaves or that we condone it, but spiritually the Universe calls us to experience others beyond what their personality demonstrates. We navigate, not in a holier-than-though mindset, but in a loving, compassionate, and understanding way that still includes honesty, boundaries, and respect. In other words, seeing the bigger picture with Aunt Sally doesn't mean we feel bound to sugarcoat our words, ignore her, or even accept what she says. Then, what could we do?

We may walk away in recognition that what she said reflects her own mirror of judgment. We might tell her calmly and firmly that we don't like how she is talking to us. We could later write a letter to communicate our feelings and/or hold her in love and light (removing ourselves by depersonalizing the comments) because we know that she is unhappy or depressed. To witness her illusionary layer as a human being - personality driven and pained at that moment - and still care for ourselves by setting limits with her offers self-love as well as compassion. This is not to say that any reaction we may have is wrong, returning to the premise that every situation is a lesson. Any reaction grows ripe with opportunity for us to examine, explore, and release. These situations show us our inner world, though our ego loves to blame our outer world or counterattack to release our inner critic. The more we work with releasing the beliefs that created and feed our ego, the more empowered and freer we live. Let me offer a personal example.

For years, I spent my life immersed in a belief that said, "I am lesser than others." I felt trapped in an unhappy marriage and relationships with family fraught with conflict and abuse. I felt unloved, unprotected, and powerless. The deeper layers of my childhood, lurking below the surface, created one circumstance after another that left me feeling beaten down. That is…until I changed. The marriage had run its course. I felt uncomfortable setting boundaries with family and friends. I didn't value myself as a woman or mother. Improving my life seemed beyond my control. With time, the fog of my expectations cleared; I began to really see people with the personality trends they wore and stopped hoping for different behaviors. So, learning to accept others where they were, warts and all, helped me live in the present. At times I even chose to move on, knowing some relationships needed to end. As I gradually released the old messages from childhood, I began to truly value myself and take responsibility for my life on all levels. Steadily practicing self-acceptance, I learned to embrace all of me - the good, as well as what I thought was unlovable. Through therapy, psycho-spiritual studies, spiritual retreats, reflection, journaling, meditation, dedication and vigilance, I grew. And yes, I'm human and still find myself in challenging days, slip into judgment, get irritated, etc.… Now, I can think, *I know what to do with this. It has something to teach me.* Still, I remain on a life-long project of embracing Self, integrating the self of form with the highest, most loving Self of Divine Light.

While my journey illuminates some challenging belief systems, it's not beyond the range of transformation we all face. We are all called to shed the beliefs about ourselves and our world - the negative, prejudiced, rigid, unloving parts of our personality patterns that lock us away in a fortress of our own minds and hearts. Furthermore, let's not be fooled to think that walking away solves every situation. It certainly, however, can play a part in changes we may encounter. The decision about my marriage, though challenging, came with some of my most rewarding lessons, all possible because of my deep desire to grow. And while I'd like to report the process as painless, I can't. Nevertheless, it remains a priceless part of my journey.

Not all lessons are so involved and complicated, though they may tend to appear as such. Some will be much simpler, and our painful memory of them may gently fade like old ink on paper. Others will leave their impressions so deeply because they transform the very substance of our being and propel us forward in ways we couldn't imagine. All of them move us magnetically toward our true Self and the acceptance of our Oneness with all things, one baby step at a time.

To decode our operating beliefs, many chapters offer assistance - exploring the Drama Triangle (**Transforming Drama**), the messages we received as a child (**Message in a Bottle**), our inner child (**Meeting Peter Pan** and **Visiting Never Land**), and the operation of our inner critic (**Shedding Perceived Failures** and **Snow White and The Evil Queen**). Reviewing previous journeys for deeper meaning may also prove helpful.

To delve deeper, let's explore two dynamic (and often subconscious) beliefs that we all tend to hold. These can be more easily seen looking at the heart of the Drama Triangle:

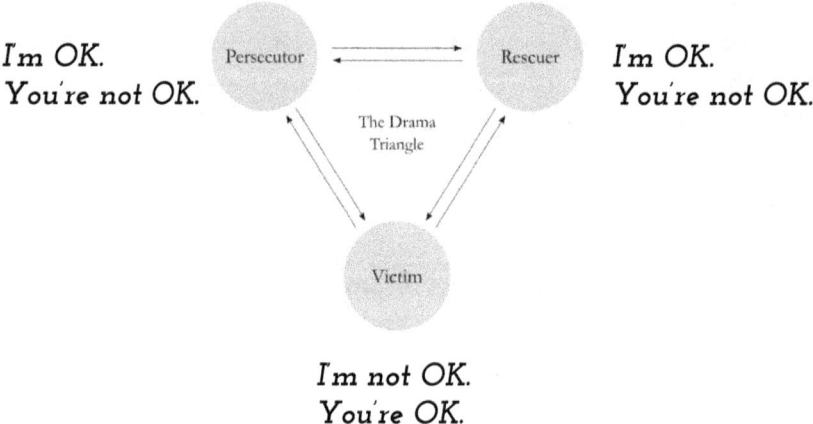

Recalling from our study of the Drama Triangle, all conflict or drama involves three roles, the Persecutor, the Rescuer, and the Victim. Each role operates from two primary beliefs regarding self and others identified in the statements next to each role in the above diagram. The Victim, for example, is seen as incapable, lacking intelligence or understanding, and needing parenting when viewed from the Rescuer position. On the other hand, from the Persecutor position, the Victim needs critical reprimand or punishment. We can see that the Persecutor and the Rescuer hold the beliefs of "***I'm OK. You're not OK***", which corresponds to their view of the Victim. When we take on either the Persecutor or Rescuer roles, we see ourselves as superior, more knowledgeable, and/or more competent or view others with criticism and/or lacking competency. From these roles compassion, love, and other's abilities to navigate life go missing from our mind.

On the other hand, when operating from the Victim, the "***I'm not OK. You're OK.***" mindset projects into the world as the belief in being flawed. This begets punishment from perceived wrongdoing or perpetuates an attitude of lack - lack of competency, strength, resources, or intelligence. As such, the core beliefs of the Victim draw Persecutors and Rescuers because the Victim views others in a superior light. Remember, however, in any one interaction between any of these players, oscillation between roles is common, so in any situation players can flip back and forth, demonstrating a myriad of attitudes all predicated on the subconscious belief of being or not being OK.

How do we move beyond the Victim, Persecutor, and Rescuer roles? Leaving these old characters behind means moving in all interactions to belief and practice of "***I'm OK. You're OK.***" - off the Drama Triangle. Thus, we relinquish our judgment and condemnation, attitudes of lack and lesser than, and our need to save people or punish them.[35] This is part of the very work of soul-discovery, the journey of growth for all travelers of these pages. This is the work you have been doing. By now, however, we can also see that the movement to feeling OK and seeing others as the same seems way simpler in theory, but not always as easy in our very humanness.

So now what? Reading this chapter may have already brought to mind many events, situation, or transitions - the big lessons experienced as life celebrations or life crises (marriage, childbirth, adoption, death, divorce, injury, sickness, etc.). Exploring the many layers of our consciousness, we can discover the operating beliefs that cause us to manifest both loving as well as challenging circumstances. Reflecting on life, we can also realize that the experiences around them mark change - the before, during, and after - growing through all that occurs.

We don't have to look very far to find opportunities for personal development, nor do they have to be major events. Day-to-day living shows us the way. All that's required is a willingness to listen, pay attention, feel our full range of feelings and emotions, and stay present. All the evidence we require is within us. All the power to change our lives rests there, too.

---

[35] The Official Site of the Karpman Drama Triangle (2005). The Karpman Drama Triangle family of sites. Retrieved March 18, 2015 from https://www.karpmandramatriangle.com

Journey I: Reflections

Spend some time in your sacred space reflecting on the chapter material.

What are your thoughts and feelings about all you read?

How does the mindset of "I'm OK. You're OK." feel to you? What impact do you imagine adopting this belief would have on your relationships?

Journey II: Lesson Review

After setting aside time to center and meditate in your sacred space, ask for help with this journey.

Allow life, in whatever way you experience it, to show you where to look. Everyday interactions, the ones that have occurred and the ones we imagine, hold everything needed to begin this process.

Take a situation, event, or recurring interaction. Write down everything you experienced from the details of the event to your thoughts and emotions about it and/or reactions.

Allow yourself to experience the emotions elicited by the event. What is the feeling under that surface reaction? Write about any fear, anger, guilt, sadness, etc. under your surface reaction.

Make note if this event occurred in real time or in your mind as an imagined argument, interaction, or situation.

Journey III: As Within

Journal about the following in relation to **Journey II**:

What is the dominant feeling? Dominant thought?

Taking the basic beliefs of the roles demonstrated in the Drama Triangle, which belief below feels most applicable to the situation you are examining? Why?

- I'm OK. You're not OK.
- I'm not OK. You're OK.

How can you link this with what you learned about childhood messages? Your inner child?

Does this illuminate a pattern your life - a pattern that is reflected in the situation/event you wrote about in **Journey II**? Write about the pattern.

Journey IV: So Without

Spend time centering in your sacred space. Ask for assistance from your Higher Self to gain clarity and understanding for this journey.

Reflect on "…as within, so without…" What are your thoughts and feelings about this spiritual premise?

Consider what you uncovered in **Journey III**. How might the pattern or your beliefs influence what situations you have currently or previously manifested?

Write about any insights.

Journey V: Releasing Outcomes

Spend time in your sacred space relaxing and centering. Take a challenging situation currently in your personal world and envision what you desire as the highest and best for everyone involved. Paint an image in your mind of what that situation would look like in that loving energy.

Now connect with each person in the situation one by one, heart to heart, and imagine them all wrapped in white, pink, and yellow light. (See **Wynebgwrthucher** in **Volume III**.) As you remain connected, feel the peace, joy, love, and understanding surrounding and permeating each individual including yourself. Keep a vision of all as competent, loving, and capable. Affirm an awareness of the Truth within each person. Ask your Divine helpers to cause you to be aware if some action on your part is necessary, intending to only be truly helpful for everyone's highest good. Pay attention to how you are guided.

If drawn, say a prayer to release any pain related to your involvement in the situation, placing the outcome in the hands of Source. For example,

Source of All Life within me,
I place into your hands this situation and those involved,
affirming the highest and best for all.
Thank you for holding us in Your perfect love, light, truth, and joy.
Indeed. And so, it is.

Write about your journey using this tool. Over time, pay attention to the energy of the situation and those involved. Every time your negative reactions about it or the people in it surface, return to the steps above and repeat, holding only loving, life-affirming thoughts and feelings.

What changes have come to your awareness as you've continued to practice this? How?

Notes:

Oh, Merciful Heart!

*Forgiveness is the fragrance that
the violet sheds on the heel that has crushed it.*
— *Mark Twain*

When we try to make sense of it all - our immediate world and the world at large - answers to our individual and unified purpose often appear elusive. The existential strife and striving to find meaning in our world can leave us feeling frustrated, lost, and defeated. As a result, we may turn from one source to another, searching for clarity and meaning.

While perhaps we assume that answers to such questions must be complicated and difficult, surprisingly, what we seek is generally simpler than we realize. Plainly put, our purpose here is to learn that we are Spirit, connected in perfect Oneness with each other through God/Source/Universal Power and to live in accordance with that truth. Remember, we are God. Not *THE* God but part of the vast cosmic web of life. Every living thing is an individualized aspect of Life, of Source/God, energetically joined through a giant network of invisible, vibrant, living strands. And while plants, animals, and minerals remember their true essence as Spirit, the vast majority of us as humans forget. So, we continue our journey to uncover the purpose of this grand adventure - to remember the way Home...*in and through us.*

How do we experience being God living in human form? Through love, of course... through the love that is the very fabric of our being, the creative energy of the Universe, the substance through which all things are birthed. Chapter by chapter, this series of soul-discovery encourages each reader to experience the many facets of love. Showing respect to our body, appreciation of our senses, care of our inner climate, practicing gratitude, allowing creativity, embracing the present, counting blessings in life, and recognizing beauty (to name a few) are all avenues of expressing, experiencing, and growing in love.

Perhaps the most challenging part on this soul-discovery came from looking anew at various and sundry life lessons. These are the situations and events that seem to shake the ground beneath us but are rife with profound, internal growth opportunities, especially learning to love ourselves. I know many of you must be thinking, "*How could I have explored love through those lessons - through the struggling, the difficulty? I find love through what's fun or interesting or enjoyable, but the rest…?*" Frankly, yes…through all of it - the lighter aspects that nurture and carry us, the meatier obstacles that require more effort and dedication, and finally the lessons that send us to the closet searching for hip boots and waders. All have a role in turning us toward love as we grow through life's dance of opposites - from impatience to patience, coldness to compassion, illusion to Truth, victimhood to power, fear to courage, attachment to letting go, and judgment to acceptance. In other words, through our experiences, we learn about life, evolving through the negative to find the positive. And over and over we arrive at the doors of our heart, throwing them wide open to embrace ourselves and others with the sweet arms of love.

What is the key to opening the heart's doors when the lock appears rusted with pain and misery? What makes love possible when anger is blocking the way? Forgiveness. Forgiveness is a healing balm - it soothes our fresh and raw wounds, softens the hardened scars of the past, and clears our path Home. We forgive others to release them and ourselves from the prison built by blame; we forgive ourselves and embrace our humanity, accepting that we did our best with what we knew at the time. Ultimately, we offer forgiveness to Source, which appears as an outside force that sent pain our way. Certainly, God/Universal Power/Source doesn't need forgiveness for something Him/Her/It would never do, but we may need to go through the process of forgiving God and then ourselves for tossing the responsibility There.

While human impatience strives toward immediate results, forgiveness is a process - one that we've explored through other chapters in earlier volumes. Through the triumphs and struggles, we forgive and extend love to others and ourselves. One step at a time, as we gradually let go of shock and denial and navigate through the hurt and anger, we begin to release our fear, attachments, judgments, and blame. Eventually, we forget the pain of the experience and the gift of the lesson emerges. There we rest in the knowingness that we learned something valuable.

Forgiveness is one true purpose of being here, a major highway Home as the Route 66 to remembering our Divinity. Forgiveness brings us to expressions of love as the signposts, the forks in the road, and the people we meet along the way until we see that everything outside us is merely a reflection of our own consciousness. We grow in compassion and understanding for others first, and then for ourselves. Believe it or not, these are the ways we practice being God. Every time we love someone despite their faults or have the courage to not be stopped by fear or offer compassion to ourselves when we make a mistake, this is the energy of God in us expressed.

So, let's be love, through forgiveness, traveling Home one step at a time. Journey with me into the heart where love abides.

Journey I: Forgiveness Survey

Join me for a review of people in your life who call for forgiveness:

1. Make a list of 3 or more people in your life who cause a negative reaction in you (disappointment, irritation, anger, sadness, etc.).

2. If you have difficulty identifying a person close to you as family, friends, or co-workers, consider minor negative reactions regarding unknown people in your life encountered in casual, day-to-day interactions.
   Ex: on the bus, driving about, in the grocery store, at work, or in your neighborhood.

3. For each person identified, list the qualities or behaviors they possess that you find most challenging. What do they do that elicits your negative reaction or attitude?

4. Reflect on what it would feel like to forgive each person on your list.

5. Can you step back and see the person with eyes of compassion?

6. Journal all your reflections.

Notes:

The Soul-Discovery Journalbook

Journey II: Forgiveness Meditation

 Below is a meditation for forgiveness. To listen to the recorded version, use the QR code that takes you to the Om page of www.pathways2innerpeace.com. If you don't have access to the internet, consider asking a trusted friend to read the following until you are able to walk through the process on your own.

Set aside at least thirty minutes in your sacred space. Shift your focus now inward. Begin by taking several cleansing deep breaths, centering yourself. As you sit quietly, just focus on your breath going in and out...in and out.

As you allow everything to drop away, you find yourself in an all-white space. Everything is bright and clean, light and buoyant. This is a peaceful, safe, healing space where you can relax. Take another deep breath, allowing your mind, emotions, and body to just be. As you rest in this space, a soft pink light comes down from above your head and surrounds your body. You can feel the energy of this light warming your heart, opening it gently like the sun encourages a flower to unfold its petals.

Set your intention for forgiveness and allow the space for this energy to align. No reaching is necessary. Know that this comes from your heart as you wait patiently in this sacred space of healing.

Now, in your mind's eye, a group of people enter your white space. The soft hum of their voices become louder and louder until they come into focus. All walk toward you; familiar faces emerge as friends, family, loved ones, acquaintances, and work mates. From the group, one steps forward, and you become immediately aware that they desire forgiveness and healing.

Ask the Holy Spirit to work through you to release any negative attitudes toward this person. Ask that the Holy Spirit helps you let go of this freely and replaces whatever is removed with love and forgiveness.

Now step closer to this person; your eyes meet. The soft pink light that fills this space swirls around you both, cradling, hugging, and soothing. Your heart feels open and you say to them:

*I want you to know how I feel about _____ (situation). I felt
_____ (emotion) when you _____ (action).
I release my feelings of _____.*

*I love you as one heart, one soul, one Spirit to another.
I am grateful for the lessons you agreed to bring me.
I accept the lessons and allow them to be my gift.
I forgive you and let you go in peace.
Thank you for meeting me and listening.*

The negativity, like a gray cloud swirling around you, dissolves, floating away from you both and upward into the white space. It fades until it is completely nothing. In its place a yellow radiance mixes in luminous ribbons with pink and white light, encircling both of you as it dances and weaves healing energy.

Allowing the feeling of openness and forgiveness to take root, offer a gesture of good will and love - a hug, handshake, or pat on the shoulder. Know this healing energy ripples out in ever-increasing circles and everyone receives its loving touch, reflecting the great Cosmic connection we share.

Wave goodbye to all the group as they turn to leave. Everyone fades into and becomes subsumed by the wispy white space; voices grow fainter and the outlines of shapes disappear. Take a nice deep breath to allow all the energy to settle into each cell of your being, retaining the feeling of peace, love, understanding, and forgiveness deep within.

Return your awareness to your physical surroundings, bringing the feelings of love and forgiveness with you. Open your eyes when ready.

Turn to **Journey III** to reflect on this meditation.

Journey III: Reflections

Journal your experience with **Journey II**.

How do you feel after this meditation? Make sure to write about the shifts in your attitude, thoughts, and feelings after this experience.

Repeat the meditation in **Journey II** with the same person until *all* feelings of anger, pain, blame, resentment, and sadness dissolve and are replaced by total forgiveness.

Journal your experiences.

What lessons do you believe this person brought you? What is the gift?

Has your relationship with the person in the meditation changed in any way since this journey? How?

Journey IV: Forgiving Yourself

Repeat the same meditation listed in **Journey II**. Instead of choosing another person, make yourself the person who steps out of the group.

Connect with the you at the age or timeframe related to a situation that you feel warrants your forgiveness.

If you desire a more general forgiveness, you can connect with any age, including the present you. Ask that all be done for your highest and best, trusting that where you are drawn is perfect.

Journal your experience.

Know that these exercises may require many, many repeats. Though ideally, we may feel that once and done is best, remember that forgiveness is a process that requires our patience and gentleness.

Return from the Looking Glass

Since love grows within you, so beauty grows.
For love is the beauty of the soul.
— *Saint Augustine*

Your self-love is the flower that opens its petals, sharing its beauty with all the world. Consider all the ways you have grown to appreciate yourself - your body, intellect, creativity, warmth, expression, and truth…the many facets and layers of you and You, embraced through all your journeys in their varied ups and downs.

To witness your metamorphosis in self-love, we return to a few of our first journeys.

Journey I: Selfie

Paste a current photo of yourself to the right or in your journal. A simple image printed on paper is fine. Now draw, color, or paste a frame around your image, decorating as you see fit. Be sure to write your name, the date of the photo, and your nickname.

Journey II: Draw

Draw a self-portrait using any media you desire. Again, add a frame, your name, date, and nickname.

Journey III: Reflections

Return to your sacred space, taking time to center and relax.

Reflect on how you feel after completing **Journeys I** and **II**. Journal your experience.

How have your overall attitudes about yourself changed as this book series comes to completion? Are you more accepting, less critical, gentler, and loving? In what ways do you witness this?

What do you notice comparing your photo here with the first photo from **Through the Looking Glass** in **Volume I**, at the beginning of this soul-discovery series? Do you look more relaxed, happier, healthier, etc.?

Ask a trusted friend to compare the two photos to witness any changes, recording here what they share.

How do you feel about the changes they witness in the photo or in your life? Are they similar to what you see?

At Journey's End

Every one of us has in him a continent of undiscovered character.
Blessed is he who acts the Columbus to his own soul.
— *Author Unknown*

You've done it! You've navigated your own soul-discovery, acting the Columbus to sail a sea of learning, re-learning, forgetting, forgiving, and forging anew. How you've flourished!

Traveling companions, metaphysical reflections, and the increasingly longer and deeper soul-discovery helped deliver you here, although you did all the dedicated hiking. This chapter brings to a close a great adventure, a journey to your self and your Self. Know that all remains within you to provide support, reference, and nurturing, even if at times your memory might say otherwise. Practicing what you have learned and putting it to use day to day is where the magic continues to happen. The tools and journeys that are now part of you lead to new trails and exploration, drawing many more adventures as other life challenges and new lessons present themselves. Your life is ever evolving. The journey you take continues to peel away layers, revealing the Light of your true Self. This is an ongoing process…the process of embracing your Self to live it!

What you've gained through your participation with this volume and series provides a companion in ongoing soul-discovery for life. Remember, returning to recollect or repeat chapter exercises is not failure but dedication to the path, which may feel necessary until we are able to sustain and remain connected to our Self at all times.

Take a moment to acknowledge all your work and courage. Write or draw about how you've grown. Here is the space to celebrate and acknowledge your authenticity, chutzpah, and dedication. Reflect on your biggest triumphs and what you take with you as your life adventure continues.

An Intimate Journey into Self

Hold a celebration with friends and family to acknowledge your graduation. Create something intentional to ground your changes, like purchasing a special gift for yourself, going on a trip, or letting your outward appearance herald the shift within.

Celebrate your embrace of the new!

Anything that annoys you is for teaching you patience.

Anyone who abandons you is for teaching you how to stand up on your own two feet.

Anything that angers you is for teaching you forgiveness and compassion.

Anything that has power over you is for teaching you how to take your power back.

Anything you hate is for teaching you unconditional love.

Anything you fear is for teaching you courage to overcome your fear.

Anything you can't control is for teaching you how to let go and trust the Universe.

— Jackson Kiddard

Thank you

Thank you for all the energy, time, focus, courage, and care you put forth on your soul-discovery. Every step of unearthing, growing, and evolving reaches out like the rays of the morning sun that radiate over the horizon, gently touching each blade of grass, tree, and flower. We are One, you and I... learning, connecting, and remembering.

Many blessings on your path of continued soul-discovery.

May your light shine, brightly.

Peace and infinite love to you.

Epilogue

The Soul-Discovery Journalbook publication completes my part of a five-year journey of soul-discovery to merge with my Self. It's hard to believe that I dedicated so many years to bring this work to completion. In many ways it was like having a child that I carefully carried through pregnancy, gave birth to, nurtured, fed, clothed, disciplined, mentored, and still deeply love. Now it's time to send the "child" into the world to be whatever it needs to be. So, **The Soul-Discovery Journalbook** adventure in its totality remains far from finished because this creation grows and lives on in and through you.

As a feeling of gratification surfaces, questions from my inquiring mind also arise like the bubbles in a newly opened bottle of seltzer. Did I cover everything I intended? Did I miss something vital? Did I emphasize the most essential parts of growth and soul-discovery?

While I affirm that all is as it needs to be, to address any lingering introjections, I leave you, precious reader, with a few closing thoughts:

- Don't underestimate the power of a hug, a beautiful way to give and receive love. If the importance and value of this connection seems missing, a quote from the well-known family therapist Virginia Satir captures it:

> We need 4 hugs a day for survival.
> We need 8 hugs a day for maintenance.
> We need 12 hugs a day for growth.

- Tending to yourself is like landscaping - an overgrown and weedy garden can feel too big to tackle, especially when we ignore it over time. Persistently and gently pulling the weeds of your negative attitudes through daily attention to thoughts, feelings, and habits makes the process less overwhelming. Showing yourself ongoing gestures of self-care keeps you lovingly fed and assists you to grow strong and beautiful in your Truth.

- The shadow side is not who you are! The personality trends, patterns, and ways you approach life are tied with your belief system but have nothing to do with the innocent, eternal Self of you. Your temporary reality in the flesh through journeys in personality offers lessons to discover and embrace the Self - the Truth we all seek.

- I can't say this any better than A. A. Milne:

> Promise me you'll always remember:
> You're braver than you believe,
> and stronger than you seem,
> and smarter than you think.

- Said the Universe to Its Child, "I give you the gift of your mistakes. May you lovingly dust off the dirt of disappointment, soothe your bruised heart with compassion, and courageously step forward with grace."

- You are beautiful, and your growth impacts all the world.

Blessings, love, and light,
Adriene

Appendix

Resources

Resources below include books on spirituality, psycho-spirituality, psychology, and metaphysical topics. While this list is far from complete, it includes rich reading and studying sources to continue and/or enhance your development.

<u>Sacred Garden Fellowship</u> (SGF) - founded and directed by Reverend Penny Donovan and Donald Gilbert, MSW - is a non-denominational spiritual community dedicated to helping others transform daily life challenges. This nonprofit organization offers a primary source of study materials for the author and where she attends retreats and serves as a co-facilitator. Teachings from SGF include over four hundred lectures on spirituality from Master Teachers in spirit, channeled through deep trance medium, Rev. Penny Donovan. Below is a just a short list of materials that provide additional reading to supplement topics presented in this book series. Materials inventory and MP3 recordings are available through www.sacredgardenfellowship.org. Publications marked below (*) may be purchased on Amazon.

<u>Teachings of Archangel Gabriel:</u>

I AM GABRIEL: Lessons from an Archangel - Book 1 and 2 **

Introduction to Practical Spirituality *

Healing: Select Lessons from Archangel Gabriel *

Angels, Spirit Guides, and Other Entities: Select Lessons from Archangel Gabriel *

The Christ Within

Karma and Love

Reincarnation

Perfect Trust

The Power of the I Am

The Emotional Plane: Its Pain and Power

Prayer and Meditation

The Anatomy of a Miracle

Teachings of Master Ng-on Kar:

True Detachment

Meditation and an Empty Mind

The Gifts of Our Mistakes

Chakra Energies: We Are Eternal

Teachings of Master Yeshua

How We Create Our Lives

The Crucifixion's Deeper Intent

Living from the Higher Self Now

The Importance of What We Are Here to Do

Other Channeled Teachings

These powerful texts provide valuable teachings whose principles and concepts are reflected and/or quoted in this book series.

A Course in Miracles: Original Edition, Helen Schucman

A Course of Love: Combined Text, First Receiver Mari Perron

The Pathwork of Self-Transformation, Eva Pierrakos

Additional Spiritual and Metaphysical Sources

This list reflects books referenced within these pages and include favorites of the author in no particular order.

Everything I Wanted to Know About Spirituality but Didn't Know How to Ask: A Spiritual Seeker's Guidebook, Peter Santos

A New Earth: Awakening to Your Life's Purpose, Eckhart Tolle

The Life and Teaching of the Masters of the Far East (Vol. 1-6), B.T. Spalding

The Wise Heart, Jack Kornfield

The Art of Forgiveness, Lovingkindness, and Peace, Jack Kornfield

The Art of Spiritual Healing, Joel Goldsmith

Practicing the Presence, Joel Goldsmith

An Open Heart: Practicing Compassion in Everyday Life, The Dalai Lama

The Four Agreements, Miguel Ruiz

Heal Your Body: The Mental Causes for Physical Illness and the Metaphysical Way to Overcome Them, Louise Hay

Through Time into Healing, Brian Weiss, MD

Animal Speaks, Ted Andrews

The True Power of Water, Masaru Emoto

The Energy Healing Experiments: Science Reveals Our Natural Power to Heal, Gary. Schwartz, Ph.D. with William L. Simon

Vibrational Medicine, Richard Gerber, MD

Fictional Books with Spiritual Truths - a small sampling of fictional books recommended by the author that metaphorically explore spiritual laws.

A Wrinkle in Time, Madeleine L'Engle

Harry Potter (any of this series), J.K. Rowling

The Alchemist, Paulo Coelho

Siddhartha, Herman Hesse

The Way of the Peaceful Warrior, Dan Millman

Psychological Sources:

Recovery of Your Inner Child, Lucia Capacchione, PhD

What Do You Say After You Say Hello?, Eric Berne, MD

The Dance of Anger, Harriet Lerner, PhD

Toxic Parents: Overcoming Their Hurtful Legacy and Reclaiming Your Life, Susan Forward, PhD

Why Is It Always About You?: The Seven Deadly Sins of Narcissism, Sandy Hotchkiss, LCSW

A Man's Guide to Women: Scientifically Proven Secrets from the "Love Lab" About What Women Really Want, J. G. Gottman, PhD et al.

Spiritually Themed Movies:

Avatar - learn about how all life is connected through Eywa in this beautiful story about humility, Oneness, and true love.

Star Wars - this classic series stands on spiritual truths and the connectedness of all life through The Force.

What the Bleep Do We Know - a documentary-style movie that addresses the connection between quantum physics, consciousness, and spirituality.

Heal - a film with well-known practitioners addressing the power of the human mind to heal the body.

Samsara - a documentary that takes viewers to twenty-five countries to visit the varied worlds of sacred grounds, disaster zones, industrial complexes, and natural wonders; the film visually speaks to the range of human experiences of the earth plane to spiritual ones.

The Secret Life of Trees - a beautiful documentary about the interactions of trees with all forest life; speaks again to the connectedness of nature.

The Way - an inspiration story about a father trying to reconnect with his deceased son through a spiritual journey on El Camino del Santiago.

Siddhartha - based on the novel *Siddhartha* by Herman Hesse about a young Indian man who embarks on a journey to find the meaning of existence.

The Celestine Prophecy - based on the book by the same title about spiritual evolution and ascension.

Ram Das, Fierce Grace - an authentic look at a spiritual leader's experience with physical illness.

Into Great Silence - An examination of life inside the Grande Chartreuse, the head monastery of the reclusive Carthusian Order in France. Winner of six awards.

Internet Resources

www.acourseoflove.org
www.astrohealing.net
www.grief.com
www.institutehearthmath.org
www.manifesthealing.com
www.rewire.com
www.rewireme.com/explorations/rollin-mccraty-closing-gap-heart-brain/
www.rewireme.com/explorations/power-emotional-attitudes-upon-entire/
www.pathways2innerpeace.com (author's site)
www.pathwork.org
www.sacredgardenfellowship.org

Artist Attributions

Mandala creation displayed in **Journey I** of Mandala created by Visnezh - Freepik.com
Patrick Broderick, Rotodesign, http://www.rotodesign.com

Glossary of Terms

Abstract mind - the energy of pure knowingness fed by our Higher Self in tune with Source.

Akashic records - the collective energy (vibrational field) of the soul memories of all beings. (See **Soul, Soul Memory**.)

Alter ego - the most negative aspect of our personality and ego that holds hostile, aggressive, violent, selfish, and shameful or guilt producing desires.

All-That-Is, Divinity, Divine Source, Source, Mother-Father God, God, Universal Power, Cosmic Energy - these terms all refer to the same creative force of the Universe that knows all and feels all; a source of our own Divine Nature and the God within; we are an individualized aspect of this energy, lovingly contained within and intimately connected to Him/Her/It.

Astral plane - a dimension that all living things pass into as they leave their physical body; the realm of emotions where our Spirit travels when we sleep; the vibration our consciousness visits when we daydream, imagine, dream, or do guided meditation.

Astrology - the ancient study of planetary influences on earthly existence.

Aura - the energy field expressed by all things; holds our physical health, thoughts, attitudes, feelings, emotions, unresolved issues, and beliefs.

Awareness - a state of knowingness beyond what may be identified by concrete mind; a deep feeling that surpasses the lower vibration of words, images, or other logical thoughts and reaches into our Divine Nature and Union with Source.

Chakras - seven energy centers that attach from the etheric body into the physical, linking our form to the mental, emotional, and spiritual bodies; these are ordered from one to seven as follows: root, sacral, solar plexus, heart, throat, third eye, and crown chakras.

Christ - the unconditional love aspect of Source; the highest aspect of our emotional body, which is our Feeling Nature; an energy we all have as Children of God, often labeled as Son, or Son of God; the collective energy of the Christ is all of creation in Unity with Source as the Sonship; frequently thought of as Jesus Christ, the man who attained Christ Consciousness.

Christ Consciousness - the knowingness that all aspects of creation are part of and connected to Source; the recognition of God/Source/Universal Power in all things.

Concrete mind - the aspect of our thinking consumed with planning, logic, figuring, and thoughts regarding our daily earth life; works in conjunction with our ego.

Consciousness - an internal state that addresses where our thoughts and emotions lie at any given moment.

Discernment - the employment of higher perception without the assessment of ego thinking and beyond the vision of what we see as appearances with our physical eyes; a bridge from higher consciousness to awareness.

Divine Helpers - the guidance, assistance, encouragement, support, and love from angels, our Higher Self, and those who have passed over as guides and friends/family in spirit.

Ego - the vibration of fear created by us to sound the alarm bells for danger; works with our lower vibrational thoughts through judgement to facilitate separation and lack of love; an operative energy of our personality that uses our soul memory to block us from knowing our Divinity.

Emotional body - a range of esoteric energies from the purity of feelings (Feeling Nature) through the lower energies of emotions; the higher aspect of our emotional body intermingles with our mental body.

Empath - a person who is more intensely affected by energy and thereby absorbs it, wears it, or expresses the energy of those in direct proximity or what's held in the ethers.

Etheric - the energy beyond the physical plane that carries our planet's collective consciousness from Earth and all that exists on her.

Etheric body - an exact replica of our physical form; serves as a bridge from the physical to our mental, emotional, and spiritual bodies.

Feminine energy - the nurturing and sustaining energy of all beings regardless of gender, reflecting one aspect of the whole of our Divine creative flow within; feminine energy gives masculine energy direction and purpose in order to make whatever we pour energy into manifest.

Higher Self - our True Nature; the Divine energy within each of us accessed through stillness and connection to our Holy Nature.

Holy Spirit - the action arm of Source in us that bridges our Christ (Self) with our soul; an integral part of us as a transformative power that knows the limitations we believe and the Truth of our being; the Divine energy of comfort and peace.

Inner child - an aspect of personality held in place energetically by our childhood experiences; the appearance of more than one inner child represents fractures of the collective energy of our childhood/adolescence; an inner child appears at a particular age due to childhood events and the child's accompanying perceptions.

Intentions - the powerful combination of thoughts powered by emotions; the directing conscious and subconscious energy behind all we manifest in our life; intentions that are subconscious are always more powerful because they operate often beyond our awareness.

Intuition - the energy of knowing without how or why we know as an aspect of our Divine energy; intuition pours from our solar plexus, helping to give rise to gut feelings and an impression of something beyond our five senses.

Judgement - the energy of fear perpetuated by our ego that separates us from others and Source; the conscious or subconscious evaluation of self or others as right, wrong, good, and/or bad instead of understanding/witnessing their wholeness; seeing without the vision of the Higher Self in a state of unbalance.

Karma - the lower aspect of the Law of Cause and Effect; karma is created when we feel we must pay back, balance, seek revenge, etc. on deeds done to us or those we do unto others; karma is an act of balancing and re-balancing driven by guilt or revenge.

Law of Attraction - like attracts like; positive attracts positive energy; negative attracts negative energy.

Law of Cause and Effect - what goes around comes around; the lowest aspect of this law is karma.

Law of Polarity - all things have an opposite on all energetic levels; to work with this law is to remain in balance.

Magic - the manipulation of energy.

Manifest/Manifesting - exercising our creative abilities to bring into the physical plane that which we want or desire; this includes objects, events, experiences, and situations; the sustaining of energy through our thoughts and feelings in order to bring objects, events, and circumstances into existence; the generation of action energy (**masculine energy**) that is nurtured and sustained (**feminine energy**) long enough to create in the physical plane.

Masculine energy - the energy of action, doing, and initiative; everyone contains masculine energy regardless of gender, as it reflects one aspect of the whole of our Divine creative flow within; feeds feminine energy, offering what may be sustained in order for what we desire to manifest.

Mental body - a spectrum of vibrational energy ranging from concrete mind to abstract mind; intermingles with the higher aspect of our emotional body.

Metaphysical - known, experienced, or existing beyond the realm of physical form through our typical five senses.

Mindfulness - the practice of maintaining a non-judgmental state of heightened or complete awareness of one's thoughts, emotions, or experiences on a moment-to-moment basis.

Non-judgment - the practice of evaluating situations, events, objects, or people as good or bad, right or wrong, etc.; releasing the thinking influenced by ego to move beyond duality toward wholeness.

Observing - the act of watching our thoughts, emotions, feelings, beliefs, or attitudes in order to be able to step beyond the influence of ego and personality trends and align with our Higher Self. (See **Witnessing**.)

Oneness - our natural state as a Child of the Divine; the expression of Union with all of life through the collective energy of Intelligent Force/God/Source.

Past-lives - previous incarnations of ourselves who appear to have occurred in a time continuum of dates earlier than the perceived present moment; we all have many past lives where an aspect of our Spirit incarnated to learn, grow, and help us return Home.

Psycho-spiritual - the blending of psychological and spiritual transformative experiences and interventions to create that which is both psychological and spiritual, but a distinctly different experience greater than the sum of its two parts.

Reincarnation - the recycling aspect of life by which a portion of any Spirit decides to return to the earth plane to learn and evolve in consciousness; reincarnation occurs with humans, plants, and animals, but only within the species.

Soul - an energetic recording device that logs thoughts, feelings, emotions, body sensations, experiences, events, situations, and dreams in our life from the beginning of time to the present and into the future; the soul knows the Truth of our being as well as the misperceptions and illusionary aspects of our consciousness. (See **Akashic records**.)

Soul knot - an energetic tangle in our soul created by our reactions to distressing, traumatic, or problematic situations; current beliefs affect the creating of soul knots, especially when previous events become re-activated by current ones.

Soul memory - the collective information of our entire history held by the soul from the moment of our creation out into our future. (See **Soul**.)

Spirit - the pure aspect of a life created by Source, imbued with the same creative, joy-filled, loving, knowingness as Source/Mother-Father God; this includes humans, animals, plant life, and minerals.

Spiritual Energetic Protection - the formation of an energetic shield through loving thoughts and feelings, angelic help, and a barrier created in our mind that buffers us from negative energy.

Spirituality - an individual's experience of connection with that power, energy, love that is Source as Source knows us to be in truth.

Veil - an appearance of separation between the earth plane or physical plane and all other planes of existence, which include the etheric, astral, and higher spiritual dimensions; disincarnate spirits exist across the veil, typically in the astral plane, having discarded their physical form.

Witnessing - the act of paying attention to our internal experiences in regards to situations or events; watching how we feel and think about anything in our life in order to move from a state of discomfort to healing; when employed as a mindfulness practice, it involves non-judgment and the movement past the influences of our ego. (See ***Observing***.)

About the Author

Adriene Nicastro is an intuitive, psycho-spiritual therapist, ordained minister, healer, teacher, and author. In 1993 she graduated from Hahnemann University with a Master of Science in Group Process and Group Psychotherapy. Adriene began studying the teachings of Sacred Garden Fellowship (SGF) in 2008 and subsequently embarked on a journey to share them with local groups. Through a blend of metaphysics, psychotherapeutic techniques, and spiritual healing, she guides individuals through deep levels of transformation that integrate spiritual development and personal growth. Adriene privately holds sessions, workshops, and groups locally and internationally. For more information on sessions, classes, workshops, and other materials, please visit www.pathways2innerpeace.com.

www.ingramcontent.com/pod-product-compliance
Lightning Source LLC
Chambersburg PA
CBHW080608170426
43209CB00007B/1366